FREE WILL, CONSCIOUSNESS AND SELF

FREE WILL, CONSCIOUSNESS AND SELF

Anthropological Perspectives on Psychology

Preben Bertelsen

Berghahn Books
New York • Oxford

First published in 2005 by
Berghahn Books
www.berghahnbooks.com

© 2005 Preben Bertelsen
First paperback edition published in 2006

All rights reserved. Except for the quotation of short passages for the purposes of criticism and review, no part of this book may be reproduced in any form or by any means, electronic or mechanical, including photocopying, recording, or any information storage and retrieval system now known or to be invented, without written permission of the publisher.

Library of Congress Cataloging-in-Publication Data
Bertelsen, Preben.
  Free will, consciousness and self / Preben Bertelsen.
      p. cm. -- (Studies in the understanding of the human condition)
  Includes bibliographical references and index.
  ISBN 1-57181-661-5 -- ISBN 1-84545-313-1 (pbk.)
  1. Free will and determinism. 2. Consciousness. 3. Self.
  4. Evolutionary psychology. I. Title. II. Series.

BF621 B47 2003
150.19'8--dc22

2003057871

British Library Cataloguing in Publication Data

A catalogue record for this book is available from the British Library.

ISBN 1-57181-661-5 hardback
ISBN 1-84545-313-1 paperback

Contents

List of Figures		vii
Preface		xi
Introduction	General Anthropology	1
Chapter 1	What is General Psychology?	23
Chapter 2	What is Anthropological Psychology?	47
Chapter 3	The Distinguishing Traits of Human Beings Seen From the Perspective of Natural and Cultural History	57
Chapter 4	Levels of Connectedness of the Psyche	99
Chapter 5	The Free Will	119
Chapter 6	Consciousness	143
Chapter 7	The Self and the Life Project	183
Chapter 8	An Anthropological-psychological Taxonomy	225
Bibliography		245
Index		249

List of Figures

0.1	The MAT-method.	19
1.1	The interrelation between general psychology and the specific disciplines.	30
1.2	The difference between scientific and purely pragmatic forms of knowledge.	33
1.3	How the psychologist's model (using DIT) influences and relates to a given aspect of the psychic.	36
1.4	Model of the four main elements of the knowledge-accumulating process.	37
1.5	Model of the pragmatic aspect of the knowledge-accumulating process.	38
1.6	Model of the theoretical aspect of the knowledge-accumulating process.	39
1.7	An overall metapsychological model of the different forms of knowledge.	41
1.8	The contribution of different sciences to a joint scientific conception of the human being.	44
1.9	An interdisciplinary model of the scientific examination of the anthropological domain.	45
2.1	The three anthropological-psychological approaches to the basic and universal human phenomena.	52
3.1	The development of the home base and successive developments within the areas of technology, society and culture.	60

List of Figures

3.2	The difference between standard evolutionary theory, and a theory of the individual as an active co-creator of the selection process.	64
3.3	Three stages in the evolution of humanness.	84
3.4	The development of a proto-morality and the capacity for directedness at/by others.	89
4.1	The two ways in which living organisms may be connected.	103
4.2	The distinction between non self-activated processes in nature and true self-activated behaviour.	109
4.3	Schematic representation of the relation between explanatory levels and levels of reality.	110
4.4	The difference between three views of the dynamics of organization, of downward causality.	112
4.5	The various levels of psychology, the levels of activity, and the levels of explanation belong together taxonomically.	118
5.1	The three main positions regarding the relationship between free will and scientific principles.	121
5.2	The conception of free will from the perspective of genuine compatibilism.	125
5.3	The most important characteristics of the will.	133
5.4	The basis of the will consists of the weighing up of goals against internal and external conditions.	135
5.5	The process of willing and the different states that the agent may find him/herself in within that process.	137
5.6	The process of willing – the realization phase.	138
5.7	The process of willing – the will is primarily expressed through intention.	139
5.8	The process of willing – The state of open weighing up.	139
5.9	The process of willing – the state of determination without actually realizing one's goal.	140
5.10	The various levels of free will in relation to the distinctively human form of will.	141
6.1	Intentioned connectedness and qualia.	147
6.2	The development of consciousness.	160

6.3	Three levels of psychology.	170
6.4	Levels of psychology, levels of directedness, and levels of consciousness.	176
6.5	Levels of psychology, levels of will, and levels of consciousness.	181
7.1	The intentionality, its mirroring intentio, and its idealization of the intentum.	185
7.2	Three subordinate levels of the high-level psyche.	190
7.3	Overview of the evolution of the human with special reference to the relation between mode of life, form of connectedness, and form of the self.	193
7.4	The taxonomic connection between the levels and forms of directedness of the self and of the psyche.	211
7.5	The core of personality – A.	222
7.6	The core of personality – B.	223
8.1	The self (or another psychic phenomenon) in its horizontal and vertical forms of connectedness.	227
8.2	The self (or another psychic phenomenon) from three different methodologically reduced perspectives, each providing a model of the formation of the self in terms of directedness/consciousness.	230
8.3	The self (or another psychic phenomenon) from three different methodologically reduced perspectives, each providing a model of the fundamental dynamic forces involved in the formation of the self.	232
8.4	The different taxonomies combined – A.	238
8.5	The different taxonomies combined – B.	239

Preface

This book has grown out of the fertile ground that is the basis of general psychological research in Denmark, especially at the Department of Psychology, University of Aarhus and the Department of Psychology, University of Copenhagen. The work published in the research network *Forum for Antropologisk Psykologi* (Forum of Anthropological Psychology) with amongst others: Shyam Cawasjee, Lars Hem, Henrik Høgh Olesen, Jette Fog, Boje Katzenelson, Jens Kvorning, Jens Mammen, Henrik Poulsen, Jan Tønnesvang and myself, as well as the ongoing general psychological discussion in the Danish periodical *Bulletin fra Forum for Antropologisk Psykologi* been inspiring.

I wish to express my gratitude to Shyam Cawasjee, Niels Engelsted, Lars Hem, Jens Mammen and Erik Schultz for dialogues and comments on the project. I also thank Kim Frandsen, Thomas Koester and Henning Lund for their suggestion to have the project published as a book in Danish, and to Shyam Cawasjee for many useful comments and assisting with the English publication.

Finally, my thanks to Annie Dolmer Christensen for the first translation of the majority of the book, to Sally Laird for the English language revision and valuable comments on the majority of the book, and to Joan Alexandersen Coke for translating selected paragraphs from some of the book's chapters.

Preben Bertelsen,
Summer 2000 and Summer 2003

Introduction

General Anthropology

What is it to be human?

Human existence means human co-existence; this is an inevitable part of the human condition. As human beings we co-exist; not merely in the shallow sense that we like being together, have friends, or live our lives with a partner and in groups – but in the deep and crucial sense that a condition for existing as human beings, is to be dependent on and contributing to a shared human world. As human beings we share a common existential basis. A weak (and less significant) definition of co-existence states that each of us gain certain advantages from the facts of human co-existence; we help each other to survive, and prosper in ways we could not achieve individually. In principle, one could do without this type of co-existence, and some people do in fact move away from the company of others. A stronger (and genuine) notion of co-existence states that we cannot exist as human beings without living in co-existence – whether we live in active social interaction or bring a mind formed by the facts of co-existence with us into our own self-chosen or inflicted loneliness.

Without fundamental co-existence, human beings could not preserve what gives life a genuine form of human meaning: the attachment to loved ones, social interaction, and cultural products of technological, artistic-aesthetical and intellectual kinds. As human beings we cannot exist independently of what is meaningful, without being directed toward human culture, and toward other people and their particular ways of living their lives. To be directed toward the cultural and societal forms of life that make co-existence meaningful is the fundamental human condition. This will be further elaborated in Chapters 3 and 7.

The central questions, then, are: how are we as humans able to participate in moral and societal life built on co-existence? What should a theoretical model look like that identifies and explains those core aspects of human competencies and qualities which enable us to participate in moral and societal life? How, that is, by which methodologies, on what kind of scientific foundation, and with the aid of which explanatory styles, can such theoretical models of the human condition be constructed? These are the questions which will be investigated throughout the chapters in this book.

The anthropological domain and general anthropology

I propose that humanity and human phenomena belong to the anthropological domain of the world. Human beings, their forms of existence and actions, constitute this domain. In general, the sciences that examine this domain could be termed the anthropological sciences (or at least one could speak of the parts of these sciences that deal with what is particular to humans as anthropological). The analysis of the anthropological domain is the task of general anthropology.

In this book the anthropological domain is approached primarily from the psychological perspective, and in particular from the part of psychology, which, in this book (and in Danish psychology more generally), is called Anthropological Psychology. It is a psychological discipline that spans what could be called in a more international terminology, evolutionary psychology, cultural-historical psychology and general, theoretical psychology. A central idea in this book is that this kind of psychology is reciprocally related to general anthropology. On the one hand, Anthropological Psychology contributes to our knowledge of the anthropological domain, and thereby sheds light on what it is to be human – seen from a psychological point of view. On the other hand, general anthropology, with its accumulated empirical results and theoretical models from different scientific disciplines, will offer the psychological disciplines – or at least the anthropological parts of these disciplines – a viewpoint toward the basic human condition. This will be further elaborated in Chapters 1, 2 and 8.

The basic anthropological model

Hence the project in this book is to put forward a general psychological model as a contribution to the study of the anthropological domain. This model will emerge in the following chapters as a basic anthropological model.

It will be shown that one of the basic building blocks for theories in the anthropological domain, and therefore a basic concept in the anthropological model, is *intentional connectedness*.

Proposing *intentional connectedness* as one of the core concepts of what it is to be human does not mean that the project of this book is a traditional phenomenological project, although phenomenology certainly plays a central role in later chapters, which deal with consciousness and the self. The project in this book, however, is first and foremost a cultural-historical project, conceptualising the human condition in terms of intentional connectedness, realised through human activity in its historical emergence.

The basic anthropological model proposes that human connectedness to the world has a horizontal and a vertical dimension.

The horizontal dimension of human connectedness can be explained as follows: we interpret the world, our lives, the situations we are in, and other people according to our own projects. We experience the world, and initiate and conduct our acts in terms of what we desire, strive for, what we find meaningful, good and right. We behave and act in ways that shape and produce our surroundings so that they answer to our needs and projects. However, at the same time our interpretation of the world, our experiences and our behaviours and acts are highly influenced and formed by our surroundings. People are influenced by their social surroundings; they conform to the discourses of their culture and in particular to the groups to which they belong. People comply with authorities, and strive to attune to friends, family and loved ones. In general we are influenced by the world: our mental processing, our knowledge, our opinions and attitudes are about the world and shaped by the properties of the world.

Our connectedness to the world, therefore, has two sides. On the one hand (I call this 'inside-out') we express our selves, and thereby shape and produce the world. On the other hand (I call this 'outside-in') we are shaped by the world (both as it is in itself and as it has been formed by our actions). On the one hand (inside-out) we are directed at the world, at our social surroundings and other people. On the other hand (outside-in) we are directed *by* the world. In short, the concept of being directed at/by something is proposed as a central concept in the formation of theories about the human condition. This will be further elaborated in Chapter 4 (and in Chapters 5 through 7 as well).

The vertical dimension of human connectedness. Experts on cognitive psychology and consciousness, as well as clinical psychologists and psychotherapists, tell us that a great deal of our mental processing happens automatically outside our conscious awareness. It is both mentally cost-effective and often necessary for survival that we make interpretations and act without any further considerations on the basis of rather minimal information. Fortunately a few clues ('traffic situation! Large object moving at high speed in my direction!') are often enough to make us act immediately. In terms of horizontal connectedness we are outside-in directed by those few clues about the surroundings, and simultaneously we are inside-out directed at exactly those same few clues by means of our categorical processing.

However, social psychologists also tell us that there is a flipside to the coin. Indeed the fact that we can act on the basis of automatic categorisation and social stereotyping makes complex social life possible. On entering a room with other people, it only takes a few glimpses and quick automatic processing of which we are seldom aware, for us to know a lot about the type of situation we are in, what would be appropriate behaviour and what would be out of line. However, such automatic stereotyping can degenerate into negative prejudices – e.g., unjustified negative attitudes towards individuals based solely on their membership of a certain group, which is, in itself, judged in a negative, unjust, even racist way. How do we overcome such automatic prejudiced horizontal connectedness, which not only harms the targeted people and our humanity, but harms social life and the social conditions and possibilities of humanity? One – passive – way is to hope for a reformation of our automatic horizontal connectedness, that is, passively wait for a reformation brought about by the development of cultures, societies and communities. Fortunately there is another – active – way as well. Our stereotypical ways of being directed at/by the world exist as automatic connections beyond our reach only as long as we let them exist outside awareness and thereby outside conscious control. Sometimes, and at least to a certain degree, we can overcome a negative prejudice by focusing on which sort of connectedness it represents and how we are directed at and by the victim of our prejudice. To some extent, we can overrule the automatic horizontal connectedness with more realistic, morally superior, socially more just and humane principles for our connectedness and directedness at/by our surroundings.

On the one hand (bottom-up) it is a fact that we – one way or another – are always connected to the social surroundings through our horizontal connectedness and ways of being directed at/by these surroundings. Our horizontal connectedness constitutes our being in the world and thereby constitutes us as human beings. On the other hand (top-down), we can sometimes, and to a certain degree, organise the way we are directed at and directed by the world in general, our social surroundings and other people in particular. From the top-down perspective one can say that we have some level of freedom to organize our own horizontal connectedness by giving it the directedness we want, or which we find it morally ought to have or legally must have.

In other words: our connectedness has a vertical dimension given the fact that we in a self-organizing manner can be directed at our own horizontal directedness (top-down) while at the same time being directed by our own horizontal directedness (bottom-up) (in so far as the human condition always involves us in some sort of connectivity).

This brings us to the second important conceptual element in the basic anthropological model. The first one was the concept of the horizontal dimension of our connectedness, formed as directedness at/by something. This second element is the concept of vertical connectedness formed as our directedness at/by our own directedness. In later chapters we shall see how we as social beings are often preoccupied with other people's minds and their ways of experiencing the world, their surroundings, us, themselves. We are highly preoccupied and aware of other peoples' directedness. That is, we are directed at/by others' directedness. In short: an essential conceptualization of the human condition and human possibilities is directedness at/by directedness (our own as well as others').

In itself, the basic anthropological model must, by its very nature, be abstract. Nevertheless, as shown in the examples above, the model should be useful in conceptualizing rather complex social psychological phenomena with its general concepts of horizontal social directedness at/by the social surroundings and vertical directedness at/by horizontal social directedness. Correspondingly, the basic anthropological model should also be useful in other disciplines.

Consider, for example, the phenomena dealt with in clinical psychology and psychotherapy; especially the sort of life problems that would not be seen as stemming from insanity or serious damage to fundamental psychological functionality. In dealing with such phenomena, many psychotherapeutic traditions address the client's (missing) capacity to gain insight into, and control of, his/her life one way or another. The cognitive psychotherapist will train the client's capacity to focus on and disable automatic thoughts; the Freudian psychoanalyst will try to help strengthen the client's ego; self-psychological therapists (at least the ones inspired by Kohut) will help the client to enter some sort of pastoral growth relationship in which the self can develop into a state in which it can choose its own mature relationships; the existential therapist will address the client's capacity to take responsibility for his/her life conditions and life projects, etc. In any case, what is dealt with in these seemingly very different traditions can, on the basis of the general concepts of the basic anthropological model, be conceptualized as concerned with how the client with varying degrees of freedom (vertically) can organise his/her way of being connected to life (horizontally), to the social surroundings, to others, and – in a reflective manner – to him/herself. How this should be understood is considered in more detail in Chapters 5 and 7. Obviously, these therapies are rather different in terms of their own theoretical traditions. The point, however, is that the basic anthropological model offers us some of the building blocks with which to conceptualize the human condition as approached by a variety of methods, represented by the different therapies.

These considerations, obviously, address such central questions as: how do we organize our lives? How do we make choices about the way to live and the kinds of person we want to be? Can we indeed make our own choices at all? In other words, do we have a free will so that we are able, to some extent, to make decisions about our lives and ourselves, and thereby to form our own lives and ourselves as persons? Or is everything that happens to us, or within us, determined by psychological, social and biological forces over which we have no control, and of which, indeed, we may not even be consciously aware?

What does it actually mean to be consciously aware of oneself and one's life? How do we come to be capable, as conscious beings, of taking a comprehensive look at ourselves, our lives and each other? And how, on the basis of this conscious insight, are we able to make choices that are meaningful to us and make sense in relation to our lives? What does it actually mean to be conscious of oneself as a person, as a someone or a self that can engage in freely chosen projects?

The proposal of this book is that *free will, consciousness* and *self* are central human attributes that allow us to participate in human life, and in the moral and societal network of the surrounding world. They are the core human forms of intentional connectivity, and will be elaborated in Chapters 5, 6 and 7.

Critical realistic universalism

The basic anthropological model, which will be presented in this book, is proposed as a general theoretical model of human beings and the human condition as such. Therefore this model will necessarily be proposed as a universal model. This raises the problems of universalism. Furthermore, the model proposes that human co-existent life has to be realized in a certain way, namely as a two dimensional intentional connectivity in the form of the human capabilities of free will, consciousness and self. Therefore the basic anthropological model must, one way or the other, be a critical model. Critical, firstly, in the sense that the model shows how human beings on the basis of intentional connectivity are capable of participating in a *critical* way in moral and societal life. That is, human beings do not only have the capacity to contribute to establishing and maintaining their human world, but they also have the capacity to change and improve those parts of their world that violate the fundamental principles of co-existence, and thereby the very foundations of their own existence as humans. Critical, secondly, in the sense that this scientific model of the human condition can identify societal and cultural forms of life conditions, under which human beings may be forced to live, but which obstruct their ability to flourish. Let us therefore turn first to universalism and next to critical science.

Universalism

Universalism claims that it is possible to abstract shared features from superficial differences between people, societies and cultures. A universalistic view of humans simply states that human beings belong to the same species. According to universalism, what is good is fundamentally the same everywhere, to all people, at all times. Basically, races, ethniticities and nationalities are only superficial differences that are irrelevant to the fundamental questions of what it means to be human.

Universalism can be defended in various ways. Either in a super naturalistic and dualistic manner, claiming that the world and world order is given by a miraculous or divine force, which is external in relation to the forces that rule the world. Or in a naturalistic and monistic manner, claiming that the natural order of the world can be conceptualised scientifically, and that we can identify facts about the anthropological domain as a natural part of the world. It is this naturalistic and monistic version of universalism that is proposed in this book.

Universalism can degenerate

However, it is important to keep in mind that universalism can degenerate. Universalism can degenerate into moralistic tyranny and political dictatorship, or into cultural ethnocentrism and suppression. Let us therefore take a closer look at the central objections to universalism.

Moral relativism cannot be genuinely critical

One of the problems of exporting a moral and legal system, such as one that proposes talk of human rights as a universally valid discourse, is that for those who live with another moral-philosophical or religious mind-set will regard it as utterly unfounded, tyrannical and intolerant, if they are forced to acknowledge this new system. This critique of universalism can be seen to call for *moral relativism*. Moral relativism claims that a moral system is always relative to a society or an historical epoch with its own framework for the good life. Any view of what it means to be a good and fair person, and what it means to live a good and fair life, is only valid in the very context in which it was created. Often, relativists claim, moral perception cannot even be understood outside the life contexts in which it has developed.

Individualistic relativism is even more radical: Moral perception is ultimately only valid to the individual who has acquired this perception and who has made it his/her own. Consequently, in the case of moral conflict between two people, there can be no universal moral system to solve the conflict. In the name of relativist tolerance, one is therefore left with 'you do your things and I will do mine – if you have a different view than I do, that is your choice'. In such an individualistic, relativist perspective, universalism will be considered an encroachment, exercised by one individual on another individual who has a different view. In this perspective, universalism looks like one individual's intolerant, moralistic tyranny over another.

Social relativism is a critique of individualistic relativism, but is still critical of universalism. People live in societies and depend on getting along and working together and their co-existence is organised by common rights, values and legal principles. But still, what is good and fair is relative to the given society. There are no universal values independent of the society in which the values and moral guidelines are formulated. In this perspective it will similarly be a case of intolerance and encroachment when one social system and one culture tries to elevate its own value system and moral world into a 'universal' system, applicable to other social systems and cultures.

Finally, there is *historical relativism*, which involves the notion that society is under constant historical change. There are no universal values and no universally true moral perceptions of what is good and fair outside the cultural-historical epoch, in which these are formulated.

Relativism would therefore seem to be a critical defence against encroachment of people who live their lives with cognitions, emotions and conations of their own, and universalism would seem to be a slide towards such encroachments.

On the other hand: can relativism with its self-declared tolerance be critical? Yes, at least according to social and moral relativism itself. A way of living, it is claimed, is only good and fair if it is in accordance with the way in which members of society think and feel about life, and if it accords with the developmental paths pursued by the participants. One must therefore be critical of a moral system that is contrary to, or undermines, the possibilities of realizing what the community perceives as the good and fair life. Good and fair, according to social relativists, are found through dialogue and debate amongst society's members, who are actually themselves going to live their lives directed by morality and justice. Precisely these debates create the valid social and moral constructions to the participating constructors.

However, it should be obvious that moral relativism can never present deep or convincing criticism. Consistent and meaningful consensus about 'good' and 'fair' could easily take place amongst the developers of the Nazi exterminations camps, amongst the brothers in charge of the Inquisitions' torture chambers, amongst people joining paedophile groups on the Internet, in the upper classes that own the child slaves in the Far East factories, etc. Moral relativism can never be anything but a quite uncritical argumentation for what could be called 'moral self-oscillation' – a self-confirmation that strengthens and closes rather than criticizes and opens up a given moral and legal system. If good and fair, right and just, are only a matter of consensus and consistent and meaningful discourse, then any horrendous narrative can pass uncritically in the name of tolerance and relativism. Actually, one could argue that relativism promotes itself on a Western kind of mediocre self-centeredness and individualism: 'Leave everybody alone, avoid interference, and mind your own business'.

The alternative to non-critical relativism is realistic and critical universalism. Realistic in the sense that on the basis of facts, one can argue rationally about the good and fair life. The basic facts originate from the inevitable realities in the anthropological domain. What is *critical* science? Critical science does two things: firstly, it produces scientific knowledge about what a given phenomenon is and how it can be handled, treated, changed, developed, etc. Similarly, the soundness of argumentations and claims regarding this phenomenon and the handling of it are tested. Secondly, it gives scientifically founded professionals the opportunity to develop a confident, professional autonomy to become independent, involved and significant participants in the public debate.

Critical science is, on the one hand, not unsubstantiated rationalism. Such rationalism can only be about its own inner consistency or its own narrative aesthetics and meaning. As an unsubstantiated construction, it cannot be about the real world, and cannot make a real difference to the real world's people and their life problems. On the other hand, a critical science cannot be blind empiricism, studying the phenomena without an effort to develop general scientific knowledge. Critical science must necessarily be universal because it can only be critical on the basis of scientific theories that are independent of a specific culture's discursive self-understanding. Critical science must necessarily also be realistic because it can only make a difference to the world if it is about something other than its own consistency and aesthetics. Anthropological sciences can only be critical if they are based on realism about people, human existence and existential problems.

Critical universalism can be said to be critical in its devotion to *mild paternalism*. Contrary to mild paternalism, intolerance can, in a moral sense, be defined as the rejection of other people's different ways of living, different values and different perceptions of the good life. Intolerance is the effort of forcing on them another set of values and another way of living. Such intolerance must not be confused with mild paternalism. Mild paternalism is the view that one should critically try to make a difference to other people, that one should try to influence them critically to achieve insight and self insight if it is obvious that they live according to a set of values and perceptions of the good and fair life that are clearly damaging to, and clearly have the opposite effect of, what these people intend with their values and life perceptions. Mild paternalism is a critical effort to influence another person to gain insight into his/her own good. What does 'own good' mean? It is part of a person's own good to have optimum information about the foundation of human existence as a starting point for choosing one's own existence. Mild paternalism means making a difference by being influential in creating an insight into the specific and current situation they are in, as well as, this situation's contents of real and realistic possibilities of change and choice. Mild paternalism means to take part in creating liberating, critical self-knowledge in the cultural-historical and life-historical development that has led to the present situation, and to one's current set of values and perceptions of the good and fair life. Mild paternalism is the critical and confrontational effort of giving another human being (or another society/culture) the basis for qualified, informed and self-chosen influence and autonomy.

One can – especially if one enjoys a secure life and an advantageous socio-economic position – object that such paternalism, mild or not, nevertheless is violating and oppressive, because it is the individual's right to have his/her own life projects, whatever they may be. One can – especially when one lives in (Western) surplus societies – claim that it is the individual's personal right to possess diminished self-knowledge, to make a fool of oneself, to act on the basis of misunderstandings, idiosyncrasies, slight 'madness' and personal quirks, etc. Simply because none of us are perfect, and because these small 'deviations' from the optimum human condition are part of our personal make-up, which nobody has the right to take away from us. Incidentally, it is, among other things, these small deviations and quirks that give life such a colourful diversity that makes it worth living. The reply to this claim about a right to 'quirks' must be crystal clear: Certainly! *If* these 'small quirks', 'shortcomings' and 'sillinesses' are part of the self-knowledge and informed choice one has, and part of the tolerance one has of oneself and one's own reality. Mild paternalism must certainly be tolerant (and self-tolerant) in this way. Mild paternalism is, however, critical in situations where the opportunity of gaining insight into life possibilities is not present, where people are kept in ignorance, and where external social forces or inner mental force keep people ignorant to the extent that their values and perceptions have an effect contrary to what was intended.

The central question in this book is: how are we, from a psychological point of view, able to connect to the human surroundings and how are we able to participate in a co-existing moral and societal life? The critical proposal of this book is that on the basis of the fundamental anthropological model of the horizontal and vertical dimensions of the intentional connectivities of free will, consciousness and self, we are in a position to be able to criticise forms of life that are unjust to human life conditions and possibilities.

Cultural relativism cannot be genuinely critical

Universalism and paternalism can be a slippery slope – not least when one moves into the inter-cultural field. Universalism tries to develop general theories about human existence and about the human condition. Mild paternalism is in this context a culture-critical universalism that relates critically to any culture that is destructive of the possibilities people aim towards in their own culture.

One objection to general culture theories is that they are often too abstract about actual cultural differences, or at least postpone the work on the differences until later, when the general aspects have been sufficiently worked out. The objection is that one will never get to address the actual differences, and therefore significant insights into the individual culture – and also the general aspects of a culture – are lost. Naturally, universalism must face this criticism. Obviously, the general theory must always be in contact with the concrete phenomena and the particular theories regarding these phenomena. A general theory must also be a theory about specific differences in human types of expression; it must always be a theory about specific and local problems, as well as about those actual and local problems that occur in cultural meetings and clashes. Otherwise such a theory can hardly be said to have covered general phenomena or be universally applicable.

Another important critical objection is that Western psychology (claiming universal validity) has participated in oppressive practices because of ethnocentric Western concepts. Ethnocentric Western clinical psychology has diagnosed as mentally ill what were in fact just non-Western expressions of cultures, and even legitimate resistance against Western oppression. In the name of universalism and paternalism, developmental psychology, cognitive and learning psychology and pedagogical psychology with ethnocentric Western models of development and learning, have remained ignorant about the developmental and learning paths in other cultures, with catastrophic consequences for the children and young people in the targeted cultures. Ethnocentric Western organisational psychology has been exported along with Western economic interests with equivalently catastrophic consequences for the adults, who, out of necessity, have had to work under those types of organisation.

Cultural relativism, then, reappears in an attempt to explain and critically oppose such Western encroachment and suppression. What goes wrong, cultural relativists tell us, is that Western psychologists approach other cultures with theories and concepts, which can only be valid in the culture (usually Western) that has developed these theories and concepts as part of their own self-understanding. To cultural relativists, the problem is that cultures are basically created, maintained and developed by the very efforts to formulate them, talk about them, develop artistic expressions for them, as well as produce scientific models about them. According to relativism, any culture is in that sense a self-organizing and self-constructing system. Therefore, it also follows that the self-evident concepts that help create and maintain one culture cannot be used in another culture that is created and developed on the basis of its own constructions. The concepts needed to understand cultures, including the scientific psychological theories, are always relative in relation to the culture in which they are developed.

What is commendable about cultural relativism is naturally its persistent rebellion against narrow-mindedness and tyranny including a rebellion against science – including psychology – in so far as science itself contains such narrow-mindedness and prejudice that cause encroachment and suppression. Obviously, we must remain critical of science itself. Critical science is also self-critical. It includes criticism of its own axioms, prejudices, choice of method, empiricism, conceptualisations, operations and normative aims.

However, the solution to the problem of suppression is not the cultural relativist one, which is to lock science up in its own cultural glass case and deem it invalid in relation to all cultures other than the one it originates from. Such relativist strategies remain impotent concerning criticism, because relativism must, in order to avoid self-contradiction, renounce on pointing out what is suppressive, stupid and life-limiting in another culture, and what sets the inhumane conditions for that culture's people, contrary to the life possibilities they could either have or would strive for. Cultural relativism must settle for quite uncritically and ignorantly terming another culture's own types of expression, stupidities, ideological distortions, etc. a 'different type of existence', which we have neither the prerequisites nor the right to be judgemental of, or intervene critically with.

Consequently, a claim of this book is: the road away from a prejudicial, culture-ignorant and suppressive anthropological science (including psychology) does not go from ethnocentrism to cultural relativism, but from ethnocentrism to critical, realistic universalism. We have to understand the general human condition, the possibilities and life projects in the anthropological domain, morally, culturally and psychologically, in order to be genuinely critical of life conditions that suppress, distort or limit human existence. Only a general anthropology, formulated critically and universally can help us in this regard and reveal to the culture's own members the cultural-historical and social developmental paths that have led to the suppressed life conditions and limited possibilities, and which can create the informed foundation that makes genuinely conscious and free life choices possible.

Racism is wrong! Imperialism is wrong! Ethnocentrism is wrong! Tyranny and dictatorship are wrong! Can such positions be defended only from some sort of relativist position? And must universalism necessarily lead to those evils? No. In fact, we cannot build a real defence against these evils from any relativist position, and in fact we must look for a certain kind of critical universalism to find the real defence! The point is that we are in need of the sort of critical universalist anthropological model to be constructed in this book.

Universalism: generality vs. particularity and essentialism vs. historicity

The world – including its anthropological domain – is infinitely diverse, and no general theory can include it all. Is that not a strong argument against any form of universalism? No! An argument that it is not will be spelled out in what follows.

General theories and specific theories

In a way the plurality and diversity in the field of the anthropological sciences is good because it is an effective vaccination against narrow-mindedness, and intolerable simplification that would block creativity and development of an understanding of the world and the human condition. In another sense it is bad because the very same diversity could seem to block effective progression based on knowledge accumulation. Especially, if the diversity leads to individual research enclaves, institutes, faculties and universities becoming ignorant about what is happening 'on the other side of the corridor', and failing to see the necessity of putting their research results and explanatory models into perspective, then the result is a patchwork of incompatible and non-accumulative detail studies – maybe of some interest in themselves, but rarely able to contribute to our overall understanding of human life.

Naturally, one can choose to be pleased with the diversity of theories and claim that since the world itself is (ontologically) incoherent and characterised by diversity, such scientific patchwork reflects reality quite well.

An alternative proposition is that the world is ontologically coherent (in a colourful and beautifully diversified way) and thereby, so to speak, deserves that science strives for an increasingly coherent theoretical overview. That is my view. The view is usually expressed in two versions. The first is the endeavour towards a Grand Unified Theory. The second variation states that it is not possible to develop such a Grand Unified Theory. Such a theory presupposes that science could reach a stage of definitely concluded theories, which could not, and would not, need to be further developed. In that case, the final work of formulating the ultimate Grand Unified Theory would merely consist of finally combining the finished partial theories. However, all indications point towards the idea that because the world is infinitely diversified and complex, scientific development can consist only of making our partial theories clearer and simpler. Partial theories are never final and the developmental work will never come to an end. The development of theories must take place, and does actually happen in a decentralized and distributed manner in the different evolutionary growth areas in the disciplines and research projects.

The task is, on the one hand, to look for and create the best possible conditions for this decentralized diversity of growth areas in the sciences. On the other hand, to make sure that they do not fall apart and degenerate into isolated enclaves that fail to create a shared growth of knowledge in the end.

Scientific work must be carried out from two sides simultaneously. On the one hand, science has to be empirically founded in the world. It should be anchored in myriads of specific research projects. A scientific process, which is not anchored in reality via empirical research and detailed theoretical explanations of individual phenomena within the domain of the given science, degenerates into speculative rationalism, or even worse: into unconstructive ideological warfare. On the other hand, science must also strive for unity. It has to create extensive, general, theoretical and explanatory frameworks for the more specific projects. For example, it is not at all unconstructive within physics that we see quite an extensive amount of work carried out in developing cosmologies that combine what is known about the world. Such work within cosmology and theoretical physics has decidedly important returns. For instance, new mathematical understanding is being developed, which can be part of the further development of the partial theories, and more unifying and basic explanations about the world's physical organization are being developed.

The following three scientific efforts should in principle always go together:

- The general theoretical effort to combine the general theoretical explanations of the domain of the world involved,
- Efforts to develop knowledge about real problems within a limited aspect of the domain, and
- The applied disciplines' attempts to develop applicable science, which increases our ability in practice to handle these aspects.

None of these are dispensable. Science without empirical anchoring (easily) becomes rationalist constructions without realistic obligations. Science without general theoretical efforts (easily) becomes empiricist blind fumbling in myriads of incoherent, empirical projects without drive or obligation towards collective scientific accumulation.

General and particular universalism

It was asked above whether universalism loses its grip on the world's infinite diversity – including that of the anthropological domain. Not according to the model outlined above, to which we will return in Chapter 1.

A potential problem could be a universalism in the shape of one-sided generality. The generalist effort is to try to find the most general principles and thereby strive to abstract the most general features from the plurality and diversity of concrete phenomena. A one-sided general universalism will try to formulate general concepts about moral facts in those situations in which people generally find themselves. Against this, for example, situational ethics would object that we can only understand how a person should act and why a person actually acts morally, when we understand the actual situation the person is in, and when we understand how the person is capable of perceiving this situation and how it makes a difference in the choices he/she makes.

Again relativism will certainly emerge as an attempt to solve this problem of universalism. Human activities are always relative to the specific situations in which they take place. However, what is criticized here is not universalism as such. Only a purely generalist universalism should be the target of such a criticism. The problem of general universalism cannot be solved by a total rejection of universalism's efforts to develop general knowledge about the world. The solution must be based on the mutuality outlined above between the general model's efforts towards universality with regards to knowledge about a domain on the one hand, and on the other hand the specific theories' empirical anchoring in very concrete – and particular – phenomena.

Essentialism vs. historicity

Anthropological Psychology identifies and explains its phenomena as historical and emerging entities, which means that they change over time as a product of culturally specific ways of encountering the world. In the course of cultural history, humans produce and develop (at least some of) their own conditions and possibilities, and thereby the human phenomena that constitute the anthropological domain. This means that general anthropological phenomena should always be understood as part of 'local history', existing only in a certain natural-historical and cultural-historical epoch. We always exist in a certain local historical epoch – and this local epoch may be defined as spanning millions of years, thousands of years or hundreds of years, depending on how fine-grained our models are set to be and how nuanced the forms of human phenomena and possibilities we want to identify and conceptualise.

However, is singling out such specific phenomena as free will, consciousness and self not some sort of essentialism contradicting the claim that this book represents a cultural-historical approach to human conditions and possibilities? Essentialism is often seen as genuinely a-historical, telling us that there cannot be anything new under the sun. The cultural-historical approach, however, maintains that any entity in the anthropological domain is under constant historical development. Some developmental processes take place over a very long period of time, such as the biological development of human gene pools (at least as long as no artificial gene manipulations are at work), or the development of international understanding and democracy. Other developmental processes, such as the development of technical forms of interaction on the Internet, change within a few years, even months. This means that no phenomena in the anthropological domain has a fixed essence, but it does not mean that we cannot, when looking at a certain local historical epoch, identify the developmental and cultural-historical state of the anthropological domain on the basis of some attributes current for exactly this epoch or this culture.

As will be defended throughout the book, the roots of the human condition as identified and theoretically conceptualised in the basic anthropological model – that is, the horizontal and vertical dimensions of intentional connectedness – has been here since the very first primitive animal life forms and will not disappear again (unless bombed away, gene manipulated or subsumed under some unpredictable future forms of existence). The human psyche with its horizontal directedness at/by something (especially its social surroundings) and its self-organizing vertical directedness at/by directedness (one's own as well as others') is here to stay (in this epoch).

Free will, consciousness and self will be the central human phenomena on which to anchor the basic anthropological model of the horizontal and vertical dimensions of human connectedness and the universal properties of human conditions and possibilities.

The MAT-method

The first questions dealt with above were how are human beings able to participate in a critical way in moral and societal life built on co-existence and what should a theoretical-particularistic-universalistic model look like to be able to identify and explain the core aspects of human competencies and qualities that enable us to participate in social life? The final question, to which we now turn, is how, that is, by which methodologies and on which scientific foundations and explanatory styles do we construct such theoretical models of the human condition?

Model building

This is a question of how to develop theoretical models of the human condition and of how to build such a basic anthropological model. So, this is also a book about theory building. The reader will not face massive references to empirical studies. This does not, however, mean that the book represents some sort to speculative rationalism ignorant of reality and indifferent of the obligation of any scientific theory to be founded on empirical facts. On the contrary. Nothing of what is said in this book can claim any meaningfulness if it cannot – in principle – be founded on empirical evidence. However, given the abundance of detailed studies in this area the questions must be as follows:

- How is it possible to accumulate all these different pieces of knowledge of humanity into a general theoretical model (or sets of compatible theoretical models in different disciplines) of the human condition and human possibilities?
- How is it possible by means of such a general model to reduce the complexity of the human condition and human possibilities into understandable and meaningful entities with explanatory power?
- How can we on the one hand do this accumulative work in a manner that remains founded on empirical facts of human reality and on the other hand construct such accumulated theories in a manner that offers meaningful empirical and methodological directions for further scientific investigations into the realm of human conditions and possibilities?

Although the issue at stake is general principles of theory-building, this should in no way be understood as an 'imperialistic' attempt to discredit important work carried out in other areas of psychology, as well as in the social sciences and the humanities. On the contrary: hopefully, this general model will parallel important works in other fields concerned with understanding humanity.

Neither should the book be understood as a (futile) attempt to 'reinvent' Psychology. This would not only imply an extensive description of the real world and societal phenomena and problems to which Psychology should contribute with explanations and interventions. It would also imply an extensive analysis of the institutional and disciplinary nature and history of psychology, which sets decisive frame conditions, mainstream directions, and financed fundaments for the development of Psychology, its research projects, and theories. However, the focus here is general principles for theory building connected to the general psychological question of what it is to be human, and therefore, the reader should expect no such institutional analysis of Psychology.

The MAT-method (an acronym of 'Models Abstracted from Taxonomies')

The project of this book is to present the basic anthropological model and thereby show:

1 *That the human condition and human possibilities are basically founded on the fact that humans live – and can only live – in connectedness.* Obviously, in connectedness with their surroundings, physically and biologically, but, just as importantly, with social, cultural and inter-personal surroundings. We cannot be the beings we are without existing in life-giving and meaningful exchange with our fellow human beings. To exist in a human way is to exist in a *co*-existing way. The almost infinitely diversified variations this gives rise to, demands acknowledgement and tolerance of diversity. However, to exist in a human way is also to be critically intolerant to anything which can be destructive for the very *co*-existing core of human conditions and to use forms of mild paternalism in the dialog with people living under and for some misconceived ('misconcepted') reasons maintaining such life conditions.
2 *That this basic anthropological model is a proposition for a critical realistic universalism.* Knowledge about the anthropological domain whose most significant fact (biological, as well as social, cultural and moral) is the co-existing required by connectedness. In order to be genuinely and critically protective of this general and real basis, a realistic and universalistic (general and particular) scientific approach is called for (as opposed to a relativist/constructivist).
3 *That this basic anthropological model is a proposal for psychology's contribution to general anthropology.* The basic anthropological model in this book is, as already mentioned, a psychological approach to central human phenomena, notably *free will, consciousness and self*.

The method of critical realistic universalism as proposed in this book can be described as follows. One begins by selecting certain phenomena that, for good scientific reasons, can be said to be universally human; i.e., free will, consciousness and self. One then attempts to create a theoretically descriptive and explanatory model, or a taxonomy, of these particular phenomena and the ways in which they interrelate. Once one has succeeded in developing this kind of explanatory model, the next step is to investigate the basic structure underlying the model itself: in other words, to deduce the more fundamental relations, principles and laws of which the model is a reflection. These underlying principles, it is assumed, relate not only to the particular phenomena in question, but constitute the universal principles governing our distinctive nature as human beings. By uncovering the more

Step 1	Step 2	Step 3
Identifying the phenomena	**Taxonomical arrangement of the phenomena**	**Abstraction of the taxonomic model in itself**
The first step in the procedure is to identify the phenomena based on the results of empirical sciences.	*A taxonomic model is produced by investigating the ways in which these phenomena are interrelated.*	*On the basis of this model we arrive at a general system for taxonomically arranging the other phenomena.*

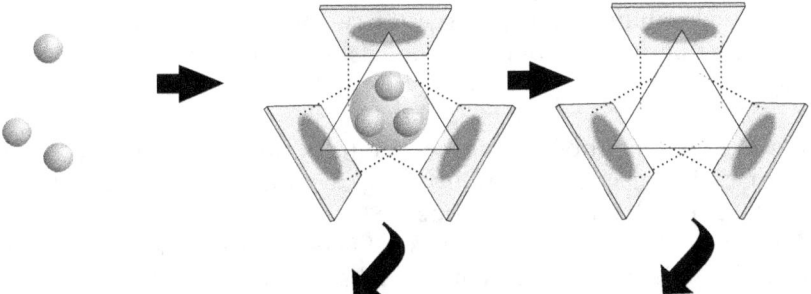

At this step, the result is a model of the particular phenomena of the distinctively human - e.g. a model of free will, consciousness and self.	*At this step, the result is a general model that psychological or anthropological phenomena <u>can</u> be organized in this way. This abstract or general model provides a general picture of the human psyche and of how to build theoretical models of phenomena in the anthropological domain.*

Figure 0.1 *illustrates the MAT-method. It also illustrates the particular project of the present book: (1) to construct a model of free will, consciousness and the self, and (2) on this basis to form a general model of the distinctive features of the human psyche, that is, a basic anthropological model of the capacities by which we are able to maintain the human condition of co-existence.*

general principles underlying the particular taxonomy, or model, one thus arrives at an overall model of the distinctively human psyche. This method is illustrated in Figure 0.1 (the results obtained by applying the method are illustrated in the various figures and taxonomies presented in Chapter 8).

The method of realistic universalism, then, is as follows:

- Certain phenomena are selected (free will, consciousness and the self) ⇒
- Taxonomical models are constructed on the basis of the *characteristics* of these phenomena ⇒

- On the basis of these models, the various characteristics are related to one another, and an overall model, or explanatory taxonomy, of these relations is developed. In this way, one can, from a psychological perspective, identify the overall structure underlying certain selected characteristics of being human ⇒
- Hereby a general model of human intentional connectivity that enables us to participate in maintaining the fundamental human condition of co-existence is constructed, which (1) in itself provides us with knowledge and understanding, and (2) suggests how we might in the future go about constructing further concepts, models and theories about the human psyche.

Overview. This method, and the result in the form of the critical-particularistic-universalistic anthropological model, will gradually unfold throughout the chapters of the book:

Chapter 1 – General psychology is defined as a discipline of psychology, which (1) identifies and conceptualises the general psychological phenomena that constitute the field of psychology, and therefore (2) defines and analyses the science of psychology – especially concerning the general principles of model building and of the relation between empirical and theoretical sciences.

Chapter 2 – briefly presents the concept of anthropological psychology: the sub-discipline of general psychology which can be defined as the science of the human psyche as distinct from other forms of psyche.

Chapter 3 – presents an evolutionary and cultural-historical account of the development of the human condition of co-existence.

Chapter 4 – analyses the different kinds of scientific explanation that can be applied in the construction of scientific theories in general and psychological theories in particular.

Chapter 5 – argues that *free will* is compatible with scientific theories and explanations and that free will can in fact exist as a principle of (animal and human) nature. It is argued that we are not just determined by forces beyond our control, but that we are able to a certain extent to form our own lives and personalities, and that our 'self' consists precisely in this self-organizing power.

Chapter 6 – presents a model of *consciousness*, showing in particular how it emerges into its complete form during the first four or five years of child development.

Chapter 7 – is concerned with creating a model of the human *self*. All three phenomena: free will, consciousness and the self are then combined in an overall taxonomy that demonstrates their interrelationship.

Chapter 8 – presents an overview of the taxonomic relations among the various psychological phenomena presented in the previous chapters. This taxonomy is then analysed as a general anthropological psychological model in its own right. This completes the project of the present book: to construct a model of the distinguishing features of the human capacity to live under and maintain the fundamental human condition of co-existence from a psychological perspective, based on the analysis of selected psychological phenomena of *free will, consciousness and self*.

Chapter 1

What is General Psychology?

The wealth and variety of psychological theories – patchwork or coherence?

The ambiguity of psychology

One may turn to the science of psychology in search of an answer to a specific question, or to learn something more about life in general and what it is to be human. But one is likely to become confused by the rich variety of approaches, theories and traditions that psychology has to offer. One seldom gets an unambiguous answer to one's question – and on the contrary risks becoming even more confused than one was to start with.

Certain theories are hard to reconcile and may even contradict one another outright. Take, for instance, the phenomenon of violence. Ask a psychologist and he or she will tell you that one possible approach to the subject is offered by social psychology. That does not mean, however, that social psychology offers an unambiguous account of what violence is. Certain theories of social psychology will tell you that acts of violence indicate a failure of upbringing – a failure, that is, to turn a given individual into a well-adapted citizen. When a person is violent, something has evidently gone wrong with his/her socialization, such that she/he never sufficiently developed and internalised strong, self-regulating norms of acceptable behaviour. According to this theory, the solution to the problem of violence lies in ensuring good individual upbringing and socialization so that from early childhood individuals are inculcated with a decent set of norms and sound morals. In contrast other theories within social psychology interpret acts of violence as attempts on the part of the violent individual to find a way out of problems which may appear, on the surface, to be her/his problems alone, but which are fundamentally social problems that society has created. According to these theories, then, the problem of violence can be solved by changing the social conditions that give rise to it. Yet a third type of social-psychological theory goes so far as to claim that there is no straightforward or unequivocal way to define what constitutes an act of violence. It all depends on the point of view of the beholder and the circumstances in which the act occurs. For example, giving one's child a beating is today regarded as a form of violence and (in Denmark) is forbidden by law, whereas a few decades ago it was considered an efficient, necessary and even caring, method of upbringing.

But our confusion does not end here – for the above by no means exhausts the theories of violence on offer. On further investigation, one may discover that the phenomenon of violence should not be approached through social psychology at all, but can be better understood through the psychology of learning. Learning theorists argue that the inclination to acts of violence stems from role models experienced in childhood. An individual raised in a violent environment will learn quite simply that violence is an acceptable way of handling certain problems. Still further theories postulate that the phenomenon of violence should rather be understood in terms of biology. Such theories regard violence as a product of 'excess pressure': aggressive drives, so the argument goes, are an essential part of our make-up as biological beings. These drives result in a continuous accumulation of energy which has to be released in one way or another. In the past we found an outlet for this energy in the sheer struggle for survival against the forces of nature. Nowadays, we may find a release for it in playing competitive sports or games or just by grumbling over bad television programmes. But if we get bored or there are insufficient opportunities to channel this excess aggression in acceptable ways, then it will manifest itself in the form of violence – or so it is argued.

So, what is one to believe?

There is still further ground for confusion. For psychology as a science is not confined to a single, unambiguous domain, but extends over at least three different scientific territories. First, psychology is one of the social sciences. As such its task is to investigate how the psyche is grounded in the social surroundings and how, for example, language, norms and identity are developed in interaction with these surroundings and with society. Second, psychology belongs to the natural sciences. Within this domain it investigates how the psyche is grounded in neurophysics and biology. Our mental activity and our consciousness are necessarily grounded in the body in general and the brain in particular, a brain which functions by means of the kind of biochemical and bioelectrical processes described by the natural sciences. Third, psychology extends into the domain of the humanities in so far as it investigates how the psyche is influenced by humanity's cultural and spiritual traditions. Our ways of understanding the world in general and human life as a whole are bound up with the culture in which we grow up. The psyche is shaped by unique and individual cultural events, such as reading a great novel that may offer us new insight or open our eyes for the first time to something we were previously unaware of. An intellectual experience of this kind may change forever one's view of what it is to be human and hence lead to a fundamental change of the self.

As a rule these various theories of human nature are formulated independently, without any attempt being made to link them together.

Thus, on the one hand, psychology can be seen to offer a wealth of approaches to understanding the immense complexity and richness of the human psyche. On the other hand, it may appear an ill-composed patchwork of theories, lacking any internal coherence or overall pattern and, worst of all, unable to provide a single clear, unambiguous, illuminating and explanatory answer to one's original question, and hence to suggest an appropriate course of action.

How does general psychology relate to this ambiguity?

Such ambiguity is of course confusing. Four possible approaches may be taken in addressing it.

The first is to assert that psychology is not a (coherent) science at all. It should be split up into various different sciences, for example, into the three areas mentioned above: the social sciences, the natural sciences and the humanities. This would not be the first time in the history of science that such a thing has occurred. We have seen, for example, how over the centuries theology and philosophy have parted ways and how psychology has separated from both these fields (as well as from other sciences) – thus resulting in three different areas of knowledge relating to human nature and human life.

The second possibility is to accept this 'patchwork' state of affairs as a scientific virtue. It might be argued that psychology never could be a coherent science, for the reality it deals with is by its very nature not a unitary or unified phenomenon, but consists of a multitude of realities. Human consciousness, for example, arguably constitutes a quite different kind of reality from the processes found in the brain. Thus – so the argument goes – it is absurd to believe that neuropsychological theories of consciousness and humanistic psychological theories relating to the same phenomenon could ever become integrated into one coherent theory: each, according to this view, is dealing with its own separate reality.

A third possibility (one that has gained currency in recent years) is to take the view that the science of psychology consists of a large number of independent theories each of which merely expresses its author's personal and cultural outlook on life. Any theory of clinical or personality psychology, such as Freud's psychoanalytic theory, represents first and foremost a personal and cultural endeavour on the part of its author to discover the meaning of existence, to navigate within the culture of his age and to find solutions to problems in his/her personal life. According to this view, psychology is nothing more than a bundle of currently held philosophies of life, views of the human psyche and attitudes towards human social life. Indeed, psychology consists of just as many theories and views as there are human beings, groups, or cultures interested in formulating their thoughts on psychological topics.

This is the viewpoint of constructionism: the view that a psychological theory is a kind of self-sustaining construction. The validity of a given theory is not sustained or constrained by its necessary accordance with reality, since reality is always something other, and far more complex in its structure than we will ever be able to grasp; besides, everything in the last resort depends on the eyes of the beholder. The primary purpose of the various different theories, it is argued, is simply to help us to apprehend the meaning of life and navigate our way through it. Thus the only constraint on a given theory is that it be perceived as meaningful and true by those who have committed themselves to believing in it. The validity of any given theory – so the argument goes – therefore depends only on its internal coherence and on whether it is considered relevant and convincing by those who uphold it.

In this sense, an individual's self and self-conception are not independently existing realities but are constructions shaped by the various theories and views – both scientific and popular – which we put forward about ourselves. The whole thing is quite obvious and straightforward, so it is claimed: without a conception of the self we have no self-conception. Our self-conception consists precisely in our conception of ourselves, or in our theories concerning that self-conception. Hence all theories of the self are in the end self-referential – and the same indeed is true of any psychological theory. None of these theories is required to be 'objectively true', in the sense of correctly depicting some independently existing reality (such as a concept of the self which exists regardless of whether or not it is captured by any current theory). A given theory is required only to be 'subjectively true', in the sense that it is perceived as true and feels right to those who have committed themselves to it.

Since psychological theories are not constrained by any independent 'reality', it follows that anyone – be he/she a researcher, a student or a layman, can collect whatever appeals to him/herself from the abundant literature available and compose a theory to his/her own liking.

Indeed, that is the very reason why there is and should be an abundance of different theories, according to this third view. Psychology cannot and should not be a unitary science, simply because human beings are different and experience things in different ways, and because psychology's mission is precisely to express this living diversity and variety. To standardize psychology, it is claimed, would be to standardize human beings.

A fourth possible conclusion goes as follows. It is true that psychology looks like a bouquet of all kinds of theories and explanations. However, this just goes to show that psychology remains constantly open and flexible in relation to its extremely varied and complex subject matter: namely, human beings and human life. Thus the many disciplines and research methods within psychology are constantly able to generate new insights. But this, it is claimed, need not prevent us from creating a more general and coherent overview. This view is based on the following premises: (1) that psychology is a science, (2) that it is possible to create coherence and unity within psychology so that it can come up with ever more unambiguous and consistent answers to our questions, (3) notwithstanding this ongoing integrative endeavour to create unity and coherence, there will always be a need to adjust this coherent overview as new theories are constantly advanced and new insights gained as a result, and (4) that finally, realism is crucial. In the particular context of psychology, realism can be characterized by the following statements:

- Reality is not just a construct. It exists independently of our theories about it.
- A theory about a particular reality is necessarily either true or false – regardless of whether our present methodological approaches are (yet) able to determine whether it is true or it is false. However, it is possible for different, equally true theories and models about the same piece of reality to exist, since these may focus on different aspects of the same reality. Among several theories and models that are equally true, one model may nevertheless be more effective than another, in so far as it renders the aspects of reality in question more intelligible and corresponds more directly to our intuitive understanding. If the purpose of the model changes, its truth value may also change.
- A's psyche, including A's conception of or theory about him/herself, exists independently of B's possible theory on this matter – and B's theory about A's psyche (and about the human psyche in general) can, in principle, be determined as true or false. The truth value of B's theory, however, does not depend solely on the fact that it is true.
- The development of psychology as a scientific discipline within a culture can (at best) contribute to the development of that culture's self-understanding and of the psyche of the individuals within it. In this sense, psychology changes its object by intervening in its development – or to be more precise, it changes that part of the psyche that is particularly concerned with self-conception and the conception of others. Nevertheless the psyche exists, as we shall see, as a complex and layered

reality, part of which moreover remains unalterable (or not at least alterable purely by theory and discourse).
- Psychology as a scientific discipline cannot be composed or constructed according to personal convenience, but is constrained by the reality of the psyche and hence by truth criteria.

It is this view of psychology – the realist view – that will be defended here. And, as we shall see, the very purpose of general psychology is to make psychology a coherent science.

General psychology in relation to the other disciplines within psychology

The task(s) of general psychology

The task of investigating the nature of psychology and ensuring its coherence as a scientific discipline is undertaken by general psychology whether this is viewed as (1) an independent discipline alongside the other disciplines within psychology (e.g., developmental psychology, clinical psychology, and so on.) or (2) as a discipline practised by any researcher or practitioner to the extent that he/she is concerned with and reflects on his/her knowledge and profession, and on how his/her individual theoretical or professional contribution is connected to psychological knowledge as a whole.

On closer inspection, however, the task of general psychology turns out to be twofold. On the one hand, as we have seen, its purpose is to ensure the coherence of psychology, in part by developing an overall model of the discipline: a metascientific model which shows us the different forms of knowledge created by psychology, and (1) how these forms of knowledge deal with reality, (2) how they have been created, and (3) how together they form a coherent whole. It is this kind of metascientific model of psychology that will be examining in what follows.

On the other hand, further inspection reveals another, albeit closely related task. As we have seen, the various forms of knowledge generated by psychology should ideally be combined into a coherent whole: At any event, it is the purpose of this book to attempt to confirm the hypothesis that such coherence is possible. The precondition for coherence, however, is that all the various branches of the discipline address the same reality: namely, the reality of the psyche or of the psychic in the world. This may sound obvious, and indeed it should be. But it is not self-evident to everybody, certainly not to those who think that reality is not coherent; that there are many 'realities', and that the psychic realm is itself so variable that psychology neither can be, nor should aspire to be, a unitary and unified science. The task of general psychology – and of this book – is thus to defend the view, first, that the psychic represents a single, coherent domain and, second, that this domain is also connected with the rest of the world: meaning, among other things, that our psyche does not exist independently of our brain and body. It is by means of our brain and body that we live, act and experience our existence psychologically within the physical, biological, cultural and social environment.

Whereas the different disciplines, fields of application and theoretical areas within psychology each investigate individual aspects of the psychic domain, general psychology investigates the psychic domain: it identifies the kinds of phenomena that belong to it, and what it means for a given phenomenon to be 'psychic' or 'of the psyche'. To the extent that general psychology succeeds (1) in elucidating the nature of the psychic domain, and (2) in demonstrating its coherence, it will be able to prove that (1) any discipline within psychology deals with the same basic subject-matter, and (2) all the various insights generated by psychology in relation to one or another aspect of this subject-matter therefore can and should be brought coherently together.

Thus general psychology is concerned with the psychic as such: not just with the human psyche, but with anything within the psychic domain, including the kinds of psychic phenomena we encounter in the animal realm, as well as the kinds we may see artificially produced, perhaps a few years from now, by means of digital networks, virtual reality and bio-digital couplings between living organisms and technical artefacts. This book, however, deals first and foremost with the human psyche. In other words, it deals with what is called anthropological psychology – as that branch of general psychology that specifically addresses the human psyche, or the human being seen from a psychic point of view. We will return to this. But in the first instance we will look at general psychology and, in particular, at the meta-scientific model of the various forms of knowledge within psychology.

General psychology and the specific theoretical disciplines

The specific theoretical disciplines within psychology each deal with well-defined particular domains. Cognitive psychology, for example, deals with our perception and awareness, thinking and memory as well as our language. The psychology of personality deals with how our personality is constructed and how it relates to the way we live our lives. Clinical psychology deals with psychic conflicts, personality disorders and psychological dysfunctions. Each of these specific theoretical areas has its own approach, and each of them addresses a more or less narrow aspect of the immensely complex human psyche.

Thus any given theory within one specific field of psychology does not necessarily tell us anything explicit about the conditions within another, nor does it necessarily enrich our common insight by pointing out the ways in which it contributes to, and relates to, our accumulated knowledge in other areas. Great insight might be gained, for example, by endeavouring to relate the knowledge generated by cognitive psychology, concerning our various abilities, to the understanding offered by personality psychology in relation to who we are as persons, and to that offered by clinical psychology in relation to how we manage to stay mentally healthy. Such knowledge-accumulation, however, has never been advanced as a specific aim within the separate fields of psychology; hence the apparent incoherence of psychology as a whole. Moreover, as we saw with the example of how psychology addresses the phenomenon of violence, this lack of coherence is further complicated by the fact that within each discipline we find a number of theories which may not appear immediately compatible.

One task of general psychology, then, is arguably to address this problem by investigating the underlying interconnections between these fields of study, and how the different disciplines within psychology may be brought to communicate with and enrich each other. Whereas specific disciplines of psychology investigate particular, well-defined areas, general psychology examines the possible coherence among these fields by (1) exploring their underlying connections, and (2) making these findings explicit by developing an overall, general picture of the human psyche.

Thus, on the one hand, general psychology is based on the knowledge created within specific areas of research. On the other, it aims to enrich each of these specific areas by organizing them in an interdisciplinary perspective and illuminating their underlying coherence (see Figure 1.1).

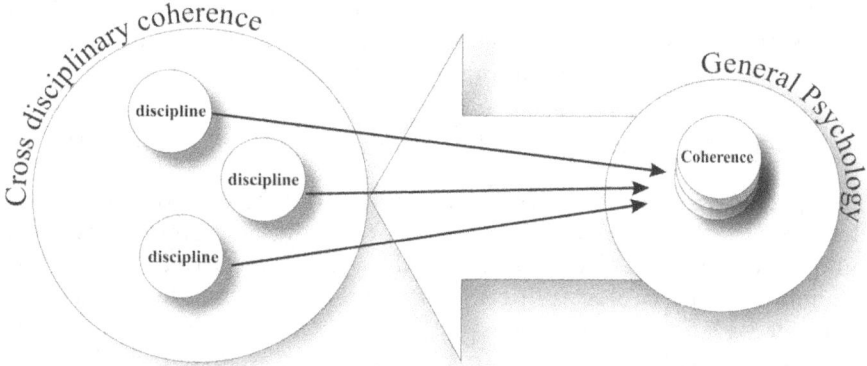

Figure 1.1 *illustrates the interrelation between general psychology and the specific disciplines (small arrows). General psychology is based on the results of the specific disciplines and endeavours to create cross-disciplinary coherence and an overview (big arrow).*

General psychology and the applied disciplines

The applied disciplines within psychology are special disciplines, each of which deals with a specific area of research: such as clinical psychology, pedagogical psychology and organizational psychology. What distinguishes them from the other, purely theoretical branches of psychology is that they have the additional task of developing practical, applicable knowledge which can be used directly by the practicing psychologist. A cognitive psychological model of human memory may be theoretically sophisticated and provide us with a true picture of reality, but it may not therefore be immediately applicable. For the clinical psychologist, however, it is crucial that the knowledge offered can be used, for example, in helping an elderly client to train his/her memory or to develop techniques that may compensate for memory-loss.

Once again we see a form of duality. On the one hand, general psychology is based on knowledge generated through practice, but at the same time, it can contribute to the enrichment of applied psychology by providing a coherent overview of existing knowledge that may function as a theoretical 'eye-opener' for the practising psychologist. General psychology can provide the practising psychologist with new concepts and knowledge that will serve to sharpen his/her sense and understanding of the processes underlying psychological practice, and thus help him/her to make his/her work more effective.

Further attempts at defining the task of general psychology

General psychology can thus be defined as follows: (1) it is concerned with the definition of the psychic realm, (2) it is based on specific theories, including those generated in applied psychology, and helps to set these in a coherent overall perspective, (3) whereas these specific theories relate to particular areas of knowledge, general psychology covers the entire field of psychology, (4) unlike the applied disciplines, general psychology is not concerned first and foremost with developing practically applicable knowledge, and (5) the primary aim of general psychology is to contribute to the development of psychology as a coherent science.

The status of general psychology within psychology and in relation to other sciences: a meta-psychological model

We will now attempt to give a more precise definition of the status of general psychology within the field of psychology as a whole by applying an overall model of psychology as a science.

Two different forms of knowledge

Knowledge provides *theoretical insight* and suggests possible courses of action. Theoretical knowledge enables us to understand and explain (and sometimes predict) why something is the way it is, or why it acts as it does. Useful or practically applicable knowledge enables us to influence, manipulate and change the nature of a given thing or the way in which it functions or behaves. Knowledge which meets the criteria of scientific truth is not necessarily useful; likewise, useful knowledge is not necessarily true. As a hypothetical example, let us say that a man from a non-technological culture may believe that the reason he can create fire by striking one stone against another is that the spirits of the stones are fighting and thus producing sparks. He may even know that it takes certain spirits, in the form of certain stones, to emit sparks. This knowledge may help him in his search for the right kind of stones, and in this sense is undoubtedly useful, but it does not meet the criterion of scientific truth. It is not true that stones are inhabited with spirits of fire, nor is it possible by means of such concepts to reach a deeper understanding/explanation as to why sparks are emitted when one stone strikes another. Yet this kind of concept does make it possible practically to predict what will happen when stones of a certain kind strike one another, and in that sense can be regarded as useful.

Or let us take the example of a body therapist who states that she works on 'harmonizing the psychic energies of the body'. If the client has too much 'energy in his/her head', she may help him/her to 'relocate some of it to other parts of the body'. It may very well be that this kind of terminology helps her to work in ways that are actually useful to her client. It is, however, highly doubtful whether this kind of 'psychic energy' exists as a physical phenomenon.

These considerations show us that various forms of knowledge can be found. Some are purely pragmatic: they serve merely to suggest some effective form of action and in this sense are primarily seen as useful, whether or not they are true in the theoretical sense of the word. Other forms of knowledge, by contrast, are purely theoretical in the sense that the requirement we make of them is that they be true in a theoretical sense, whether or not they are useful or applicable in practice. It could be said that the applied disciplines within psychology – or the applicable elements of the discipline as a whole – represent both forms of knowledge. They are bound to deliver operational knowledge which is neither mere metaphor nor a fumbling, pragmatic attempt at to formulate theory, but which is scientifically valid and based on scientific truth. In Figure 1.2, an attempt is made to illustrate the distinction drawn between scientific/academic knowledge on the one hand (consisting of both the theoretical knowledge generated by the particular disciplines and the applied elements of that knowledge) and, on the other, purely pragmatic knowledge.

What is General Psychology?

Scientific conceptions
- *must be theoretically true, whether useful or not*

Applied scientific conceptions
- *aimed at guiding or determining practical intervention*

Pragmatic conceptions
- *required only to be useful, their truth values are of minor significance*

Figure 1.2 *illustrates the difference between scientific and purely pragmatic forms of knowledge.*

Anchoring tools (DIT)

Regardless of the form in which our concepts, models and theories are presented, they share in common the requirement that, in order to be scientific, they must address some element of reality – they must, in short, be anchored in reality. 'Anchoring' means that our knowledge is not sheer speculation but is about reality and connected with it. 'Knowledge' concerning the number of angels that can stand on the point of a needle is not real knowledge in the sense that it is not concerned with anything real. Anchored knowledge, by contrast, enables us (1) in general to become aware of certain aspects of reality, and (2) to explain and/or intervene in and change these aspects. The process of anchoring is carried out by what one might call Data-Identifying Tools (DIT). Such tools may, for example, take the form of questionnaires, interviews, therapeutic discussions with a client, or laboratory experiments. Each represents a particular way of obtaining basic empirical knowledge, or data, concerning psychic phenomena. The tools identify certain aspects of reality and capture them as data. When our knowledge is based on the data identified and captured by such DITs, it is said to be empirically anchored: that is to say, it is about something and is not just a form of insubstantial speculation on something which may not exist at all (for instance spirits of the fire, angels or 'energies').

Models and hypotheses

Once these data have been collected, the process of knowledge formation proceeds to a draft collation of the material gathered and a preliminary investigation of the patterns and relations which these data appear to reveal. On the basis of the data collected, in other words, an attempt is made to construct a model of that part of reality (for example, some aspect of a client's life) which has been identified and captured by the DITs. A model represents a picture of a small segment of an always far more complex reality: a segment small enough to create a clear and concrete overview of the relations posited. Because these models are necessarily concerned with such small segments, the researcher will often end up with a whole array of models relating to different segments. Let us suppose that one model indicates 'that the client feels trapped in far too narrow a framework in his/her life, and that is why anything he does, and the way he generally relates to other people, seems like an attempt to rebel against and confront these frameworks'. Let us then suppose that another model of the same client indicates 'that the client has a need for security and tries to establish secure and solid frameworks around his life; which is why he goes in constant search of such frameworks, continually trying to establish them for himself – or making other people establish them for him'.

As can been seen, such models may in the first instance appear to contradict one another (although they may in fact be quite easily reconciled within a more general theory, such as, for example, that setting frameworks around oneself serves, for better or worse, to shape one's identity). What is important to notice here, however, is that such apparent contradictions are acceptable at this stage of the process because it is important, at this level of knowledge formation, to relate openly and flexibly to the complex reality one is confronted with, and not jump to conclusions by forming delimited or delimiting theories.

The next stage of the process entails developing, on the basis of the preliminary hypotheses put forward by the different models, a more coherent theoretical explanation for all the various relations which these models suggest ('the client's ambivalent behaviour in relation to 'frames' may be explained by the dual nature of identity formation, which is at once anchored in a strong connection with and attachment to the social environment, and yet secures for the individual a unique personality and personal autonomy').

Gradually, as yet further models of this kind are advanced, they will help clarify the direction which the investigation should take in explaining the domain of reality in question. The models thus provide an overall perspective from which to investigate the given phenomenon. They function, in this sense, as a set of practical hypotheses relating to this phenomenon, which the researcher can test out by selected DITs.

Thus, the process of investigating psychic phenomena involves the creation of hypothetical models. These may be effective in some areas and quite misleading or wrong in others. A more precise picture of the situation can be found in Figure 1.3 (the letters A, B, etc., below all refer to this figure).

(A) The investigation may, for instance, reveal aspects of the human psyche which were not in any way predicted by the model. The researcher will therefore have to extend the model to accommodate these aspects. (B) The human personality may be expressed in ways which precisely accord with the hypothesis – in which case this part of the model/hypothesis will be verified. (C) Some of the assumptions put forward by the model in relation to the human personality may not be verified in practice – they are not a real part of the human psyche. This means that this part of the model is invalid and must be removed. (D) Most parts of the human personality may not be covered by the model at all; nor in any way revealed by the actual investigation or by the Data-Identifying Tools applied. These aspects of the personality cannot be captured by the model in question or by the methods used in collecting data.

The models thus play a dual role in the process of knowledge formation. Seen from one end of the process, their role is to function as hypotheses that direct and determine our DITs. But if we look at the process the other way round, their role is to provide a more elaborate empirical basis on which to develop explanatory theories. In what follows, this dual role will be captured by using the word(s) 'model/hypothesis' in order to emphasize that, one the one hand, this form of knowledge is characterized by models and, on the other, by hypotheses.

The same kind of duality can be seen in the relation between theories and models. Seen from one end of the knowledge formation process, a theory is formed on the basis of the various models put forward about the phenomenon in question. The theory is advanced as an overall explanation for the general patterns and regularities underlying, and expressed by, these models. Seen from the opposite end, however, a theory constitutes the

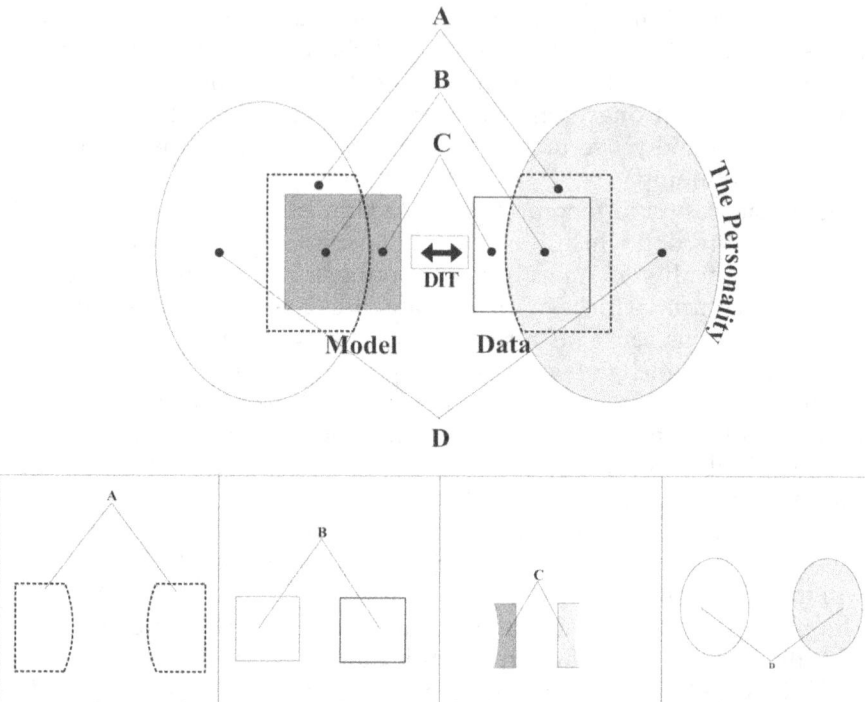

Figure 1.3 *illustrates how the psychologist's model (using DIT) influences and relates to a given aspect of the psychic, e.g., the human personality, and how the personality is thus reflected in certain aspects which may then be considered empirical data. It also shows how the draft version of the model (the dark grey square) will very probably have to be adjusted in some respects to fit the emerging picture of the area of personality in question. These adjustments will finally result in a changed model (the dark grey/broken line A+B) corresponding to the area of personality (the light grey/broken line A+B) from which responses/data have been received.*

overall perspective within which these models are formed as hypotheses about possible relations. A certain theory of identity, for instance, will be made explicit through various hypothetical models as to how identity is actually expressed (alternately as a constricting framework and as a framework that offers stability, security and structure).

Finally, we find the same duality operating between general psychology and the various theories advanced in particular fields. On the one hand, the overview provided by general psychology, and the insights it offers into the psychic realm, are based on the explanations advanced by the various, empirically-anchored theories in each different field. On the other hand, this general overview serves to put the, specific, theoretical and application-oriented research projects undertaken within each field into a larger perspective – indicating the ways in which the researcher may be able to relate his/her particular, detailed study to other areas of research, and present it in a form that will reveal its underlying congruence with other fields of psychology.

This congruence is shown in Figure 1.4.

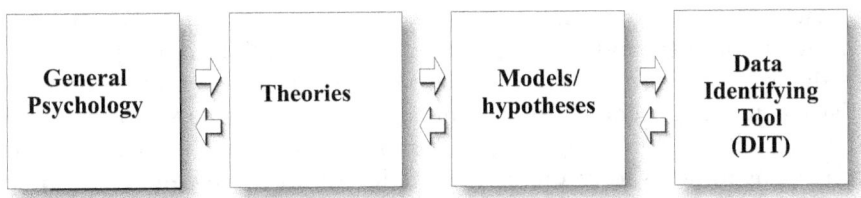

Figure 1.4 *Model of the four main elements of the knowledge-accumulating process.*

Knowledge formation from a pragmatic viewpoint (POM)

Let us take a closer look at knowledge formation from a pragmatic viewpoint. Pragmatic knowledge is the kind of knowledge that is more or less implicitly and tacitly generated by the practising psychologist as his or her clinical experiences and skills develop. Here we are mainly concerned with two levels of concept formation. On the first, empirical level the psychologist forms an immediate and concrete conception of his/her client and of the process which he/she and the client are mutually involved in. In other words, he/she establishes a pragmatic model which serves concretely to direct his/her actions in relation to an actual client. This kind of model may be called a Pragmatic Operative Model (POM).

At the more abstract level, the psychologist forms an overall conception of what psychological practice means in general. This overall conception is often referred to as the psychologist's repertoire or 'tool kit', from which he or she, according to the situation in question, may fetch a suitable tool of intervention or POM.

On the basis of his/her tool of investigation or DIT (interviews, therapeutic sessions, questionnaires, etc.), the practising psychologist forms a specific model/hypothesis of the therapeutic process, interview, consultation, etc., in question and of how it should be conducted. This model/hypothesis then serves to guide the practising psychologist in his/her subsequent actions and interventions in relation to the client. Depending on how the client responds in practice to these interventions, and on the consequent direction which the process takes, the practising psychologist will either be able to confirm that his/her model offers a useful picture of the client and the therapeutic process involved, or will be obliged to discard or adjust the model because the client has taken the process in a direction which renders the psychologist's model irrelevant. Thus the practising psychologist's model has not so far served to generate appropriate actions and interventions, and that the model/hypothesis of the process and the client must therefore be adapted or changed. This is the precise situation illustrated in Figure 1.3.

Each time the practising psychologist develops his/her sense of the therapy in progress and adjusts his/her actual conceptions of the process he or she is involved in, he/she will also be given an opportunity to develop his/her more general view of therapy and of human beings (and him/herself). Thus the psychologist's pragmatically constructed models/hypotheses form the basic material for anchoring and developing his/her general practical repertoire and underlying view of human beings.

On the other hand, it is through the perspective of this general repertoire and view of human beings that the practising psychologist sharpens his/her sense of the particular process with each client and becomes aware of new aspects in the interaction between him/herself and the client. Thus the practising psychologist is able to refine his/her tools of investigation in the light both of general psychology and of his/her own general repertoire, as illustrated in Figure 1.5.

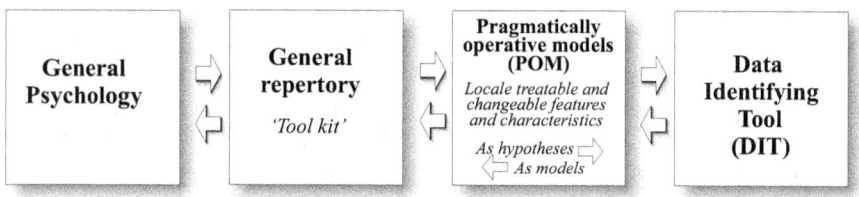

Figure 1.5 *Model of the pragmatic aspect of the knowledge-accumulating process.*

Knowledge formation from a theoretical viewpoint (TOM)

The same considerations, treated above in connection with the pragmatic formation of models and hypotheses, may be equally applied to the formation of theoretical knowledge, in which the emphasis is placed on the scientific truth of a given theory rather than its practical usefulness. Moving in one direction (from empirical data collection to theory) we see that the data collected by means of DITs provide the basis for forming theoretical models of possible relations. These models may then in turn provide the basis for more general, unified theoretical explanations, which, again, are based on the patterns and regularities which have emerged from empirical study of the area in question. Moving in the opposite direction, we see how our theories provide the direction for, and put into broader perspective, the research designs and DITs we develop. It is on the basis of such theories that we put forward hypotheses which can be tested empirically. This kind of hypothesis formation represents precisely the operationalization of these theories: they are, in other words, put into operation through the construction of models of relations which can then be investigated empirically, hence the term Theoretically Operative Models (TOM). On the one hand our data, gathered by means of DITs, will lead us to put forward a TOM that may form the basis for theory development. On the other hand, our theories lead us to put forward TOMs that function as hypotheses, which in turn point to and enable us to choose concrete DITs. See Figure 1.6.

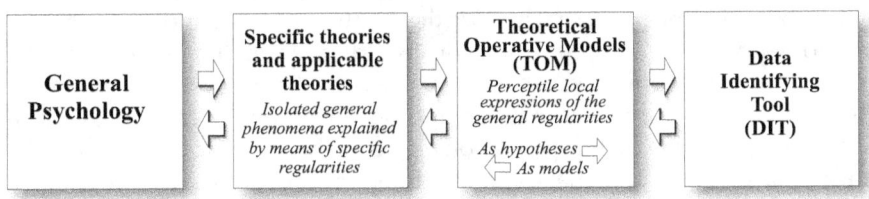

Figure 1.6 *Model of the theoretical aspect of the knowledge-accumulating process.*

Theory, general repertoire and general psychology

The general practical repertoire of the therapist or consultant is based on the overall notion that there are aspects of the human being and his/her life which are susceptible to treatment and can be changed in practice. As we saw in the introduction to this chapter, psychology offers a wealth of such application-oriented ideas. Clinical psychology, for example, offers numerous different theories as to which aspects of the human being can/should/ought to be treated; likewise organizational psychology has a multitude of ideas as to which aspects of organizations, and of the human relations underlying them, can and should be addressed. Together, these ideas from the various branches of applied psychology offer a multi-faceted picture of those features of the human being that are in general susceptible to treatment; not necessarily treatment of the kind that is applied to illnesses, but treatment in the sense of actions and interventions which influence the life of a human being and will result in change.

Just as psychology offers a great array of application-oriented theories, so too it offers a multitude of special theories, each of which undertakes to provide a general explanation for one or other aspect of human nature or human life. Thus each of these special theories identifies and explains a general human phenomenon.

Together this variegated bundle of application-oriented repertoires and special theories forms the basis for a more coherent conception of the human being and human life. By extracting what these theories and repertoires tell us in common about the underlying laws of human life, and about what aspects of the human being are susceptible to treatment, we can form the basis for a more integrated general psychological concept of the human being and of human life.

Methodical reducibility, ontological irreducibility

Each model, each theory and each discipline approaches the overall object, the human psyche, from its own perspective, and grasps different aspects of it. This is bound to be the case when we deal with a complex and multi-faceted phenomenon. No specific research project, or scientific theory, or practical method of intervention can cover every aspect. This is true not only for psychology, but for any science. The world is always far more complicated, rich and varied than can be grasped by one specific theory or, for that matter, by any one science. We then make a methodological virtue out of acknowledging the abundant variety and inexhaustibility of the world, and respectfully admitting that our models and theories will never grasp more than certain aspects of this complexity, and that this is exactly what they are meant to do. We make a virtue, in other words, of the fact that our models and theories are methodologically reductionist, and try as best we can to identify the ways in which they are so, and which (few) aspects of the whole they focus on.

It is therefore important at this juncture to point out that this necessary methodological reductionism does not entail an ontological reductionism. Although we are obliged, within a specific discipline, to approach reality (in this case the psychic domain) by relating to a specific aspect of it, this does not of course imply that the entire domain consists of this one aspect. To take one example, neuropsychology (in common, for instance, with personality psychology or social psychology) adopts a methodologically reductionist approach, and is indeed obliged to do so. But it would be foolish purely on this basis to claim, as ontological reductionists do, that the psyche *is nothing but* those processes of the brain that neuropsychology makes manifest. One should not confuse one's own field of research with the entire world.

Concluding methodical considerations concerning general psychology

The precondition for (1) rendering the various forms of our knowledge coherent, and (2) enabling the true insights produced by theoretical research, and the useful repertories of the practising psychologist, to be productively combined, can be described as follows:

- both theoretical concepts, and those generated in applied psychology, should be validated by the same kind of anchoring process, that is, by using the same anchoring tools (DIT)
- this fundamental empirical anchoring must take place within the same overall perspective: it must be directed by the same basic view of the human being and by the same paradigmatic approach towards the actual content and direction of scientific, psychological work.

These conditions of psychological research can now be put together in Figure 1.7, which illustrates an overall meta-psychological model. Such a

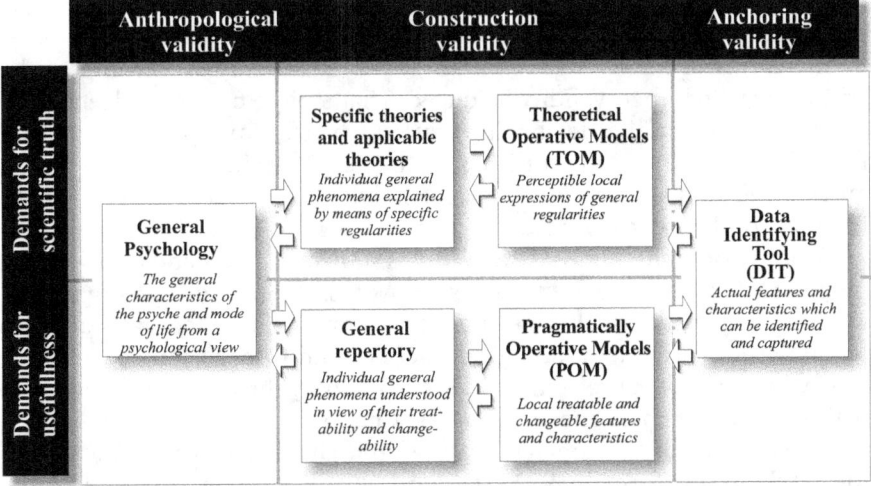

Figure 1.7 *To the farthest right of the figure we see the most purely empirical form of knowledge, the data identifying tool (DIT). Just to the left of the data-identifying tool we find the models which can be formed on the basis of the data collected. Seen from right to left these form the basis for the development of theories. Seen from left to right they represent hypotheses which can be tested by means of empirical investigation. Next to the models we find the specific theories and application-oriented theories. Each of these theories explains an individual/separate aspect of the human. Farthest to the left we find the general and overall picture of the distinctive human constructed by general psychology. In the figure, the different forms of knowledge have thus been arranged according to purpose c, whether they are designed to meet the requirement of usefulness or of truth, and according to the criteria by which their validity is judged.*

model can in the first place provide us with an overview of the different forms of knowledge described above; and, second, provide us with a dynamic research model showing the different ways in which these forms of knowledge are created.

In Figure 1.7, the various forms of knowledge are arranged vertically according to whether the requirement of truth or of usefulness has been paramount in their development. The point of the model is to show that the level closest to empirical methods – the tool of investigation – as well as the level which is most distant and abstract – general psychology and its view of human beings and science – are in each case subject both to the demand for truth and to the demand for usefulness. Figure 1.7 illustrates how general psychology and DITs (vertically) embrace both areas: that of usefulness as well as that of truth. By contrast, the special theories, the application-oriented theories and the theoretically operative models and hypotheses must be true, but are not necessarily useful, while the general repertoire and the concrete, pragmatically operative models and hypotheses of the practising psychologist must be useful, but not necessarily true.

The forms of knowledge are arranged (horizontally) according to the criteria by which their validity is judged. That a piece of knowledge is valid means that it actually deals with that which it claims to deal with. The firemaker's concept of 'fire spirits' is, in this sense, pragmatically valid (in so far as it makes claims about a practice in which fire is actually produced); but it is not theoretically valid.

The development of the research tool is subject to a demand for what one might call 'anchoring validity'. In other words, the tool of investigation is required to reveal to us those elements of human nature that we want it to reveal. The decisive methodological test of our knowledge at this level – the level which is most purely empirical – is posed by the question: do we – in reality – find the phenomena we are looking for by means of our tools?

On the basis of the concrete features and characteristics we are able to identify, we can form hypotheses/models which reveal the underlying patterns that emerge among them. At this level of model formation, the requirement made of the methods used is generally called a demand for construction validity, meaning that the theory and model must be constructed on the basis of the collected data and the possible, coherent patterns revealed by them. The decisive test of our knowledge at this level is posed by the following question: is it possible to develop our empirical knowledge, data models and tools of investigation to a higher level of abstraction, offering an explanation of the implicit relations between, and underlying, the features we have identified?

Here the object in question is conceptualised (1) by its general regularities, as expressed by the illustrative models and hypotheses, and (2) by its susceptibility to treatment/change and the laws by which it can be explained.

Finally, these theoretical and pragmatic constructions are joined within general psychology, which constructs an overall, unifying, picture of the most general, empirically anchored insights within the psychic domain. The decisive test of our knowledge at this level is posed by the question: is it possible to join up the various psychological models, the more general theories and the practical repertoires, and can they contribute to our higher-level overall conception of the psychic and the science of psychology?

General psychology and internal and external compatibility

Thus the enterprise of general psychology to establish whether psychology is a science at all, and whether, if so, it can be made coherent, leads us to investigate whether psychological theories meet the following demands:

- *Empirically anchored*. Any theory within psychology must be subject to the demand for scientific truth, must be empirically verifiable, or its hypotheses must be testable, at least in principle, to see if they accord with (correspond to) reality.
- *Realism*. The underlying basis for this demand requires that any (scientific) statement about the world can in principle (though not always in practice) be identified as true or false.
- *Coherence*. Two different scientific theories about the same phenomenon cannot both be true yet contradict each other. Scientific approaches to the same phenomenon must be coherent.
- *Internal compatibility*. One demand that is not often made (and very rarely met), but still closely connected to the other two requirements, is that specific, methodologically reduced theories about the same ontologically irreducible piece of reality must be *compatible*. This means that the various special theories must be formed and formulated in such a way that (1) their coherence or incoherence can in principle be established, and (2) that they can mutually enrich each other by offering their different insights into the same phenomenon.
- *External compatibility*. To the requirement of internal compatibility may be added an interdisciplinary demand for *external compatibility* – a demand which is even more rarely put forward. It is based on the fact that the principles of methodological reducibility and ontological irreducibility apply not only to psychology and its approach to the psychic and human nature, but underlie all the various disciplines relating to human life: medicine, biology, social science, history, ethnography, theology, and so on. In fact, each of these scientific approaches in itself represents only one perspective on human nature. Even the most general theoretical formulations offered by each science provide only one, epistemologically reduced view of the ontologically irreducible human being.

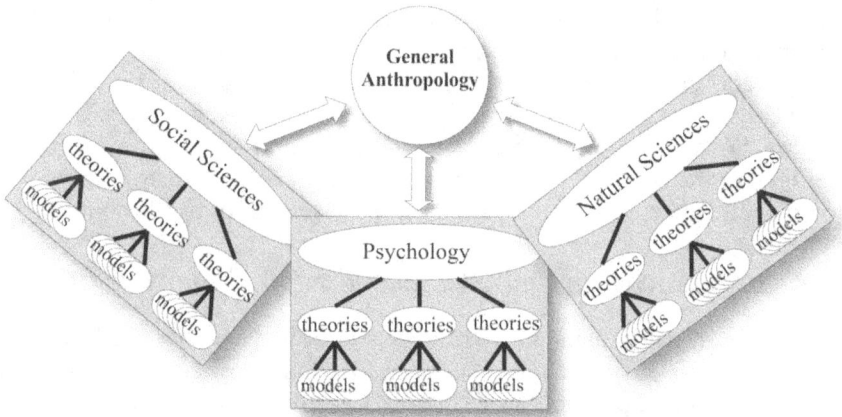

Figure 1.8 *The white double arrows illustrate that each of the different sciences contribute to a joint scientific conception of the human being.*

Thus it is evident that it would promote our interdisciplinary understanding of the human conditions and possibilities, and the accumulation of a unified body of knowledge on the subject, if each science had a general theory (general psychology, general medicine, etc.) which (1) attended to the internal compatibility of its own theories and thereby constructed a general theoretical conception of the human within the science in question (based on its particular perspective and those aspects of human life which constitute its field of study), and (2) endeavoured to formulate these general insights so that they were rendered comparable with and able to enrich and be enriched by other general theoretical concepts of human life within the other sciences. In short, it would be advantageous to formulate the general theories so that they would ensure external compatibility with other scientific approaches to the human.

In the light of the concepts of internal and external compatibility, general psychology can now be placed within a wider landscape encompassing many different domains of science, as illustrated in Figure 1.8.

Interdisciplinary science, general anthropology and general psychology

The above reflections lead us to how the anthropological domain can and should be researched interdisciplinarily.

The anthropological domain should be explored from various scientific perspectives. Each of these specific sciences are defined by their own set of methodological approaches, their own set of epistemological interests and their own set of practical tasks, which they are to help solve.

Each of them bases these specific sciences on a number of decentralized growth layers. Growth layers which are different because they have different tasks, interests and methods – and therefore look at the same domain from different perspectives. That they are decentralized and have different tasks means that one science does not present theoretical explanations and pragmatic directions of action that are immediately transferable to another. Or we cannot from the position of one science direct what should be the current explanation and pragmatic task solving in another science.

So the individual sciences do not 'disappear' in such an interdisciplinary project. On the contrary, they preserve their identity which is founded in the special perspective's interests of cognition and the special practical set of tasks. This marks each their angle of approach. Through the different approaches the individual science can show us aspects of the anthropological domain, which another science has not yet grasped, but should be able to approach. Thereby, the different specialized sciences mutually help each other to increasing insight of the anthropological domain.

The precondition is that the scientific work in these decentralized growth layers is made compatible. Only on that basis can a common general

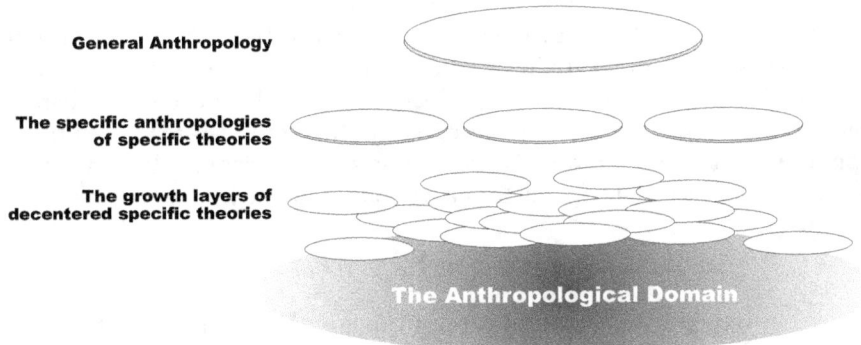

Figure 1.9 *An interdisciplinary model of the scientific examination of the anthropological domain. The decentralized special scientific growth layers are each given by their epistemological interest and each their practical tasks within the anthropological domain. Via internal and external compatibilities they constitute the respective special sciences' general anthropological models, which can then again be constitutive in a general anthropology. This general anthropology can, via a common general set of epistemological interests and task-solving strategies, have an organizing effect on the special sciences' anthropologies and the decentralized growth layers.*

anthropology be developed. This general anthropology can be shaped as a basic anthropological model, which bottom-up is constituted by these decentralized growth layers. This basic anthropological model is itself realistically scientific because it relates to the domain, on which the decentralized, constitutive sciences each focus. Looking top-down it is organizing, which means that on the basis of general common tasks, interests and methods, it provides a theoretical insight into each of the growth layers.

In this interdisciplinary view, general psychology is to be understood as the connecting link between particular psychological approaches to the anthropological domain and general anthropology. For this see Figure 1.9.

Accumulated definition of general psychology

The rich variety of psychology

We have now reached the end of Chapter 1. Considering the multitude of approaches, branches and viewpoints offered by psychology, it can be positively characterized by its openness and flexibility towards a rich and complex object area. The task of general psychology is to form an overall view of this immense and innovative scientific universe as it continues to emerge. General psychology depends on, and draws material from, its extremely extensive and varied domains, and can never therefore be a reductionist project which seeks to dismiss certain approaches or narrow down this vivid and fecund scientific field. Rather than despair over this 'chaotic' and incoherent science, general psychology must recognise in this multi-faceted domain the opportunity, not to get trapped in closed and narrow scientific doctrines, but, on the contrary, to relate openly to the complexity of the human psyche.

The task of general psychology

More precisely, general psychology can be defined as the area of psychology which deals with the coherence of psychology internally as a science through studying the general and universal aspects of the human psyche, and which endeavours externally to formulate psychology's relation to the other sciences relating to human life in an endeavour to promote our joint accumulation of knowledge.

To the extent that general psychology, as we have argued, is anchored both empirically and practically in reality (see the above statements as summarized in Figure 1.7), the task of general psychology must be undertaken, not in an insubstantial and speculative way, but, on the contrary, through the use of sound scientific methods.

Chapter 2

What is Anthropological Psychology?

Anthropological psychology in relation to general psychology

The object of general psychology is to investigate what it means to say that a given phenomenon is psychic; to identify, in other words, those characteristics which distinguish psychic phenomena from those that are non-psychic. One area within general psychology deals in particular with the human psyche and with those features that distinguish it; on the one hand from artificially produced (or, for that matter, potential extraterrestrial) psyches, and, on the other, from the animal psyche at all levels – from primitive early forms to the highly advanced mammals and primates, such as the bonobos whose psyches closely resemble our own.

Any endeavour to develop descriptive models and explanatory theories about those characteristics that distinguish us as human beings can be said to belong to the field of anthropology – insofar as anthropology is understood as the science of the specifically human. Anthropological enquiries can in this sense be found within different disciplines. The anthropological elements within a given discipline deal with the human characteristics from the particular perspective of that discipline. For instance, anthropological biology is concerned with human biology, and anthropological philosophy is concerned with those areas within philosophy which pertain specifically to human beings – in the fields of ethics, philosophy of life, and so on. Anthropological psychology looks at the human being from a psychological perspective. The task of anthropological psychology is precisely to solve the most fundamental questions of general psychology – what is the psyche and is psychology a coherent science at all? – by endeavouring to develop theoretical models of human nature and human life from a psychological perspective.

In addition to being defined by its object – the specific characteristics of the human psyche – anthropological psychology can also be defined by its method. To a great extent anthropological psychology seeks to understand the object in a historical perspective; as we will see, its approach is also cross-disciplinary (in the sense that it involves different branches of psychology) and interdisciplinary (in the sense that it relates to other sciences which similarly endeavour to define what it is to be human). Finally, anthropological psychology is methodologically pluralistic: drawing, in other words, on a large number of different methods.

In the version of anthropological psychology presented here, however, the main common feature of these methods is that they are historical/processual as distinct from essentialistic.

The historical dimensions

The historical perspective

To take an historical approach to a given phenomenon means to seek to identify, to describe and to explain theoretically how this phenomenon has developed over time. In contrast to an essentialistic approach, which sees the phenomenon in question as given or created once and for all and essentially unchangeable, the historical approach assumes that the essence of the phenomenon will continuously change and develop. One example of this approach is the theory of evolution, which argues that a given animal species does not have an immutable essence, but is subject to constant change and evolutionary development as it continuously adapts to its environment. Reindeer, for instance, are descendants of mammals which bore very little resemblance to the reindeer we know today. These prehistoric mammals in turn were descended from the reptiles, which themselves were descended from fish that lived in coastal waters and were able occasionally to crawl onto land, moving around by means of specially developed fins which would later develop into terrestrial animals' legs and even birds' wings. If the evolutionary processes are left undisturbed (without any interference, that is, from human beings – probably a utopian prospect these days), the reindeer, as we know it today, will no doubt develop into an animal species which will have very few essential features in common with our reindeer, and in due course none at all.

Similar reflections arise if we consider the evolutionary development of mankind (we will return to this topic in the chapters that follow). Seen in a historical perspective, the essence of mankind was not 'given' once and for all, but has changed over time. Biologically as well as psychologically, the evolution of man took place in three major stages: from the mammals to the primates and then to the early hominids, bipeds who moved around the African savannah approximately four million years ago. From there the line split into various different branches, one of them resulting in the early Homo sapiens, a species which then developed into a rich diversity of races spread over more or less all continents.

As we have suggested, it is not only biological phenomena that gradually emerge and are subject to change. The same applies to cultural phenomena: they too are not 'given' and unchangeable but develop gradually into phenomena that bear very little resemblance to those from which they originated. For instance, the set of daily routines practised by a group of human beings in prehistoric times – a tribe or a group in some settlement, let us say – may originally have been carried out on the inclination of one particular individual, attuned though this may have been with the activities of the other individuals in the group. Gradually, such routines become habits: they are carried out in the same way over and over again. In turn, these habitual forms of behaviour may develop into norms, in the sense that an individual would attract attention if he or she failed to follow the habitual pattern. In other words these routines, which could previously be explained in terms of the individual's internal inclination to do things in a certain way (as opposed to his/her externally attuned inclination to conform to a certain pattern), should now rather be explained in reverse, in so far as these particular routines are now carried out as a result of established external norms. Here, then, is a small instance of a cultural-historical development in which both a given phenomenon – routine – and the dynamics which account for it, develop and are qualitatively modified.

In time, many of these norm-based routines may come together to form a cooperative system of division of labour. Within such a system, normative forms of action solidify into established institutions – religious, socio-economic, administrative and so on. An institution, in this sense, represents more than simply a set of norms guiding the routines of daily life. It serves, over and above this, to bind together the myriad routines and activities of daily life that are part of what characterises human life. Again, the historical perspective shows us how a purely essentialistic view – that human nature is given and immutable – misses the point. The emergence of a particular institution, for example, may have its origins in the inclination of various individuals to honour or to demonstrate their respect for other, more powerful figures within their community and to provide for the weaker members of the group – the young, the sick, the old. This inclination gradually develops into a normative expectation that the community will behave in certain particular ways: that weaker individuals will be properly cared for; that certain members of the group will be honoured and respected; that ritualised funerals will be carried out, and so on; and these practices, alongside others, will together develop into a religious institution, determining the community's overall discourse as to how individuals can/should/must live their social life, and how they can/should/must reflect upon it.

On the psychological level, as well, we see how certain phenomena develop. If we look at the development of different animal species, we will find, for instance, that the cognitive capacity for spatio-temporal directedness is not a given quality established once and for all in this or that species. Seen from an evolutionary perspective, the ability to direct oneself in space and time must have been more important to mammals living in the eco-niche at the top of a tree than to snails creeping along the ground (to mention just two extremes). We must also assume that the capacity for spatio-temporal directedness among primates living in the woods was brought to the savannah by the first hominids. In the savannah, these cognitive capacities enabled the hominids to form 'cognitive maps' of the landscapes they traversed: noting where the good, berry-bearing shrubs were to be found and in which season they bore fruit; and recording places in which to sleep and rest, to eat and gather food, safe – or relatively safe – from beasts of prey. Further, we may assume that these cognitive capacities formed part of the basis on which the early human beings also began to understand their personal and family relations. Such capacities allowed them to memorize for themselves, and between themselves, who was related to whom, who was indebted to whom, and so on. Again we see a developmental, historical relation between the simpler and the far more developed cognitive phenomena, even where the latter bear very little 'essential resemblance' to the former.

As we can see from the examples above, any historically developed phenomenon (be it biological, cultural or psychological) is based upon earlier forms. These forms are constituent parts of the developed phenomenon: that is, they form the basis upon which the newer and more advanced forms have developed – a basis these forms depend on and without which they cannot exist. Ultimately, a specific socio-cultural institution, such as that administering, for example, the Mesopotamian city-state's irrigation system (determining where ditches needed to be dug between the river and the fields, when they should be opened, to whom the water should be allocated and when, and so on) is based on the already-established routines of daily life (the cultivation of land, the digging of ditches, etc.). Without these constituent routines the overall administrative institutions would not exist at all. On the other hand, these constituent routines and daily activities cease, in the process, to be based merely on the inclinations of particular individuals, but are unified and organized by the institution. The practical routines which individuals carry out in their daily lives – routines which indeed support and maintain human life – are initiated, formed and directed at goals in ways which cannot be sufficiently explained merely by looking at each individual's biological or psychological make-up and inherent abilities. To account for the human urge to initiate and coordinate the myriad activities within a cooperative, division-of-labour society, in order to form a community with a unified social and cultural life, and to explain the ways in which this process comes about, we need to look beyond the level of individual action to the level of the institution. In other words, a theoretical explanation must draw upon those very principles of organization that came into existence with the emergence of the institution itself.

The same reasoning can be applied to psychological phenomena. The individual is able to navigate and manoeuvre within his/her social environment because he/she has the psychic capacity to identify and recall the various relationships implied by kin, community, cooperative labour and economic commitments that define his/her social landscape. This ability is constituted by cognitive phenomena such as memory and the capacity for spatio-temporal directedness (the ability, broadly speaking, to locate oneself in space and time and within a network of social events and relationships). At the same time, the individual's ability to navigate and manoeuvre socially cannot be explained solely in terms of these constituent abilities and the laws that govern them. Any explanation must take into account the overall social life (including the institutionalised life) which organizes these constituents. For the individual's constituent abilities are formed and developed through practice, as he/she uses them in the service of specific social goals; and they are organized according to principles to be found not at the level of individual psychology, but at the level of social consciousness and socially-formed life projects.

Thus the historical perspective must also include a conception of the mutual relationship between the constituent parts and their organization. More advanced forms are characterized by the fact that they have, on the one hand, developed from and are constituted by more elementary forms; but on the other, they differ from these constituent forms in so far as they have developed their own organizational principles, uniting and organizing the constituents to create higher-level entities – as when all sorts of daily activities are united and organized in institutions.

This conception of the mutual relationship between constitution and organization is fundamental to the anthropological model of human nature and human life which we will elaborate in the chapters that follow. In Chapter 4, we will see how this concept of constitution/organization is central to the historical approach; and we will use it (in Chapter 3) to illustrate the evolution of specifically human qualities, looking specifically at free will (Chapter 5), consciousness (Chapter 6) and the self (Chapter 7).

There are three dimensions to the historical approach in anthropological psychology, relating respectively to natural history, cultural history and life

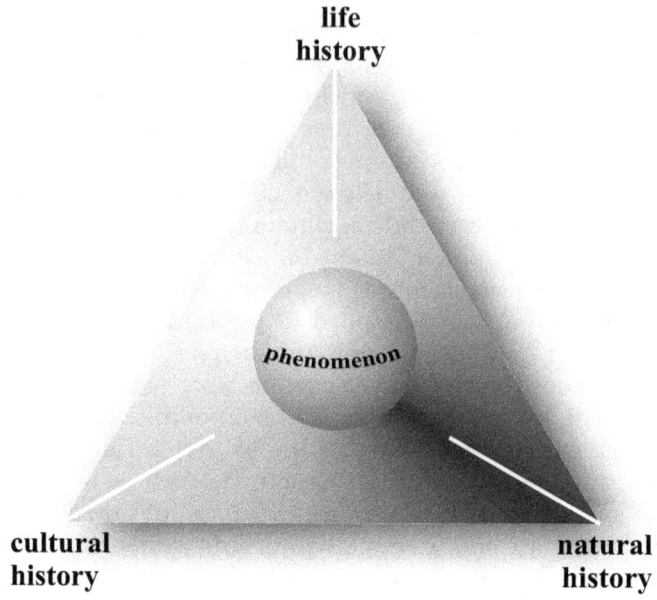

Figure 2.1 *illustrates the three anthropological-psychological approaches to the basic and universal human phenomena.*

history: Any human psychological phenomenon must be understood from all three perspectives; for, as illustrated in Figure 2.1, a complete theoretical explanation of the phenomenon requires all three explanatory dimensions.

The natural history approach

To look at human characteristics from the perspective of natural history is to consider the ways in which our nature as human beings, including our potential for development, relates to, or is determined by, our basic physical and biological constitution. We cannot ignore the (at least present) fact that the way we are, and the way we experience and relate to the world, is at least partially determined – and limited – by the immanent potential of our biological bodies (and not only by the brain, as brain researchers like to tell us, but by the entire body, including its capacities for relating and acting). But over and above our investigation of the role played by the biological organism in determining our human characteristics, we look, from this perspective, at the evolutionary development of those characteristics: at the ways in which our nature as human beings relates to the fact that we are also mammals, and, even more fundamentally, to the fact that we are biological, not artificial, creatures. In the future general and anthropological psychology will doubtless have to take into account our increasing ability to alter and tamper with our fundamental biology – genetically as well as 'bio-digitally' – and consider the implications of this – for better or for worse – for our development.

The cultural history approach

To look at human characteristics from the perspective of cultural history, is to consider the ways in which culture both sets the boundaries, and provides the opportunities, for human development. From this perspective, in other words, we look at how culture has influenced our development historically, and how cultural changes may in the future affect our course as human beings. The cultural perspective also takes into account the similarities and differences in the ways in which fundamental human characteristics are expressed within different cultures, at different times and in different places in the world. The aim is thus also to distinguish between those phenomena that are particular to a certain culture or a certain historical epoch, and those that are universal: that is, characteristic of all human beings, irrespective of the particular cultures or times in which they are raised.

Thus, on the one hand, the historical approach deals with our constitutions as socio-cultural beings in the widest sense. All over the world, for instance, the viability of a culture depends on the prosocial behaviour of individuals – for example, on their willingness and ability to keep a promise. Even the most militant and individualistic culture (not only the military cultures of the past, but also, for example, the urban culture of America as manifested in the offices and corridors of lawyers' firms) would perish if there were no mutual trust that the alliances and deals one entered into would be honoured by partners or opponents. We can thus assume that this willingness to keep promises, and other forms of prosocial behaviour, are a part of our cultural-historical constitution. If we go one step further and look at how democratic cultures function, we may describe this prosocial constitution in terms similar to those of Habermas' universal pragmatics: One must speak the truth (especially with regard to promises and agreements), one must be authentic, and one must act responsibly and decently towards one another.

These universal principles of behaviour (universal at least as far as democracies are concerned) may nevertheless be expressed in very different ways within different cultural and subcultural discourses as to what constitutes the good life. For example, these universal principles will be embedded in a very different form of cultural life depending on whether one lives in a local community in the far north of Norway or among politicians in Berlin. The fundamental cultural-historical question, however, is how to define the relationship between the constituent parts – the fundamental principles of behaviour, in this case – and their organization within a particular setting. Is the relationship such as to let us argue that human beings are fundamentally alike, and that the cultural differences are insignificant ripples on the surface of this basic similarity? Or is the relationship such as to force us to acknowledge that human beings differ so greatly in terms of their cultural discourses, and in terms of the socio-cultural and institutional frameworks in which they live, that universal human characteristics, in so far as they exist, may be virtually left out of account, since they evidently play so little explanatory role in our understanding of human behaviour?

The life history approach

This approach deals, in the first instance, with the ways in which the particular life history of a given individual shapes his/her being and development. In particular, it deals with the way in which each individual, by means of his/her life history, develops into a reflexive personality with the capacity to make choices and exercise free will: a personality, in other words, that demonstrates not only re-active forms of action and behaviour, initiated in response to external influences, demands and requirements, but that, on the contrary, leads a proactive and prosocial life of its own, based on the personal organization of its natural-historical and cultural-historical constitution. How, in other words, does the individual, as a result of his/her life history, develop into a person who has a life project and who feels morally and socially committed to the fellow human beings that surround him/her (whether at the immediate personal level or at the level of social institutions). This life history approach means looking backwards as well as forwards: on the one hand uncovering retrospectively the particular developmental forces and opportunities that have shaped the individual's personality, and on the other investigating the ways in which the individual's present circumstances and opportunities may shape his/her future life and development as a personality.

Cross-disciplinarity, interdisciplinarity and methodological pluralism

As we discussed in detail in Chapter 1, general psychology must be (1) cross-disciplinary, in the sense that it is based on the psychological insights offered by all the different disciplines within psychology; it must be (2) interdisciplinary in the sense that it is based on the insights concerning the human psyche, its interaction with the environment, and the conditions in which it operates which are offered by related sciences, and, finally – in view of (1) and (2) – it must be (3) methodologically pluralistic, basing its insights on the variety of empirical methods and explanatory models found both within the different disciplines of psychology and within the various related sciences.

Obviously, this applies to anthropological psychology too, in so far as it represents a part of general psychology. Thus our insights into the specificities of the human psyche derive from all the disciplines of psychology. To mention only one example: organizational psychology may tell us something about how the different organizational structures within which the human being lives his/her productive and active life may shape our development as human beings and influence our behaviour. At the same time, anthropological psychology must endeavour to present organizational psychology with a unifying and relevant picture of the human psyche: one that identifies and describes the fundamental capacities of human individuals to enter into, sustain and innovatively contribute to the organizations they are involved in.

As we also emphasized in Chapter 1, this endeavour, on the part of anthropological psychology, to offer unifying explanations is not an attempt to 'occupy' the various disciplines within psychology. On the contrary, anthropological psychology concerns those general conceptions and fundamental explanatory models which researchers themselves form within their own disciplines, and use as the basis on which to build their theories. Secondly, it concerns those conceptions that arise between the disciplines, since the different disciplines may profit from each other's insights concerning a given phenomenon. One example of this may be seen in the mutual, cross-disciplinary effort to develop cumulative knowledge based on insights drawn from both social psychology, with its focus on the social interactions of individuals, and personality psychology, with its focus on the individual's reasons for action.

Similarly, anthropological psychology is bound to be interdisciplinary in the sense that it can so evidently profit from, and contribute to, the ways in which the various sciences identify and explain the different characteristics that identify us as human beings.

In the chapters that follow, this historical, cross-disciplinary, interdisciplinary and methodologically pluralistic approach will be presented and applied in an endeavour to form a general taxonomy of concepts and theories regarding the defining characteristics of human beings as seen from a psychological perspective. We will look at these characteristics in general, and at certain selected phenomena: *free will, consciousness* and *the self*, from the three perspectives outlined above: those of natural history, cultural history and life history. We will also approach the subject from the perspective of a number of disciplines within our field – first and foremost social psychology, personality psychology, cognitive psychology and developmental psychology.

Chapter 3

The Distinguishing Traits of Human Beings Seen From the Perspective of Natural and Cultural History

How did the modern state of human consciousness – including free will and the capacity for self-awareness – come into being? The basic questions is: How do new species evolve? How did mankind evolve? And how did the distinguishing traits and characteristics of our species develop? Evolutionary theory tells us that new species evolve as a result of new forms of biological interaction between organisms and their environment. These interactions or modes of life may change as a result of changes either in the organism itself, or the environment, or both: (1) Genetic mutations may occur and be present among a proportion of a population, altering both the anatomy and the behaviour of certain individuals of a species. Under changed environmental conditions, such variation may confer an advantage to these individuals enabling them to enter into new interactions with the environment, thereby ensuring they live both sufficiently long, and sufficiently well, to reproduce themselves, i.e., pass on their advantageous genes to the ensuing generations. (2) The environment may change in ways that call for new anatomy and new behaviour if a given species is to survive. The individual members of a species will always differ to some degree; and those individuals which, because of their particular anatomy and behaviour, are best able to adapt to the gradually changing environment, will tend to live longer and healthier lives and thus be in a better position to reproduce. Thus it will be primarily their genetic material that gets passed on. In this way the species as a whole will gradually change in tandem with the environment. Changes of this kind may occur, for instance, when climatic changes – such as those which happened at the beginning and end of the Ice Age – bring about alterations in the ecology of the area where the species lives. New modes of life may also arise as a result of changes in the mixture of species within the local ecology – thus, smaller animals or plants that had previously constituted the species' food may disappear, or dangerous new predators may come to inhabit the area.

Between five and ten million years ago, climatic changes in Africa had (according to one theory) a crucial impact on some of the ape species living at that time, as the dense forests which they had formerly inhabited gave way to open woodlands and steppe. In this new environment the food consisted primarily of berries from shrubs of various heights, and the fresh leaves and top shoots of shrubs and small trees. In order to survive, it was necessary to gather and eat large quantities of this kind of food. Thus it became an advantage to be able to walk at an even pace while picking berries, gathering them in the hand and eating as one went – in other words, to be able to forage. Alternative kinds of food were provided by occasional fresh carrion and small animals. As we have indicated, evolutionary theory tells us that a given species will always be affected by the pressure of natural selection: those individuals that are optimally adapted to the environment, in terms of their anatomy and behaviour, will be in the best position to reproduce and hence pass on their genes. In the example above, we saw how certain species of ape were forced into a foraging mode of life in the open savannah. As a result of natural selection, the genes of those who were best able, in terms of anatomy, to walk upright and hence keep their arms and hands free to gather and carry berries, leaves and carrion became dominant: thus the ability to walk upright became a characteristic of the species as a whole. This change to an upright posture that freed the hands for purposes other than walking is considered to have been a decisive step towards the development of the human species. The adaptation was probably almost complete some four million years ago – if not earlier – and resulted in the small hominid Australopithecus afarensis ('Lucy' was one example of this early hominid).

In the following section we will look at how the distinctive traits of the human species developed over the past four million years. The model illustrates the evolution of these unique human traits in terms of the development of successive modes of life – from the centred through the decentred to the individuated mode.

The centred mode of life

Centred behaviour

Human beings' first mode of life (which may have developed around 1.6 million years ago when Homo erectus arrived on the scene) can be described as centred. What characterises this mode of life is that the activities of each individual are to a great extent initiated and regulated by the activities of the entire group, meaning that each individual is fully aware of what the other individuals are doing. When, for example, the group sets out to forage, the procedure will be as follows: everyone will join the expedition and everyone will move in a particular direction. That is why each individual – and the entire group – depends on the individuals staying sufficiently close to each other in time and space that they can keep track of one another by using their senses. Not that all of them will do exactly the same thing. The individual's own way of doing things is prompted and regulated by the doings of other individuals or of the entire group. This means, for instance, that a certain 'division of labour' may occur. Thus when chimpanzees hunt in groups, each individual within the group has a clear-cut role and function. Goodall (1986) describes what happened when she was observing four small monkeys in a tree. Suddenly a young chimpanzee climbed a tree nearby – far enough away that the small monkeys would not run away, but close enough to catch their attention. While the small monkeys were preoccupied with the first chimpanzee, another young chimpanzee meanwhile stole up into the tree where the small monkeys were sitting, rushed up to one of them and broke its neck.

The execution of this kind of 'task' does not necessarily call for any inner, self-conscious understanding of the task on the part of the individual performing it, nor even, indeed, for a conscious insight into what the other members of the group might intend, think or feel in this connection. All that is required is (1) that the individual has a 'sense of the occasion' and that his/her attention is focused on what is going on (there is a hunt 'in the air'), (2) that each individual can be motivated by the situation to direct his/her behaviour towards the common cause of the hunt, and (3) that each individual pays attention to what the others are observably engaged in. If individual A moves stealthily to the right, individual B will move to the left – not necessarily because B has any conscious insight into A's intentions, but because it is implicit in the scheme and dynamics of the hunt that the hunters should spread out and encircle the prey. Thus, once a hunt is 'in the air', the 'right' movement for any given individual, at any given moment, is determined by the movements of the group as a whole and his place within it.

This mode of life, which revolves around the observable behaviour of all the group members, means that one individual need not necessarily understand that the behaviour of another individual is based on mental conceptions and ideas. It is enough that the individual be able to perceive what is actually happening in the group in sufficient detail that he/she is able to sense when, for example, to make an equalizing move to the left when the other(s) move(s) to the right, and so on.

This set of established behaviours – encompassing everything from the particular dynamics of a given situation (e.g., the hunt) to an overall mode of life – thus constitutes the centre around which the behaviour, and general

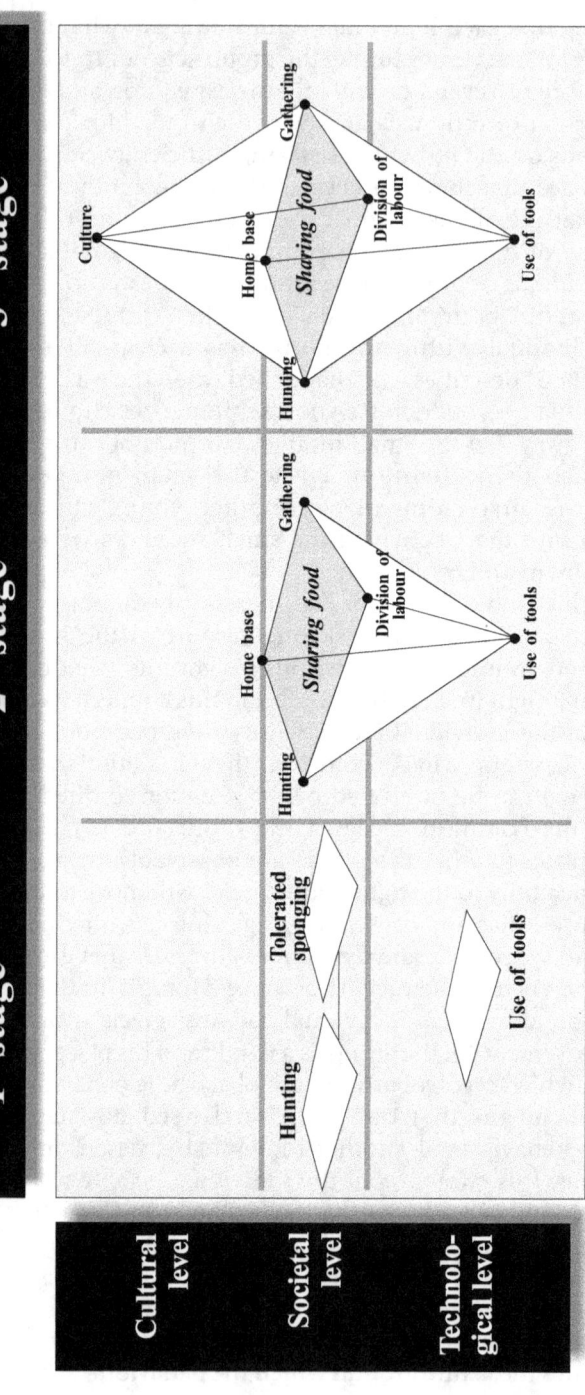

Figure 3.1 *illustrates the development of the home base and successive developments within the areas of technology, society and culture.*

life-style, of all the individuals within the group revolves. This is why we refer to this mode of life as 'centred'.

To get a more precise picture of the development of a specifically human mode of life – and hence of the development of modern man, we may look at the home base scenario described by Isaac (1978). Physically speaking, a home base is an area within the landscape which the group will return to because it provides shelter, security and a feeling of safety, and because it also makes it possible for the group to have a social life apart from its food-gathering activities. The group may stay there for a day, a couple of days or an entire season and use it as a base to set out from on hunting and gathering expeditions and to return to in order to consume the food.

Home base life

According to Isaac (1978), the development of the home base mode of life may have occurred in three stages (see Figure 3.4, a free adaptation of Isaac's figure, 1978: 102.). Here, the three stages have been put into an overall scheme, showing the developments occurring at each stage in the areas respectively of culture, society and technology.

At the first stage, we find hominids who probably lived in much the same way as the modern chimpanzee. The key features of this mode of life, for our purposes, are the hunting behaviour of the group and the fact that individuals within it display a certain limited tolerance towards 'sponging': that is to say, one individual may in some instances voluntarily give away some of his/her food to another individual in the group. Among predators who live and hunt in groups, the sharing of prey is important to the survival of the group. In the case of chimpanzees, food is quite seldom given away; in so far as food is voluntarily shared, however, it is most frequently given by a female to her infant, or, less commonly, by an adult male to an adult female. Another characteristic feature of this mode of life is also the occasional use of tools – for example to facilitate the hunt or the removal of meat from carrion.

At the second stage, the hominids definitively move beyond the level of the higher primates to achieve a genuinely social mode of life (see Figure 3.4, level 2, which shows an upended pyramid: the hatched base of the pyramid illustrates the social level). Several new and more highly developed features can be observed here, the most important being that the hominids now live in a home base, and there is a division of labour between the sexes – with the males hunting and gathering carrion, and the females and young gathering plants, berries and nuts.

These new features are both motivated and facilitated by the systematic sharing of food. The sharing of food in the home base is at once made possible and demanded by the division of labour, which allows both hunting and gathering to be pursued more intensively. Likewise, this qualitatively new kind of social life renders the further development of tool use and technology both possible and essential.

At the third stage, it is clear that the development of a social mode of life provides, in turn, the basis for the development of a cultural level (a subject that we will return to later).

It is evident, thus, that each new stage of development gives rise to an emergent level that is at once based on elements present at the previous stages, yet serves to organize, them in a qualitatively new way.

In the first stage (which could be seen as emergent in relation to the rest of the animal world) we find three key elements: hunting, tolerated 'sponging' and the use of tools. These elements are not integrated; they do not work together in any systematic way, but remain parallel elements which together constitute the given mode of life.

At the second stage of development, however, where we see the emergence of a social mode of life, a degree of organization has also emerged, centred around a qualitatively new feature: the systematic sharing of food. The 'old' elements have been refined, no longer co-existing merely in parallel, but bound together and organized on the principle of what will best secure a mode of life centred on the home base and the sharing of food.

This organization of the group's activities in turn lays the basis for a new mode of life and the creation of a new structure of social life among humans: one that includes a technological infra-structure. If we proceed to the third stage, we see that the social and technological elements present in the preceding stage now work together to constitute an elementary form of human culture with an organized system of habits, norms and institutions.

The home base scenario is a complex model, which attempts to relate a number of central developmental dimensions – social, technological, psychic, biological and so on – without giving one dimension precedence over another. The developments within one dimension are not seen as the cause of developments within the others; rather, developments within each of the respective dimensions both allow and entail one another– each dimension so to speak 'lifting' the others.

The development of the distinctive human traits in the homebase mode of life, seen from the perspective of evolution theory (based on Laland et al. 1999)

Standard evolutionary theory typically offers a passive picture of evolution. The environment or the species 'happens' to change; if the species' adaptation is successful, new modes of life will emerge. However, many species actively influence their environment and adapt to it in ways that optimize their reproductive success. For instance, the spider spins a web, the beaver builds a dam, and so on. The interaction between the organism and the environment in turn changes as a consequence of the species' active influence upon the environment, and in this sense the species' own activity affects the process of natural selection itself. Thus, for example, the spiders now singled out by natural selection – those that will have the best chance of passing on their optimalised gene pool – are those that spin the best webs, that are most adept at moving around them, that choose the best locations for them, and enjoy the best camouflage while waiting for their prey.

The recognition that organisms relate actively to their environment, themselves constructing niches which optimise their chances of survival and reproduction, leads to a more complex picture of the process of natural selection, and of the ways in which it can be influenced, than that offered by the standard model.

As we have seen, some of these niches are created by genetically programmed behaviour (as when the spider spins its web). This is the genetic part of the niche construction.

In other cases, a niche is constructed as a result of the fact that many species (including the first hominids) are capable of learning optimal behaviour in certain situations. The young members of the species may, for example, get training through imitative play, and will gradually learn more as they acquire experience. In this sense their behaviour is determined not just by their genes, but by what they have learned as well. This kind of ontogenetically acquired information cannot in itself be passed on genetically – learning is not hereditary. However, if the acquired behaviour is an active factor in optimizing the individual's chances of survival and reproduction, it will in turn influence the process of natural selection to the individual's own advantage. For instance, chimpanzees build nests for resting, and they learn from experience how to do this most efficiently (which trees in the area are most suitable, what material is at hand, etc.). Similar, though more complex, learning processes must almost certainly have played a role in the hominids' design of their home bases. Perhaps these gradually developed from nests to 'wind shelters' and finally to actual 'huts' or 'tents'. In addition, the very ability to learn from one's interactions with the environment, to respond to it flexibly and to develop appropriate behaviour, is in itself an advantage when it comes to survival – and while the content of one's acquired learning is not hereditary, the ability to learn and to improve one's learning skills may be passed on genetically.

As was illustrated in Isaac's model (Figure 3.1), the home base and the mode of life which arises from it also form a culture – albeit in a very primitive and elementary form. Indeed, the formation of a culture represents a third way in which the species may actively influence the construction of a niche (the first two influences being those of population genetics and

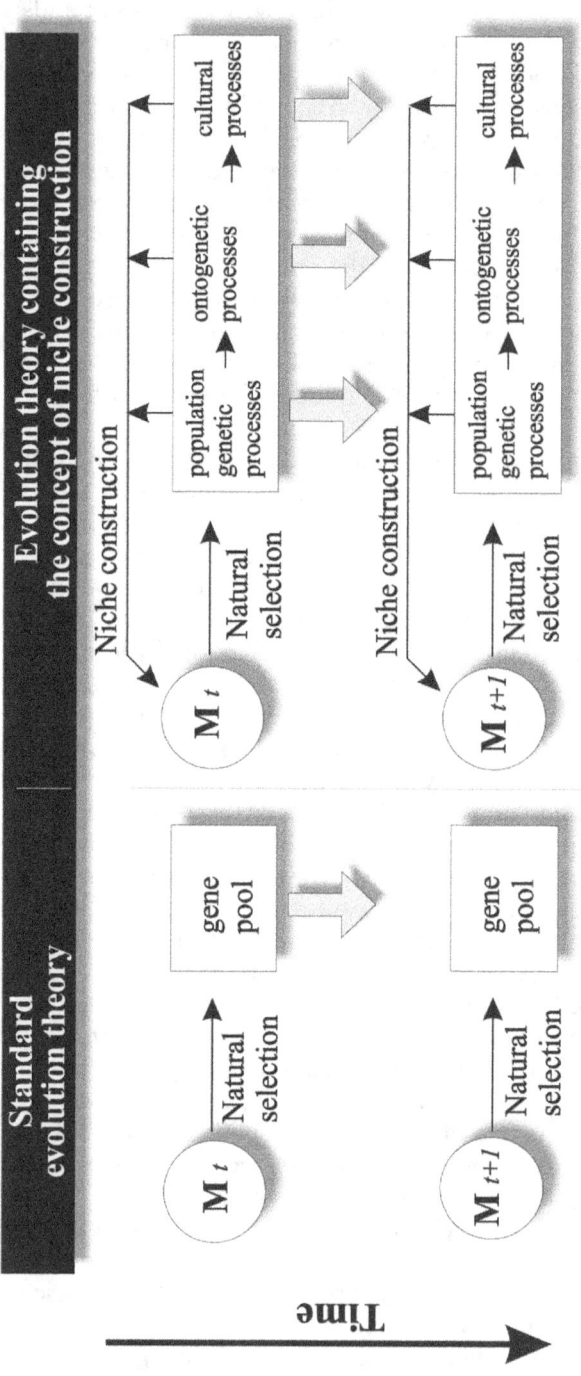

Figure 3.2 *illustrates the difference between standard evolutionary theory (which assumes that the individual is passively subjected to natural selection) and a theory of evolution based on an understanding that the individual is an active co-creator of the selection process (following Laland et al. 1999).*

ontogenetic processes, see Figure 3.2). The crucial point here is that the existence of a culture, however elementary, among a species or a group within that species means that the individual no longer learns in isolation to optimise his/her own behaviour, but benefits from his/her predecessors' learning through the acquisition of the group's culture. Culture, in other words, means that acquired behaviour is passed on to the offspring of the species. In the case of animals, each newly-born creature must begin from scratch, on the basis of its genetic background, to get to know the world and to acquire optimal behaviour. The novelty in the case of human beings, by contrast, is that one generation's accumulated learning can be passed on to the next generation through its appropriation of a transmitted culture, so that the child does not have to begin all over from the beginning.

Culture can be defined as the sum of all that which has meaning for us: it represents the fund of meanings that surround us in our everyday lives. A church in the middle of the townscape has a meaning to us, whether we are atheists or Christians or adhere to some other religion. The church symbolises the religious aspect of life and is associated with the principal events in our personal lives. On a smaller scale, an object such as a barbecue has a meaning as well. It signals a certain mode of life, a certain kind of culture, a relaxed conviviality, and the sharing of good food, red wine and small talk with neighbours on a warm summer night. On an even smaller scale, the barbecue fork has a meaning in its own right as well. It is part of, and refers to, the barbecue culture. When it is used (see Wittgenstein 1971) – perhaps for the first time – by a $2^1/_2$-year-old, it acquires yet further meaning. Perhaps the parents will show their child how to use the barbecue fork, and the small child may experiment with the use of it. In this way he/she acquires a bit of knowledge about how the fork can be used to prong, lift and move the meat around. The child thus learns something about the object itself as a tool. At the same time, he/she learns something about other kinds of things; for example, that the nature of meat is such that one can prong it, lift it, and so on, while, on the other hand, the vase of flowers or the dog are not things that one ought to poke with a barbecue fork. Finally, the child learns something about him/herself: namely, that he/she is someone who can wield a tool and thus behave in a certain way in relation to the surrounding world.

All this is implied in the meaning of a barbecue fork – and a similar range of meanings is implied in any of the cultural objects, or activities, or artefacts that fill our lives: thumb tacks, Rembrandt paintings, vibrating sanding machines, scuba diving, love affairs, elections, and so on. It is because these cultural creations have meaning that we are able to gain insight into the surrounding world through use or practice in the broadest sense. These artefacts have a meaning in themselves: they give meaning to how we live our lives, to what we can be and do. Moreover, they give meaning to something beyond themselves, in the sense that they give us insight into how the world is constituted, and how it can be treated, influenced and changed by the way in which we use our artefacts (see the data-gathering model in Figure 1.3, Chapter 1). It is not only objects that mean something. Our way of doing things also has a meaning. On the small scale (to return to the barbecue night) we may have certain habitual ways of, for example, grilling the meat. On a slightly larger scale, we may have a number of habitual routines associated with hosting a barbecue night (opening the wine bottles in advance, arranging a salad buffet, allowing the children to play when they have had eaten their hot dogs, and so on.). The barbecue night with the neighbours has become an institution – meaning a small slice of a life or a mode of life. On an even larger scale we find those social institutions which together constitute the framework for our lives (marriage, school attendance and so on).

Thus, on the one hand, the meaningful cultural artefacts that shape our lives and give us insight into the world consist of objects in the broadest sense (tools, art, knowledge, and so on) and, on the other hand, of institutions (again in the broadest sense of the word). Together, these institutions show us how we can/should behave and what our lives can/should be like, while at the same time giving significance to our lives: they show us both the framework of our existence and what can be done with it (see also the two aspects – theoretical and pragmatic – of the overall research model, as illustrated in Figure 1.7, Chapter 1).

But let us return to the origins of the human species, to the hominids and their centred home base mode of life. Simple and elementary though it was, the hominid's home base, and the life that revolved around it, was nevertheless far more meaningful than the lives of other species, and in this sense represented an early form of culture.

The home base contained artefacts whose meaning – both as such and in relation to the world – could be acquired or appropriated through use. Through this appropriation of meaning, the knowledge and experience gained in relation to being and doing, and the institutions which encompass this experience, could be passed on from one generation to the next. For example, the act of throwing a spear could contain the following meanings: that a spear is something that can be thrown, that the human anatomy is well-suited to throwing spears, and that animals are vulnerable to them. In addition, the spear is part of, and in itself implies, a more general form of activity, namely, the institution of hunting and the manner in which it is carried out. Thus the home base and the life associated with it consisted of a series of culturally meaningful artefacts, such as the institution of hunting, which were important for the existence and behaviour of each individual. The lives and activities – or the being and doings – of each individual within each new generation, could thus be said to have *centred* around the culture of the home base mode of life.

Within this mode of life, we may distinguish between two general domains: the technical/scientific and the social. Each domain gives rise to particular kinds of meaningful artefacts (both objects and institutions), on the basis of which the overall culture develops.

Within the technical domain, we see the development of both manufacturing tools and cooking utensils: stones were used to cut meat and to crush marrow bones, and in due course tools began to be manufactured for these purposes from stone or flint. Further on in this process of technogenesis, specific tools – in the form of flint knives and axes – were developed for hunting prey as distinct from preparing food. Much later we find, among the products of technogenesis, huts, houses, and the entire infrastructures of settlements or villages; as well as knowledge (science) relating to the cultivation of nature. In general terms, then, the development of technology can be said to give rise to those cultural meanings – in the form of objects and institutions – which regulated the existence and activities of each individual within the technical sphere.

At the same time we see the development of the social dimension of the homebase mode of life which, at the beginning, revolved around the consumption and sharing of food that had been gathered and brought back to the home base. In studying sociogenesis – the development of the social domain – we also look at the social life which arises through interrelations among kin, through pair bonding and through other kinds of relationships emanating from the structures of the home base group. Finally, we look at the complex principles behind these family relationships and the institution of food sharing, and, not least, at the development of language as an essential tool to secure, express and quarrel over these things. In general terms, social development, or sociogenesis, can be said to give rise to the creation of culturally meaningful objects or institutions, which constitute the centre of each individual's existence as a social being and regulate his/her life and activities in the social sphere

The development of a culture presupposes the development of a corresponding psychic capacity on the part of the individuals who share it both to appropriate and to contribute *to* that culture. Technogenesis and sociogenesis cannot take place, in other words, without a corresponding psychogenesis. (1) The individuals must possess the psychological capacity (cognitive, emotional and conative) to be able to use and live within the culture and let him/herself be directed by it. (2) The individuals must also be psychologically predisposed to feel motivated by and interested in living according to the home base mode of life, and to do their utmost to sustain the home base and the life that revolves around it. They must therefore be predisposed to use their capacities to acquire and appropriate the cultural, technical and social meanings that arise from the home base mode of life – and, in their own interests, they must be predisposed to direct their own existence and behaviour at the home base centre and allow themselves to be directed by it. (3) Last but not least, they must be innovative and open minded: able not just to acquire the given culture, but also to contribute to the adjustment of it, should it become unbalanced in relation to the surrounding environment: to contribute, in other words, to the optimalization of the culture within that environment. Thus, individuals must be able to learn, not only in the sense of acquiring what is given and passed down to them, but in the sense of reacting intelligently and open-mindedly to the challenges presented to them, so that they are able to make innovative contributions to both the technological and the social domain.

Evolution works by recycling. The fins of fish turn into the legs of terrestrial animals, the forelegs of such animals become birds' wings, and so on. This 'recycling' process is also seen within the social and psychic domains. The biological imprinting which makes goslings follow the first moving object they see after they are hatched, even if the latter is just a cardboard goose, can also be found at a more developed level in the more complex attachment of young mammals to their mother. Most members of the cat family (except lions) grow out of this 'infant-like' attachment and live a relatively isolated life as adults. Among animals who live in flocks or herds, however, this attachment is transposed in adulthood into a form of social bonding with the flock or herd. Chimpanzees are gregarious animals that display a very advanced and differentiated form of social bonding behaviour. Such behaviour evidently originates from the attachment of young chimpanzees towards their mother, and can easily be identified, for example, in the social bonding behaviour displayed by adult chimpanzees when grooming one another. The same kind of innovative 'recycling' can be seen in the evolution of more complex forms of social bonding in the home base mode of life developed by the more advanced hominids.

Because of its cognitive and social complexity, the home base mode of life called for individuals to develop the conative and emotional capacity to sustain and contribute to it by striving actively to be helpful, considerate, caring, ready to share and so on. Moreover, it called for the development not only of basic emotions such as joy, curiosity, anxiety, aggression and dislike (which other mammals also display), but also of more complex emotions which contribute to the sustenance of the home base community: for instance, love of others, caring for one's neighbour, being proud of one's children, one's partner and the group, being ashamed of breaking with the social community, and feeling guilty at not living up to expectations.

Together, these cognitive, conative and socio-emotive forms of connectedness make up the individual's deep social centeredness. And it is precisely this deep sense of connection that ensures (1) that the individual's behaviour is both directed at others and in turn steered by the overall behaviour of the group; and (2) that the support and maintenance of the home base is the primary motivation behind each individual's every action: he/she gathers food in order to sustain the life of the home base; the same goes for his/her efforts to show food-sharing behaviour, and so on. This deep social centred connectedness thus constitutes the deep ethic for each individual, co-directing any form of individual behaviour, whatever other factors it may also be impelled by (for example, the location of berry-bearing shrubs).

Several other examples may be given of human psychosocial capacities and dispositions which can be traced back to earlier species, and can still today be seen in chimpanzees. Take, for instance, the chimpanzee's ability to differentiate between the in-group (his/her own group, to which he/she relates in a socially binding and attached manner), and the out-group (other groups of chimpanzees) to which he/she relates to in a reserved manner: with curiosity, but also with a latent hostility. Young male chimpanzees often patrol the group's territorial borders and will not refrain from attacking isolated individuals from neighbouring groups (sometimes even killing them), if they feel they are sufficiently strong to tackle them successfully. Within the in-groups of gregarious mammals, meanwhile, social behaviour is expressed not only in various forms of 'socializing', but in the establishment of hierarchies: with individuals fighting for dominance, leadership and the right to mate. Chimpanzees and bonobos may even try to disrupt these 'institutions' by cheating and deceiving (for example, a female may sneak off to mate with another male while the dominant male, who has established the right to mate with her, is otherwise engaged). Human behaviour, and that of home-base-dwelling hominids, can be seen in numerous ways to have deep roots in the biology and behaviour of other earlier species. Here, however, we will focus on those aspects of natural history, cultural history and life history (see Figure 2.1 in Chapter 2), which enabled the hominids to develop a mode of life centred on the overall mode of life and culture of the home base.

We may now return to the evolutionary model illustrated in Figure 3.2. The model shows that a central, dynamic factor in the evolutionary development of a species, including that of mankind, is how the species relates actively to its environment. We have seen how this activity influences the process of natural selection, both through biogenesis, the gradual changing of the gene pool, and through ontogenesis, the experience and learning acquired by the individual during his/her life history. Likewise, we have seen how the techno- and sociogenesis of a species may also affect the process of natural selection, through the transfer of established meanings from one generation to the next.

In the case of humankind and the home-base-dwelling hominids, two aspects of psychogenesis can be seen directly to have influenced the process of natural selection. (1) The centred, home-base mode of life both required, and made possible, the development of genetically based psychological capacities and dispositions, including an openness to learning from experience and a capacity to innovate. In this case, the psychogenesis is passed on via biogenesis: the psychic preconditions for being able to live a within a home-base community, and to contribute to and develop this mode of life, are hereditary and will thus lead to the genetic development of the human line. (2) However, a specific culture, and the meanings it gives to particular activities and modes of life, is indeed passed on from generation to generation: the ability to operate effectively in both the social and the technological sphere, and general knowledge about life and the world, are accumulated from one generation to the next through the passing on of human artefacts, whether in the form of objects or institutions. These artefacts are then appropriated anew by each new individual as he/she learns through his/her own life experience. In other words, psychogenesis, understood as the development of capacities, dispositions and innovative ability occurs not only through inheritance, but through cultural learning – or, to put it another way, the psychological capacity of the individual to lead a centred mode of life is not only inherited, but culturally formed and acquired.

The centred human in relation to the modern human

In what follows, we will use the natural- and cultural-historical scenario outlined above to show how the distinguishing traits of the modern human being emerged, looking in particular, at the development in the human species of free will, consciousness, and self-consciousness or the self.

As we have seen, the development of the home base mode of life and its associated culture, elementary though this may at first have been, played a crucial evolutionary role in the emergence of the human species. It was this mode of life that both required and made possible the development of the human line, both biogenetically and psychogenetically humanizing the species. This process of humanization resulted in part from a latent element in the gene pool, and in that sense can be seen as a development within natural history. But it was also the product of the cultivation of each new generation of the home base community, and in that sense should be seen in terms of cultural or life history. Genetically, each new individual is endowed with the necessary capacities to develop distinctive human traits; in addition, however, each individual is humanized through the process of cultivation and of his/her acquisition of meaning.

Where the mode of life is centred, there is no someone whose conscious task it is deliberately to cultivate the human qualities (in Chapter 6 the notion of a someone will be further elaborated). Rather, the process of humanization occurs anonymously: it is implicit in the fact that the individual's life is centred around the homebase – both around the meaning of objects and institutions, but also around the implicit meanings contained in the existence and activities of other individuals. By the very fact that his/her life is centred around these anonymous meanings (anonymous in the sense that they are not self-consciously willed or communicated), each individual will acquire the humanizing culture by means of which his/her biogenetic and psychogenetic potential for humanization is realized.

It follows that the centred mode of life neither demands nor makes possible any real, voluntary choice of mode of life. Indeed, it leaves very little scope for choice even in specific actions. To be sure, individuals may, in their actions, pursue different inclinations. Just as we can observe a dog getting up from his sunny spot on the terrace and heading for his bowl instead of visiting the neighbour's dog, so we can imagine a hominid sitting down in the middle of foraging to gaze about the steppe, rather than heading straight on for the next berry-bearing shrubs. But the pursuit of such inclinations is not the same as the exercise of genuine free will; nor does the centred mode of life require, or allow for, the development of free will.

For an individual to have a sense of connectedness with the centre does presuppose, of course, that he/she possesses an elementary consciousness: that is, an ability to create mental models. Thus the home-base-dwelling hominids needed to be able to develop models of the landscape around the base so that they were able, when foraging, to navigate and manoeuvre effectively towards familiar places. Similarly, they must have been able mentally to model the events involved in a group hunt so that each of them would be able to navigate and manoeuvre in relation to each other and the prey. But this centred mode of life does not require them to develop more complex and advanced abilities, such as the capacity for consciousness of other individuals' consciousness, or for self-awareness – the sense of oneself as a conscious being engaged in forming models. It is sufficient that the individual be able to attune his/her models to the social life and activity of the group.

Thus, any variations that exists in the behaviour of individuals within this home-base mode of life is attributable not to free will – that is, to an ability to make genuine choices on both the small scale (in particular situations) and the large scale (in life as such) – but rather to the pursuit of individual inclinations.

The individual's life and life projects, in this centred mode of life, is directed first and foremost by the mode of life of the home-base community as a whole and by the events and dynamics which that mode of life involves. Consciousness exists in the form of mental models of the landscape, but not in the form of self-consciousness. Consequently, the humanizing project – the cultural-historical and life-historical realization of human potential – does not exist at this stage as a conscious, willed project, nor was it in any sense explicitly formulated in terms of religion, ethics or a philosophy of life. It exists only in the sense that it is anonymously embedded in the meanings of the centred culture itself.

Yet, anonymous and vague though it was at this early stage of human development, this humanizing project can nevertheless be called an ethical project in so far as it related to how individuals should live, and how they should behave, in order to sustain the common home-base mode of life. It may therefore be seen as a form of socially centred ethical code – that is, an anonymous directive issuing from the very nature of the home base, its culture and its organization of meanings – concerning what constituted the good life and good activities.

The decentred mode of life

What were the underlying factors that led to the development of human life from this basic, socially centred mode of life to the modern mode which both demands and makes it possible for human beings to develop (1) life projects, meaning free-willed and self-conscious projects for a person's individual life; and (2) mutually humanizing projects, meaning projects for mankind in general? What intermediate, transitional form may human society have taken in the development from one mode to another, and what factors made this transition both possible and necessary? Most researchers agree that the division of labour was a crucial factor in this transition. The division of labour means that large and complex forms of behaviour are divided into smaller constituents, which are then shared by several cooperating individuals. For instance, the complex procedure of fishing may be broadly outlined as follows: the production (by one individual) of traps made from woven twigs, the setting of traps (by another individual) in streams or on a seashore far away from the home base, the cleaning and drying of the fish by yet another individual, and so on.

This particular mode of life can be called de-centred in the sense that there is no longer a single centre determining the behaviour of the entire group, but rather a number of centres for different types of activity. Each subdivision of the overall activity (for example, fishing) has its own subcentre (one for the production of traps, one for trap-setting, one for drying fish, and so on). The unifying centre which, in the centred mode of life, had determined the behaviour of the group as such can also be found in the decentred mode of life, to the extent that there is a collective and cooperative effort to sustain the life of the community. The maintenance of the community and of life remains the ultimate organizing principle behind all the community's activities. Nevertheless, the community as a whole has now been divided into smaller groups, each of which has its separate sub-centre and sphere of activity.

For this kind of decentred labour-divided mode of life to work successfully, each of the separate spheres of activity must operate according to the following two principles: First, each of these activities must be undertaken cooperatively, that is to say, it must be directed at a common, overall goal (for example, to catch fish and share them). Second, those involved in these separate activities can no longer direct their actions by attuning them to the observable activities of other individuals who are immediately present in time and space. Once the individuals in the group, and their individual activities, have been divided in both time and space, some other medium must be found for maintaining the individual's sense of directedness towards, and attunement with, the overall existence and activities of the group as a whole. In one way or another, the individual must 'carry' this sense of the common goal within him/herself when engaging in this or that decentred activity. The overall system will break down if the individual merely follows his/her own inclinations as soon as the group or other cooperating individuals are out of sight (the out-of-sight-out-of-mind principle would not be adequate). The individual must be able to maintain a sense of the overall goal and of his/her necessary contribution towards it even when acting in isolation.

In order to achieve the ultimate goal – to establish, sustain and continue to develop the collective life of the group – the individual's separate activities must still be directed by a fundamental socially-centred code of ethics. Now, however, the individual must be able 'carry' or 'keep hold of' this fundamental code even when separated from other members of the group in time and space. This will mean both (1) that overall cooperation, and hence the group's common mode of life can be maintained, and (2) that the different activities within the division of labour are attuned with and directed at one another in a pragmatically useful way. Operating as it still does on the individual's sense of connectedness with the group as a whole, this decentred mode of life thus also requires the development of a moral code, which is pragmatic in the sense that it serves to coordinate many different partial activities and aspects of the overall life of the group. Thus, over and above the basic ethics of the centred mode of life, the decentred mode of life requires an organizing decentred moral code to coordinate the activities of the group as a whole according to the general principles of a division of labour.

Like its predecessor, this decentred mode of life does not require, or make possible, any real choice of mode of life. Still, it does require and allow for something beyond mere inclination (each centred individual's inclination to do this or that in relation to the activities and existence of the group as a unity). In the decentred mode of life it become possible and necessary for the individual to exercise what might be called preferences, for it allows for – and calls for – individuals to have different abilities, capacities, levels of experience and degrees of learning, and hence to prefer one kind of work over another among the different functions set by the division of labour within the community. Thus, although the individuals within a group are still unable to make the kinds of choices made in a modern society, the variation in their activities is now the result of more than simple and momentary inclination. The inclinations have developed into preferences.

In this sense the decentred mode of life also demands and makes possible a further development of the individual's mental capacity. It is no longer sufficient that the individual be able to form models based either on pure memory or simply on reactions to events in the here-and-now (for example during a group hunt). The decentred mode of life, with its ever increasing division of labour and separation of activities in time and space, now also demands that each individual – in order that he/she can direct his/her individual activity to the optimum benefit of the group – be able to imagine and anticipate an overall activity (for example, the production of tools, the catching of fish, the sharing of prey) which has not yet taken place. In other words, the individual must be able to form anticipatory mental models on the basis of which he/she can judge how and when to incorporate his/her preferred activity within the overall procedure.

Two general points may be made about the nature of these anticipatory decentred models. The first is that the individual must be able to 'carry them within him/herself' regardless of his/her immediate surroundings.

Second, whereas individuals living a centred mode of life are generally required to grasp only one model – of the activities of the group in the here-and-now – individuals living a decentred mode of life must be able to form many partial models, each of which anticipates a separate aspect of the unified activity and mode of life of the group. Mentally, they form connections with their environment through numerous, parallel models of behaviour corresponding to different activities within an increasingly complex division of labour, and they are able to alternate between one kind of model and another.

However, not even this decentred mode of life (which, as we have seen, is still based upon, and includes elements of, the earlier, socially centred mode) yet corresponds to the mode of life of modern humans, which is characterised on the psychic plane by free will and self-consciousness. These capacities are not required by the decentred mode of life – though the basis for them has been laid, as we have seen, by the fact that a division of labour requires the exercise of real preferences (as opposed to momentary inclinations), and by the fact that the individual must be able to grasp and retain a variety of different mental models.

Moreover, at this stage in the cultural-historical development of the distinguishing traits of human beings, we cannot speak of someone, having a conscious, willed project to 'humanize' the group as a whole or to influence it in some particular direction. It is true that the individual is now able to appropriate and retain a mental model of what constitutes the good for the community as a whole, and of how his/her spatio-temporally separate activity is cooperatively connected with the overall activity of the entire group (the settlement or the clan). However, this notion of what is good or right is still fundamentally defined by a socially-centred code of behaviour that is generated anonymously by the activity and culture of the entire group. The mental models carried by individuals living this decentred mode of life are still directed by, and derive their meaning from, the actual performance of the activities they engage in, the tools they use in these activities, the goals implicit in them, and the existence and activities of their actual cooperative partners. The moral code generated by this decentred mode of life is still in this sense anonymous. It is implicit, for example, in the meaning of producing traps, and there is therefore or someone, deliberately and consciously to set about promoting a certain, correct kind of human behaviour (for example, with regard to attuning one's own preferences and partial activities to those of others). Both on the large scale (maintaining the decentred life as such) and on the small scale (producing the trap in the absence of the fisherman who will use it), the 'human project' is still only implicit in the accumulated meanings of the decentred culture, be these in the form of artefacts (objects and institutions) or in the form of mental models of present phenomena, memories of past experiences or anticipations of future goals.

It is difficult to give a date to the emergence of this decentred mode of life, because it must have been potentially present, almost from the outset, in the centred mode of life that preceded it. We can see this if we look, for example, at the behavioural patterns of gregarious animals (for example, lionesses, male and female wolves and, occasionally, male chimpanzees) when engaged in hunting. As mentioned above, an elementary division of labour can be observed here in the fact that a number of small groups of individuals contribute in their own ways to the overall goal of the hunt. But in its crystallized and explicit form as a distinct new mode of life it probably emerged quite late in relation to the millions of years in which the centred mode of life prevailed. Judging from archeological finds, the centred mode of life was extremely conservative. For millions of years there was scarcely any change, for example, in the way that stone tools were produced; in other words, the culture of tool-production hardly changed in this period. But from around 60,000/40,000 B.C. until 20,000 years B.C. – the period to which we can date the clear emergence of a decentred mode of life – we can see that there was a veritable explosion of cultural artefacts. During this period, which saw the emergence of modern mankind, Homo sapiens sapiens, entirely new and advanced cooking utensils and hunting implements appear in myriad shapes and variations. Likewise, this period saw the emergence of genuine settlements with sophisticated tents and huts, and proper graves in which the dead have been placed in certain positions with flowers and objects next to them. Last but not least, all kinds of different art objects, such as cave paintings and figures carved out of bone, begin to appear on the scene.

This explosion of cultural artefacts – which expressed the rich variety of separate activities that had followed the division of labour – indicates that the decentred culture was now flourishing. Embedded within it, however, were the seeds of a new culture in which the meanings that directed the individual's life were not merely the anonymous products of the culture, but in part at least expressions of individual creation. Artistic artefacts could be said to represent meanings for meaning's sake. In his creations or representations, the artist attempts to 'extract' or abstract the meaning or the essence of some part of reality – thus in painting a hunting scene, for example, he/she distils the essence of what it is to go on a hunt. Artistic expression thus provides us with a medium through which we are able phenomenologically to model and hence experiment with meanings. The challenge of art, and the opportunity it gives us, is not simply to represent meanings that are already given and handed-down, but innovatively to experiment with the creation of meanings.

Likewise, the fact that we find evidence, from this period, of proper burial of the dead indicates that life itself, that fact of being alive, of being, had come to have a meaning of its own.

To a much greater extent than hitherto, the participants in this culture had come – especially in their art – to grapple and work with meanings in themselves. The decentred culture was thus pregnant with a new culture, a new mode of life in which the meaning of life in general, and the meaning of being human in particular, was not just anonymously implied by cultural artefacts or by the mental models which individuals operating in a decentred community needed to 'carry with them'. On the contrary, these meanings could now be treated independently as objects of contemplation (if only contemplation of the meaning of the art object). The external observation of the process of artistically modelling and experimenting with meanings is a necessary prerequisite for that internal process of modelling, experimenting with and contemplating models of meaning in which the human phenomenological consciousness consists.

It is this which provides the key to the third, individuated mode of life to which we will now turn.

The individuated mode of life

The next major step in human development – which would ultimately lead to the emergence of modern man as a volitional, conscious, self-reflecting being capable of creating his/her own life project – probably occurred around 10,000 BC, again as the result of climatic changes at the end of the last major Ice Age.

During this period the early humans ceased to live only by hunting and gathering and began gradually to rear animals, grow various kinds of crops and settle in villages. The agrarian revolution had begun. We can see from archeological finds how villages developed during the period from around 10,000 to 6,500 BC. In the beginning, the houses in these villages tended to be homogeneous, or at least showed no sign of social stratification into classes or of differentiation according to the nature of the work in which most of the population was engaged (for example as peasants or artisans). From around 7,000 to 5,500 BC we find evidence both of intensive farming and of differentiated buildings and burial places (chieftains' farms and the graves of wealthy people which bear witness to some form of social stratification).

The earliest real towns or city states date from around 4000 BC. A town is more than just an overgrown village. It is the centre of an entirely new mode of life, the polis. In the towns we find large religious centres, rich people's houses, areas of poverty, warehouses, artisan quarters, and so on. The town represents the centre of the surrounding area with its many villages, large or small. During the period 2900 to 2400 BC, in the city-state of Uruk in the Middle East, the population reached approximately 100,000! The surrounding area had a range of ten kilometres.

Logan and Saunders (1976, here quoted from Jolly and Plog 1987) point to four characteristics of the city state: urbanization, that is, the concentration of a growing population in a relatively small area; specialization: a specialized division of labour among peasants and artisans of all kinds; stratification: the division of the population into classes according to wealth and social status; and centralization: the formation of a bureaucratic centre of power which coordinates the myriad activities and events generated by the community.

The fact that large sectors of the population were engaged in specialised activities, each of which generated its own mode of life (albeit within the unifying framework of the city state), together with the growing stratification of society and the centralization of political, military and religious power, led to a dramatic proliferation of different modes of life, each of which in turn could be subdivided into different aspects. Quite literally, life for different individuals was no longer the same. Furthermore, the distance between the various occupational groups and classes, and the distance between the individual and the centre of power, had now become so great that individuals seldom experienced spatio-temporal proximity with those outside their immediate circle, except at occasional feasts and other events arranged by the central authorities.

The common life of the community was still sustained by a fundamental, socially centred morality, and the life of the new, urban communities still relied on the more advanced cooperative/pragmatic morality of the decentred community. The problem with these basic ethical codes, however, is that they function only in the immediate environment, where individuals are still in sufficiently close contact to be able to attune their behaviour concretely to that of others and to relate to one another as individuals. In this sense they can also function within the immediate environments of the urban community – the individual family, the community of the street or of particular occupational groups. An ethical code which relies on proximity and acquaintance cannot, however, function in large, complex urban environments where some practical form of organization is needed to attune and coordinate the disparate mode of life and activity of individuals who are not in close contact with one another. The social, spatial and temporal distances involved are too great in this case for social life and activities to work on the basis of these centred and decentred moral codes alone. The solution lay in the development of what might be called a morality of remoteness: a generalised moral code based not on individual attunement to the behaviour of others in concrete social and cooperative situations, but on the profession of a certain all-encompassing idea of what is the right and proper way to behave, and what the good life consists of. Such, for example, is the allegiance expressed by an individual when he asserts his recognition of, and belief in, his/her city state as the good place to live, and one that is worth sustaining; his faith in the central powers, for whom he will if necessary give his life; and his commitment to a religious discourse that prescribes the only true way of reflecting on life.

This kind of generalised morality, which remotely regulates the individual's life, becomes even more essential when the numerous different modes of life arising as a result of urbanization lead to an even more advanced degree of individual variation. In the centred mode of life, as we have seen, individuals might vary their activities according to passing inclination, but such variations did not lead to any real differences in the individuals' mode of life. In practice, everyone lived the same kind of life. In the decentred mode of life, individuals were able to vary their activities on the basis of more permanent preferences: that is to say, they could focus on some particular aspect of the community's life, and make their particular contribution towards it according to their individual temperament or preferences, without, however, leading a fundamentally different kind of life from that of their neighbours or fellow-members of the community. With the rise of urban-style communities, however, and the concomitant increase in specialization and stratification, new opportunities arise for leading quite different lives, in which the individual's activities are guided by often radically different norms and forms of internal organization. The urbanized mode of life thus opens up the possibility for genuine differentiation in individual modes of life: an individuated mode of life.

Because these widely differentiated modes of life are so decentred, their underlying connection is literally invisible in daily life; individuals within the same society can each live their lives in their own way within their own subculture. Individuals can thus observe that others live their lives in accordance with their own sets of meanings, which may be different from one's own. Life is thus seen to have different meanings to different individuals – and the culture as a whole, including its objects and institutions, may therefore mean something different to individuals other than oneself. In other words, the mental models that others have formed of their environment, and of life itself, on the basis of their own subculture, may be quite different from those which one has formed oneself. This applies not least to the individual's ability, within the fields of art or technology, to work abstractly with meanings in themselves (an ability which, as we have seen, began to emerge already at the decentred stage of human development). In observing these differences, the individual thus has an opportunity to construct mental models of how other human beings give meaning to the world.

The fact that other human beings observably live their lives within other frames of meaning than one's own, and that they may have other models of what constitutes the good life and the right way to behave, forms the basis for recognizing that others may differ from oneself in terms of their culture, their meanings and their mental model of the world. And this experience of difference in turn provides the basis for understanding that each person is a special and unique individual with his/her own meaningful mental models of and engagement in the world.

Thus for the first time the foundation is laid for understanding that other human beings may have other values, profess other systems of belief, and form ideas of life and mental models of the world that differ from one's own (see also Jaynes 1976). And this understanding opens out a new stage in human mental development: namely, the realisation that each individual has a distinct 'inner' life which is distinct from one's own. This in turn is a prerequisite for recognising, and focusing on, the fact that such a thing as the inner exists at all, and that, in so far as the other has a unique inner life, this is true of oneself as well.

It is thus now, and only now, that a real, fully developed self-consciousness emerges – in the form of a phenomenological model of one's own 'inner' mental life and that of others.

The advanced, urbanized mode of life not only gives rise to self-consciousness, understood in these terms, but demands it: for it requires a form of organization that can direct any individual inclination or preference towards a unifying system of belief. This means that each individual must be capable of professing such belief: that is, he/she must be able to form mental models of the system to which he/she is related, and to distinguish which, among the numerous potential forms of activity and behaviour which arise in a decentred society, would accord with this system of professions, and which would be at variance or in conflict with it. In short, the individuated mode of life demands for the first time that the individual must be capable of self-knowledge: capable of forming, that is, a phenomenological model of the self – a self-model or self-consciousness – in order to be able to navigate among the complex choices offered by an urbanized mode of life and to choose the 'correct' path that accords with the overall system of belief.

To sum up: during the previous, centred and decentred epochs there was no need for any particular someone to initiate or develop some ethical or pragmatic system for organizing human existence. Individuals lived their lives according to directives concerning the optimal, right or good life which were anonymously generated by the centred and decentred meanings in the overall culture of the community itself. By contrast, the individuated mode of life both requires and makes possible an organizing ethical system which represents not merely the anonymous product of the culture itself, but rather the crystallization of some conscious, goal-directed project initiated by someone, that is, other people with their own life projects, self-consciousness, and consciousness of another's consciousness.

To be more precise, what might be called 'project human being', or 'the human project' is now implied at two levels: (1) It represents the distillation of a number of separately formulated interpretations of life and directives for living – for example, laws governing correct behaviour, religious directives concerning the meaning of life in general and the nature of the good life in particular, and accepted interpretations of the meaning of artistic works or other cultural artefacts. In other words, the human project is formulated in a meaning-giving discourse which – together with specific political, judicial and religious directives – is communicated to each individual through socialization, culture and education, and at the same time represents an object of contemplation in itself. (2) The human project is the distillation of each individual's version of this overall discourse – as a discourse for giving meaning to, understanding, explaining and regulating oneself as a self.

Such discourses, representing an ongoing project for human development at both the individual and the social level, can be seen to have emerged gradually during the individuated epoch. In the first instance these discourses took the form of myths and religious systems. As time went on, the development of the written word, in particular, meant they could be formulated and disseminated far more efficiently, over much greater distances, and to a far greater number of people than hitherto. Today, as much as ever, the written text represents a medium in which one may give material and lasting expression to one's thoughts, feelings, reflections and so on, creating an object 'outside' oneself that offers a basis for more sustained reflection. Unlike mere passing thoughts, the thought captured in writing remains before us. At the private level we know this from the act of writing a diary: by literally seeing the thoughts one has recorded, one endeavours to arrive at a greater understanding of oneself. Works of art likewise represent an external, palpable and durable expression of the artist's inner world which he/she may continue to reflect upon long after it is made. And the same goes for any scientific project, an important part of which consists precisely in the act of writing one's considerations down in order to be able to wrestle further with them (by the same token, the purpose of getting students in schools and universities to formulate their thoughts in written essays should not primarily be to check their knowledge or understanding, but to oblige them to focus on the subject and assemble their thoughts in a coherent form).

As we have seen, the process by which human beings began to develop as self-reflecting individuals, capable of engaging in a discourse that would generate new meanings, dates back to the time of the decentred mode of life, but it accelerated tremendously with the appearance of agrarian communities and city states. It was not until the emergence of the Greek city states, around 400 BC, that this self-understanding could be said to have crystallised into a conscious discourse on the self.

This gradual process of development could thus be characterized as follows: up until 400 BC, human discourse on existence was formulated primarily in terms of mythical and religious statements or directives concerning the common life of the community and the life project of the individual. Such discourses gradually became the object of political and philosophical debates, as we know in particular from the written sources of the Greek city states. To begin with, these elaborations of the discourse in debate and discussion were mainly rhetorical: the most eloquent speaker held the winning cards. Gradually, however – and especially through the influence of Plato and Aristotle – the principles of rational dialogue were developed, such that the conclusive argument was not necessarily the most eloquent but that which had logical validity. The influence of the prevailing discourse of myth and rhetoric is nevertheless still evident in Plato, who preferred to formulate his philosophical discourses in the form of dramatically staged dialogues between Socrates and various rhetoricians and/or ignorant persons: dialogues which still emanated from the same cultural universe as that of the myths, for, just as mythical and religious discourses were presented and recited by religious leaders, gurus and wise men, so Plato sought to support his discursive points by presenting them through the words of his guru or wise man, Socrates. It is only in Aristotle's writings that we find a genuine liberation from the culture of myth and rhetoric: here, the discourse is no longer presented in the form of a dialogue, but as a series of statements whose validity can be tested.

The principal contribution made by the Ancient Greeks to the development of the modern human self lay precisely in this transition from a mythical/religious, fundamentalist discourse, with its untestable claims, to a discourse of logical argument. Nevertheless, certain important components of the modern self – those relating to the will – are still missing. These will be discussed in Chapter 5.

In the following chapters we will seek to offer a more detailed psychological explanation of how, for example, free will, consciousness and self-consciousness could have emerged as distinctive human traits. The main purpose of the present chapter has been to show that these human phenomena come into being as a result of natural and cultural evolutionary processes because they were both required and made possible by human development from the centred through the decentred to the individuated mode of life.

The layered topography of the modern human

As will be evident from our presentation of the three-stage model of human psychological evolution, the various different modes of life, and the psychological developments they brought in train, did not happen in simple succession. On the contrary, we have seen how, from the very beginning, the centred mode of life was pregnant with the decentred mode, which, albeit in tiny stages over millions of years, gradually took shape and developed on the basis of the preceding mode. The centred mode of life remained the basic material from which the more advanced, decentred mode was constituted and organized.

The same duality is manifest in the relationship between the individuated and the decentred modes of life. The individuated mode is at once constituted by, yet serves to organize, the myriad different life opportunities arising from the decentred mode.

The modern human psyche thus consists of a series of layers, corresponding to the different demands made at different stages of human existence. The 'top' layer represents the stage of personal, individuated development in which the community operates on a 'morality of remoteness'. However, this layer is still fundamentally based (at both the individual and the social level) on the organization of the many different modes of life thrown up by the decentred stage. Though it is organized and coordinated by a unifying morality, life can be experienced and lived from many different and at times conflicting perspectives. At the most fundamental level, the universal human traits (and the sense of common human identity) can be traced back to the socially centred mode of life, in which a sense of connectedness was maintained and expressed by a morality based on spatio-temporal proximity. Thus, while the core of individuality can be traced back to the decentred stage of human existence, an even more central core goes back to the stage of socially centred activity. This is illustrated in Figure 3.3.

The Distinguishing Traits of Human Beings

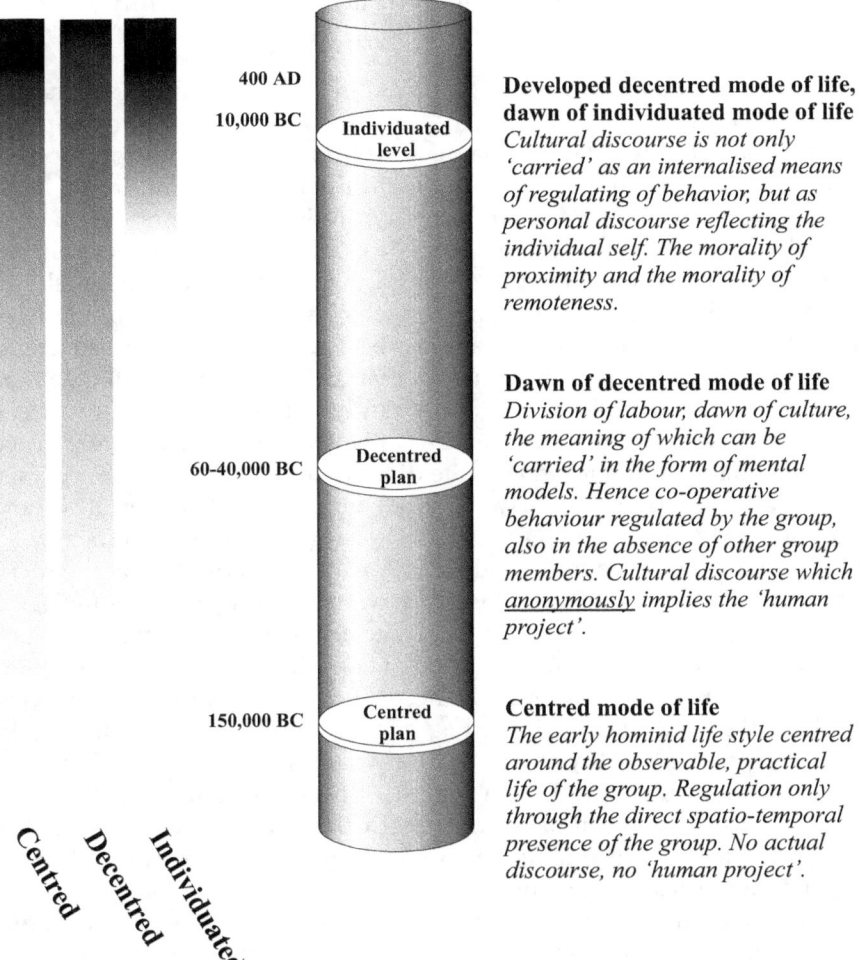

Figure 3.3 *illustrates (1) how the different modes of life overlap, and (2) how they constitute various levels in the topography of modern life.*

The development of proto-sociality, proto-morality and directedness at/by the directedness of others

As we have suggested, the mode of life of our early hominid ancestors may have resembled that which can be observed among, for example, chimpanzee groups today. We may assume from this that the expressions of sociality and morality found among chimpanzees are similar to those existing among the earliest groups of hominids. In the present chapter, morality is understood as the regulation of social interaction among individuals. This does not mean, of course, that the advanced and developed forms of sociality and moral regulation which we can observe in ourselves, in our own modern societies, can also be found among chimpanzees or hominids. But what we may assume is that the elementary building blocks for developing a social and moral life can be found among chimpanzees, and that these constitutive elements have evolved into, and been organized as, the social and moral mode of life of modern man. In this connection a distinction can be made between what might be called Morality$_A$ and Morality$_B$. Morality$_A$ represents the kind of regulation of social behaviour which occurs by virtue of the individual's natural directedness at the social group. Thus, this kind of morality, which we can observe at the centred level, requires nothing more than the ability to let oneself be directed at, and directed by the similarly socially-directed behaviour of others in the group. Morality$_B$ represents a more advanced kind of morality, in which the individual's behaviour is directed at, and by, the sociality implied by the character and personality of another individual, as the former encounters it in actual situations and over a period of time. Morality$_A$ must thus be regarded as the evolutionary predecessor of Morality$_B$, but nevertheless contains a number of evolutionary building blocks for the more advanced regulation of social behaviour.

Embarking from the Darwinian assumption that the social and moral behaviour of modern humans is the result of the evolutionary development of the species, Flack and de Waal (2000) have made several studies of groups of chimpanzees with the aim of identifying these fundamental building blocks. The assumption that the foundations of social and moral behaviour can be found among animals is in fact much closer to Darwin's basic view than popular – and distorted – interpretations of Darwinism imply. Contrary to popular lore, the basic principles of evolution, as Darwin presented them, do not imply a brutal struggle of 'each against all'. The 'brutalist' view originates not from Darwin but from Herbert Spencer (1825–1895) and was later developed by Huxley (1825–1903), who interpreted the theory of evolution to mean that both humans and animals are essentially nasty, selfish, brutal creatures, and that morality was invented by mankind to restrain our natural inclination to self-centred cruelty.

A great many studies of gregarious animals in general and of groups of chimpanzees in particular, have, on the contrary, proved that the directedness of the individual's behaviour at, and by, other members of the group is a fundamental, basic feature of behaviour – without which life in groups would not be possible at all. Among other things, Flack and de Waal investigated two types of behaviour among chimpanzees which bear witness to this tendency: food sharing and conflict management.

Most animals do not share food, but consume what they gather or catch themselves. In general this is true for chimpanzees as well, but food sharing (understood as the voluntary transfer of food from one individual to another) does occasionally occur. Flack and de Waal's studies have further shown that there is a certain principle of mutuality in the sharing of food between individuals. If A shares food with B, then B will also be inclined to share food with A (at least in the short term, meaning on the same day). On average it turns out that A and B will share the same amount of food with one another. Moreover, the studies have shown that other forms of behaviour, such as grooming, also have a positive influence on food sharing. If B has groomed A, A will be more inclined to share food with B (on the same day), whereas A will not be inclined to share food if A has already groomed B. Contrariwise, negative behaviour on B's part (such as an attack or show of aggression) will negatively influence A's inclination to share food with B. In such cases, A will be inclined to withhold food and other social 'services' from B.

On the basis of these observations, Flack and de Waal conclude that individuals in these groups of chimpanzees are able to differentiate among the various other individuals in the group with regard to their social behaviour. They are able, that is, to record and remember the behaviour of certain others in the group and the services they may have received from them, to 'evaluate' whether the behaviour of another chimpanzee was positive or negative, and in these and other ways they appear to have expectations of, or principles concerning, proper mutual and social behaviour.

In other words, chimpanzees not only display a certain general principle of reciprocity in their behaviour towards others, but evidently differentiate among those others according to the behaviour shown by each individual. Some degree of reciprocity can also be observed among other mammals living in much simpler herds or groups, but in a far more primitive and undifferentiated form. For example, buffalo or elephants living in herds show a tendency to protect from predators not only their own infants but those of other members of the herd. Such behaviour, however, represents a simple form of mutuality centred on the herd itself and what is happening to it, whereas the reciprocity displayed by chimpanzees is directed selectively at other individuals according to the behaviour they display. In this sense, the behaviour of chimpanzees represents a more advanced and developed form of centred group living than that displayed, for example, by herds of ruminants.

To avoid jumping to conclusions about the conscious mental capacities of chimpanzees, however, let us confine ourselves for the time being to saying that each individual in the chimpanzee group is able to allow its behaviour to be directed at and to be directed by the socially-directed behaviour of the other. In short: each individual's behaviour is directed at/by the behaviour of others.

This kind of formulation does not assume any advanced form of directedness at/by the behaviour of others, in which the individual would be able to reflect consciously on the social and moral 'attitude' implied by the other's behaviour. The chimpanzees' capacity to direct themselves at/by the behaviour of others cannot in this sense be compared to that of humans: we are able to direct our own behaviour according to the abstract personality of another individual (that is, according to a set of characteristics which we are able to recall independently of that person's immediate presence in time and space) and in relation to his/her 'mind' (that is to say, his/her attitude, point of view, consciousness, character, and so on).

The other type of behaviour which Flack and de Waal observed and studied among chimpanzees related to conflict and conflict management. As they point out, conflicts between cohabitating animals are unavoidable, but in so far as the existence and maintenance of the herd or group itself is essential to the well-being and survival of the individuals that compose it, it is crucial that they possess the behavioural capacity to contribute to restoring calm, balance and peace in the group, and to repair any 'social damage' that may occur between individuals.

Flack and de Waal have observed several forms of conflict-management behaviour. First, there is what may be called 'general group care'. Each individual within the group (and especially the dominant male) will in general react to unrest, aggression and conflict within the group by displaying intervening behaviour, dealing impartially with the conflicting parties regardless of his/her possible kinship or alliance with either (or any) of those involved, and irrespective of the latters' positions within the group hierarchy.

Second, there is what may be called the 'impartial reconciliation'. By various forms of behaviours (physical intervention, soothing sounds, grooming, and so on), a third party will try to reconcile two conflicting individuals who cannot handle the conflict themselves. Yet another form of behaviour involves consoling the victims of aggression.

On the basis of these studies, Flack and de Waal conclude that chimpanzees spend a lot of time and energy on managing and defusing conflicts and unrest and restoring peace and social balance in the group. Further, they conclude that the chimpanzees display a form of 'consideration for the community', although this should not be construed as meaning that the individual chimpanzee is capable of caring about, or reflecting on, the social condition of the group as an abstract unity or 'institution'. The forms of conflict-management behaviour which Flack and de Waal observed need imply no more than that each individual reacts to the atmosphere of the group in the here-and-now.

In my view, the chimpanzees' behaviour represents yet another protoform of directedness at/by the behaviour of others. (1) Each individual displays differentiated behaviour according, and in response, to the behaviour displayed by the parties in a conflict, among other things subsequently consoling the victims of aggression. (2) Each individual's behaviour is also directed at, and by, the overall directedness of the group (thus the individual's behaviour is influenced, for example, by the general disposition of the group to be peaceable or, on the contrary, restless and quarrelsome).

Similarly, Boehm (2000) has made interesting studies of the social and moral life of large groups of chimpanzees living in captivity in semi-natural environments in Arnhem Zoo, The Netherlands, and in Yerkes Regional Primate Research Centre, Atlanta. The observations show that in these environments female chimpanzees sometimes form alliances in order as a group to control dominating males who would otherwise dominate them individually. He reports, for example, the case of an alpha male that chased a sexual rival with the purpose of harming him. The females reacted with a collective, hostile 'waa bark' directed at the alpha male. The male stopped and gave up the pursuit. In the wild, an alpha male would have disregarded the disapproval of a few females, but evidently the collective action taken by a large number of disapproving females in this environment succeeded in controlling his behaviour. This form of collectivity is seldom observed among wild chimpanzees. Boehm's explanation is that, because chimpanzees living in protected areas are automatically supplied with sufficient food and other life necessities, they and are not obliged to engage full-time in foraging, and thus have surplus time and energy to devote to this kind of controlling behaviour.

The hostile and disapproving 'waa bark' is intentional, rather than involuntary, in the sense that when an individual hears (an)other individual(s) give the bark, he/she can decide for him/herself whether or not to participate in the barking. The collective 'waa bark' directed at a 'bullying' alpha male can thus be regarded as an expression of some kind of common decision on the part of the females to sanction an unacceptable form of behaviour.

Boehm also reports another, similar observation, namely that, if the dominating alpha male is too 'bullying' and displays behaviour that is too destructive to the group as a whole, this kind of female collective will often prefer to call in another male to act as a conciliator in solving conflicts between individuals.

On this basis, Boehm suggests that it would be reasonable to assume that our earliest hominid ancestors were able to display a similar proto-moral behaviour. We may conclude, therefore, that one of the first moral forms of behaviour consisted of collective social control directed at deviants in the group, above all those that posed a threat to the peace and security of the group and thus to the shared basis of the group's existence.

In terms of the present model, Boehm's observations can also be formulated as follows: the proto-moral behaviour of the chimpanzees, and hence probably also of our earliest hominid ancestors, emerged as an advanced form of centred directedness. Everybody within the group does the same: they are directed at, and by, the needs of the group as a whole, and their collective behaviour will be especially directed at/by deviations from the optimum group-centred behaviour.

Altogether, these studies of behavioural phenomena, revealing (simple proto-forms of) directedness at/by the behaviour of others, are constitutive elements in the more developed and organized forms of sociality and morality which developed, first in the form of a morality of proximity in the home base life of the hominids, and later in the more advanced form of remote morality.

As we will see in the chapters that follow, at the most advanced level of human existence – the individuated mode which characterises our existence today – this directedness at/by the behaviour of others takes the form, on the one hand, *of* a volitional and consciously thought-out consideration towards others ('I can acquaint myself with and understand what kind of person you are, what your attitude to the world, to others and to me is like, and what it ought to be like'); and, on the other, of a directedness at/by one's own inner self ('I can understand and make myself acquainted with who I am as a person and what my attitude is and ought to be'). There is, then, a social and moral dimension to this advanced form of directedness which can be abstracted from manifest forms of behaviour and reflected upon as a subject in itself.

As can be seen from the model above (see Figure 3.3), the individuated mode of life contains, in an organized form, constitutive elements which were already present at the decentred stage, albeit in a far simpler, protoform in which the individual's directedness was based on the fundamental characteristics of the overall mode of life, namely the decentred division of labour. Here, the individual directed his behaviour both by his own inner directedness (and preferences) and by those of others, but also thereby contributed to the overall, shared and cooperative directedness of the community as a whole. And this overall directedness in turn applied to the common and mutual sustenance of life on the basis of each co-operative contribution.

The Distinguishing Traits of Human Beings

This decentred stage of development, as we have seen, in turn represented an organization of the basic, constitutive elements of the socially centred stage. In its simplest form, this centredness is expressed by the directedness of gregarious mammals at/by the directedness of the group or herd as such. In its more advanced form, it manifests itself in, for example, the differentiated behaviour of group-living chimpanzees in response to the varied directednesses of other individuals. But, both in its simple and more advanced form, this centred form of behaviour shares the same basic characteristics: there is no cooperative division of labour; on the contrary, each individual does more or less the same, separately and in parallel with the other members of the group.

To sum up, we can see that a central characteristic of the modern individuated human psyche, the capacity self-consciously to direct oneself, both morally and socially, according to both one's own inner directedness and that of others, as reflected in their behaviour, is deeply rooted in the natural and cultural history of our species.

Individuated mode of life
It is only at this stage that the individual is able to be <u>directed at/by the directedness</u> of the other, as represented in the personality and the mind of the other.

Decentred mode of life
Individuals now engage in differentiated activities, but are still <u>directed at/by the directedness</u> in behaviour as such. By means of his/her activities the individual is co-operatively directed at/by the directedness in the multi-faceted contributions of the various group members.

Advanced forms of centred mode of life
At this stage, every member of the group is still engaged in the same activities, but the <u>directedness at/by directedness</u> is differentiated according to the individual's inclinations, as expressed in the directedness of behaviour.

Simple centred mode of life
Every member of the group is engaged in the same activites and there is no differentation in the <u>directedness at/by directedness</u>.

Figure 3.4 *is similar to Figure 3.3, except with regard to its focus on the development of a proto-morality and the capacity for directedness at/by others.*

Universalism

Is this individualised form of psyche and way of existence universal – or is it, with its pointing out of the decentralized and individualized aspects and the demands for self-conscious reflections and own life projects, more like an ethnocentric attempt to universalize the Western form? (a question which we will return to in Chapter 7).

No doubt the development of this form has accelerated because of two particular conditions, which are not universally widespread. First of all, the increasingly decentralized, co-operative, work-divided life in big societies. Secondly, the increasingly widespread inter-cultural exchange of goods, cultural artefacts, social institutions, etc., amongst these big societies. Big societies have developed in a number of places worldwide and at different times on several continents: Egypt, Mesopotamia, Mohenjo Daro in the Indus Valley, Meröe in Africa, the City States in China, the City States in Central America, etc., etc. Naturally not, however, with universal prevalence. Large parts of the world's population have never lived under such extreme decentralized and individuated demanding types of existence, and to some extent, still do not. Admittedly, focus here is not on a geographical universality, on the contrary, on universality in culture-historical dynamics.

The claim of universalism here is that people in any culture, in any type of society and in any culture-historical epoch are basically (1) intentionally connected to their surroundings, and (2) are mutually dependent on each other and so are co-existing beings. The claim of universalism is, furthermore, that the basic culture-historical dynamics are independent of politico-economical, cultural and religious forms, and are dynamics in the very growth and complexity in work division and mutual exchange – thereby moving from centralized connectedness to decentralized connectedness to individualized connectedness.

Finally, the claim of universalism is the culture-historical time arrow or irreversibility of the developmental dynamics: That the psyche as vertically organized horizontal/intentional connectedness, has been here since the first animal psyche and will not just disappear within the foreseeable future (unless it is bombed away, gene-manipulated and/or subsumed in some advanced over-individual cyberspace form). Likewise, I assume the vertical organisation of the human psyche, in the shape of centralised, decentralised and individualised world connections, is irreversible.

In other words, the general psyche form and life form, which the basic anthropological model is about, has come (so far) to stay. It has in its most tender germ form (where you can only talk of infinitely simple horizontal connections without any mentionable organization) been here for billions of years. In its very advanced form (where the organization has the characteristics of a directedness at/by directedness), we also see it in every human culture everywhere on Earth – regardless of the types of existences and their cultural, political, economic and religious shapes. We have, however, seen numerous examples of how decentralized and individualized types of existence and forms of psyches can develop and degenerate. There are good reasons to make sure that the basic anthropological model under development is shaped as a critical scientific model (see the Introduction). That the basic anthropological model has precisely such a critical potential, not least to the development of the Western type of existence, will be focused on next.

The age of individuation

Mobility

The individuated mode of life and mentality emerged approximately 10,000 years ago, achieved a more distinct and elaborate form in the city states which flourished around 3,000 years ago, and has continued to develop throughout the ensuing millennia, right up to the present day. Depending on the degree of elaboration required, this model of development may be divided into a variable number of epochs. Certainly, as we shall see in the Chapter on free will, the fourth century AD – the period of St Augustine – marked one distinct stage of development within this overall model.

In the present chapter we will go straight to the period of industrialisation which brought about several important changes in the human mode of life, above all through the uprooting and resettlement of large sections of the population. Initially, this process of upheaval took the form of a mass migration from the countryside to the industrial cities and, later on, from one continent to another – including, not least, the migration of many Europeans to North America. Later on, the twentieth century was characterized by rapidly increasing mobility from city to city (a trend that began at the beginning of the twentieth century, especially in the United States, but started later elsewhere, accelerating in Europe, in particular, as a result of the creation of the European Union). Throughout the previous millennia, the vast majority of people throughout the world had lived their entire lives within the same small local society and environment (the same village or the same quarter of an industrial town). Nowadays, by contrast, human beings have become hyper mobile and may move several times during their lifetime to pursue careers and job opportunities. Even in their daily routines, many city dwellers are forced into hyper mobility, often travelling great distances between their various everyday activities. A person's workplace is seldom close to his/her home, and the people he/she spends the working day with are seldom the same people that he/she will socialize with during leisure hours. And, again, they will seldom be his/her neighbours or kin.

This hyper mobile mode of life means that bonds are constantly being broken and new ones formed. A person's ties with a particular locality are so frequently broken that the concept of one's native soil, with its implications of rootedness in a certain geographical area, has gradually lost its meaning. Similarly, bonds to particular people tend to be broken or fade – and this applies as much to bonds with family as to those with friends, acquaintances or neighbours. Meanwhile, new acquaintances, friends and colleagues constantly appear. In earlier times, a person would know the local people in the community throughout his/her life, and the life stories of all the people in the community would thus be interwoven. Now, at the beginning of the twenty-first century, the hyper mobile human being in the developed world will seldom count old acquaintances and friends among the people he/she associates with every day. Similarly, ties created by a person's work are continually broken due to frequent changes of job or career, and innovations in the workplace mean that the worker is required constantly to adapt and readjust his/her activities. In former times, one's life story was something which one could – almost literally – see and feel, since one was surrounded by objects and people one had known throughout one's life. Now the hyper-mobile human being is constantly surrounded by new objects and new people with whom he/she shares no common history. A further distinctive feature of our times is that everyday tools of the household, as well as those of the workplace, are constantly being replaced as they become obsolete. This is especially so when it comes to information technology. Scarcely has a person acquired one routine than the tools associated with it become outmoded and are replaced by newly-developed forms of technology tools which, again, require new ways of thinking, and new routines.

In earlier times, the basic conditions of a person's life (in terms of his/her biological makeup, social position and so on) were seen as unalterable 'givens' with which the individual must come to terms – with whatever degree of serenity, stoicism or fatalism. To an increasing degree, however, modern human beings are able to influence virtually all aspects of their lives. To an ever-greater extent, we will be able in the future to intervene genetically and biomedically in the course of our lives. We will be able to know beforehand the genetic makeup of the children we will have, and before long we will be able to choose which child we want in advance, as well as how we want our bodies to look (through plastic surgery, muscle increasing preparations, and the manipulation of our own genes), and how we want to function mentally (through 'happy' pills, memory-improving drugs, digital brain amplifiers, etc.).

These various steps towards ever more advanced forms of individuation may be generally characterized as leading away from the form of individuation in which the individual maintains his/her connectedness with the community through professions of belief, allegiance and so on, towards a form in which he/she asserts his/her connectedness through a striving for authenticity.

From profession to authenticity

The mobile mode of life of today appears to demand of individuals that they are able, to an ever greater degree, to formulate their own values and make their own judgements of what is right and wrong. The fact that people are increasingly free, or required, to make their own choices and to establish their own values and individual life projects, means that there is a greater opportunity than ever before for the individual to differ from others in terms of these choices and judgements. Increasingly, a person has the opportunity to come into being as an individual. Whereas, in earlier times, the individual's life was framed by a professed adherence to an external and collective discourse, a person's life today is increasingly shaped by a professed adherence to one's own discourse (see also Taylor 1991). The new requirement, the new mode of life, is to be sincere to oneself, to one's own values, one's own life project. The demand made in the modern era of individuation is a demand for authenticity.

To be 'authentic' is to take responsibility for one's own life-project and for one's own mode of life which this project is intended to create, sustain or break. The demand for authenticity requires one to make one's own judgement as to what constitutes the good life and one's true directedness. In this connection, Taylor (1982) differentiates between a weak and a strong way of evaluating and choosing one's directedness. In the terminology of the present model, this difference can be characterized as follows. The weak evaluator operates primarily at the decentred level: he or she follows his/her own inclinations according to what seems the optimum behaviour in a given situation. Alternatively, the weak evaluator can be seen as someone with an embryonic or poorly developed level of individuation who allows him/herself to be seduced, without great reflection, by a given system of belief. The strong evaluator, by contrast, will give focused and thorough consideration to his/her overall values in life, without letting him/herself be distracted by the momentary possibilities and temptations of each situation. The behaviour of the strong evaluator is directed at/by certain general principles concerning what he/she should do and who he/she should be, and is alert to the possible new values that may develop on the basis of incomplete or outdated value systems.

Taylor's three evils

Taylor (1991) has identified three ways in which this modern endeavour to achieve authenticity has developed and may degenerate.

First, he discusses individualism, emphasising that the modern freedom of choice was gained by breaking away from the old guidelines imposed by an external, moral discourse. The advantage offered by this greater freedom is precisely that the individual is increasingly able to form his/her own value-judgements as to what constitutes the good and true life – especially in those complex areas of modern life where there are conflicting values, a great many possible choices, and no real guidelines as to what the right choice would be. The value of this type of individuation through authenticity thus lies in the possibility it gives us, through reflection and dialogue with others, to focus on what one can do and what one ought to do in situations where no strict guidelines are offered in advance. Which education and career should one choose? What limits should be put on genetic manipulation? Should higher priority be given to several hip operations or to one heart operation which costs the same? Should smokers have to go to the back of the queue for medical treatment? To what extent should we accept that members of another culture may treat their fellow members in ways which our own culture would judge improper, unlawful, outrageous or an infringement of human rights? And so on.

However, this new endeavour to achieve authenticity also has its disadvantages. Having freed ourselves from what appeared to be stifling restrictions on our mode of life, we may also experience a sense of loss at the disappearance of overall guidelines for life. The effort to achieve autonomy may easily turn into an individualistic endeavour and lead to a failure to appreciate the value of the social community in which one lives and without which one could not exist. At the same time, there is a tendency towards a general 'tolerance', towards the attitude, for example, that everyone has the right to live in one's country, irrespective of their views on life, their political convictions or their culture. Taken at face value, this kind of tolerance, which provides space for political, cultural and philosophical diversity, should be welcomed in the name of a non-domineering democracy – but not if this 'liberality' in fact conceals the lack of an overall view of the social and cultural problems involved, or the potential difficulties implied by conflicting values; nor if it becomes an excuse for indifference and ignorant self-centeredness.

The second danger posed by the striving for authenticity in its degenerate form lies, according to Taylor, in instrumentalism. When nothing is any longer sacred, an instrumental form of reasoning takes over. The question is no longer: what ought I to do, but rather: what is worth (my) while? A person's relationship to others will be determined principally by economic considerations as to whether or not it is worthwhile to relate to him or to her. Moreover, when there are no longer any external sanctions in the form of divine directives concerning the good life, and when the world no longer contains the spirit of God or some other divine principle, a danger exists that humans will begin to act irresponsibly in relation to nature too. Our environment – the natural flora and fauna, and even our fellow human beings – may begin to be regarded purely as raw material to be exploited for our own purposes rather than as something of value in their own right, which we are morally bound to nurture. Indeed, even our concern about the natural environment, or our attempt to consider animal rights, is in danger of becoming absurd through the degeneration of individualism into a self-centred instrumentalism.

In its degenerate, instrumental form, Taylor argues, the search for authenticity has become synonymous with the freedom to dispense with any kind of restrictive framework or social ties, and recklessly to create ourselves and our own existence in any way we choose. We experience ourselves as free when we are in full control of, and have mastery over, our own conditions of existence, and when we have optimum technological control over the surrounding world.

As a result of this instrumental, rationalist approach, the sense of moral connectedness generated by shared values and caring, concerned behaviour is put at risk. Indeed, the idea of connectedness may appear to be in opposition to our freedom to control our own lives.

The third danger, which Taylor identifies, is that of political alienation and a weakened sense of social responsibility. With the emphasis on self-realisation, and the lack of concern towards the environment in general and the social, cultural and political community in particular, the individual risks becoming locked within his/her own self-centeredness. In its degenerate form, the search for authenticity translates simply into a preoccupation with one's own existence and activities, and leads to a withdrawal from the common political, ethical and cultural responsibility for *co*-existence. The individual is liable to lose any broad political perspective or sense of social responsibility. As a result, the centres of political power (the state, the administration), even if they remain formally democratic, will tend to lose touch with their popular roots. Unfettered in this sense by the popular will, politicians will be more prone inadvertently to 'go over people's heads' and make policy decisions that fail to cater for the people's real needs. Politics is reduced to a matter of statistics and internal parliamentary struggles for power.

The cure for 'degenerate' authenticity

From the perspective of the present model, the problems identified by Taylor can be seen to result from the fact that the individuated discourse is detached from the vertical continuum of the socially centred and decentred layers of life. The cure for this detachment lies not in a nostalgic return to the safe, religious and/or ideological fundamentalism of earlier times, which was centred around a charismatic ideal. As Taylor himself emphasises, resources exist within the modern endeavour to achieve authenticity, which are both required and made possible by the modern individuated mode of life, and these resources should not be recklessly discarded.

The cure lies in developing insight into, and respect for, the vertical continuum itself: in recognising that the our current mode of life – as determined not only by individual history but by the natural and cultural history of mankind – is fundamentally still based upon the 'morality of proximity' generated by collective human co-existence at the earliest 'centred' level. In other words, the cure lies in understanding, and living in accordance with, this fundamental centredness which constitutes both one of the most essential human traits and the deepest layer in the topography of each individual (as well as in the psychological topography of the self, as we shall see in Chapter 7).

However, it is not enough simply to develop awareness of this layer of the self, as certain psychotherapeutic practices would prescribe. Nor is it simply a matter of 'becoming' or realising oneself by trying to identify the cultural – and biological roots of our existence. It is also a matter of developing or acquiring what Taylor calls the mastery of the strong evaluator: the ability, that is, to deal as an individual with the basic questions of life – the general principles of what one ought to do and who one ought to be – and to consider what new values might be developed on the basis of incomplete or outdated value systems. This is the contribution which we, in our highly individuated and authenticity-seeking mode of life today, can make to the vertical continuum, the topography of life. On the one hand this contribution consists of the ongoing organization and reorganization of the elements of one's own life and personality in an individual human discourse and a personal life project. On the other, it consists of generating still further ways of organizing and reorganizing the community where social dilemmas and conflicts of value both require and make this possible. To come into being as an individual is not just a matter of appropriating what is already given and passed down to us through the vertical continuum, but also of endeavouring, to some degree, to create new insights and to put forward value-oriented solutions to new problems within one's society. This kind of creativity, and the ability to make such choices, necessarily implies the possession of free will. Precisely how this free will can emerge within, and as a result of, human nature will be the subject of the following two chapters.

The first dimension of an anthropological, psychological taxonomy

The topography of human life, as presented in this chapter and illustrated by Figure 3.3, will be the point of departure for our considerations in the chapters to come concerning free will, consciousness, self-consciousness and the self. It also represents a central dimension in the taxonomy of the distinctively human traits which we will address in the next chapters.

The central thesis is that these different layers within the human topography are generated by the demands and opportunities arising from human life itself. The most fundamental is the centred layer, where our humanity, or our development as human beings, is rooted in the fact of our co-existence. Next comes the decentred level, which opens up abundant different facets of human life; and finally we arrive at the individuated level, where for the first time we have the possibility of organized reflection upon, and conscious development of, these human qualities, be they centred or decentred. This, then, is the hierarchically organized constitution of the human being to which psychical phenomena may provide the key. Each of these layers of life both demand and make possible certain psychic capacities, dispositions and possibilities, and each so to speak present us with existential tasks that can be solved through the development of particular psychic features and abilities. It is for this reason that free will, consciousness and the self are described and explained in the following chapter in terms of this kind of vertical topography. In other words, we will find the centred, decentred and individuated layers in the free will, the human (self-) consciousness and the human self.

Chapter 4

Levels of Connectedness of the Psyche

In the natural and cultural-historical perspective of the previous chapter, we formed a hierarchical model of the distinctive human traits, identifying the centred, decentred, and individuated layers within us. The relationship between these layers – their internal hierarchical order – was described in terms of organization and constitution, with the upper layers organizing, and at the same time being constituted by, the layers further down. In the present chapter, we will take a closer look at the explanatory power of the concepts of organization and constitution. For this purpose we must first look at the nature of scientific explanation, and determine what kinds of scientific explanations are available within the field of psychology.

Forms of explanation

Causal explanations are explanations of fundamental relations

The basic way to explain why something is the way it is (a state) or why something happens the way it does (a movement) is to refer to its cause. The white billiard ball will start to roll across the billiard table because the red ball has just rolled across the table and pushed it. One event is explained, in other words, by reference to a prior event: its cause.

Functionalist explanations are explanations of functional connectednesses

Living organisms fundamentally consist of physical/chemical substances and processes which interact in different ways. However, simple causal explanations do not suffice to explain why these processes interact the way they do rather than in some other way. Yet we can observe a system that connects these processes: they are organized according to rather well-defined overall principles. Functionalist explanations go beyond causal ones by explaining why this interaction exists in terms of its function.

A functionalist explanation is one that states that organisms are the way they are, and do what they do, because this particular state or interaction of processes has a utility effect or a function in relation to the surrounding environment. A process or a form of connection is functional if it contributes to maintaining the organism's viability, capacities and chances of reproduction. In other words, the functions of the organism are organized according to the overall principles of evolution. According to evolutionary theory, the only functional systems are those which ultimately serve the purpose of ensuring that the organism's genetic material is reproduced and passed on to the next generation. The process of natural selection means that if the structure and behaviour of the organism cannot sufficiently adapt to the surrounding environment, its chances of passing on its genetic material are reduced (see previous chapter.)

Functionalist explanations of this kind cannot be applied to physical or chemical states and events that have a simple causal explanation. There is no functional reason behind the actions of the billiard balls on the billiard table.

By contrast, a functionalist theory of general psychology would enable us, to a large extent, to explain the basic forms of human life found at the fundamental, socially centred level. The socially centred forms of directedness can be seen as functional in the sense that they helped to maintain the home base life of the early hominids: those individuals that could not adapt to living in and sustaining this common mode of life would have a reduced chance of survival and hence less opportunity to pass on their genes. Those individuals who were more directed at the home base mode of life would have a greater chance of survival and hence of passing on, to potential offspring, their genetic disposition to adapt well to home base living. Thus, in seeking to explain certain fundamental human traits, such as a centred directedness at/by the community and a capacity for connectedness, one may point to the fact that these features have (or had) a functional value for us. As we have seen in previous chapters, however, there is more to being human than maintaining a functional connectedness with the surrounding environment. The higher, decentred and individualized layers of the human self require far more complex forms of connection, involving not only functional inclinations, but the expression of preferences, the profession of certain beliefs, and the endeavour to achieve authenticity. Here the functionalist explanations are simply not good enough, for two reasons: the first of which concerns animals as well as humans, and the second humans alone, as we shall see.

Intentionality explanations are explanations of behavioural and action-based connectedness

The first difficulty encountered by functionalist explanations is that the principles of evolution are first and foremost concerned with species-specific behaviour. A rabbit, for example, is able to display a wide range of types of behaviour, all of which can be explained in terms of their evolutionary function. Thus it displays flight behaviour when a fox is nearby; food-gathering behaviour when it is hungry and there is no immediate danger; mating behaviour during the mating season, and so on. We can use a functional explanation to account for these types of behaviour and for the fact that the rabbit activates them in appropriate situations. Such functional explanations, however, are not adequate to account in more detail for the rabbit's particular behaviour in particular situations: we cannot determine, on the basis of evolutionary principles, for example whether the rabbit in a given situation will run to the right instead of to the left, or into this area instead of another area. Thus its concrete behaviour in a specific situation cannot be explained by how the rabbit species in general adapts in order to survive and pass on its genes. Rather, to account for its specific behaviour, we must look at how the individual itself apprehends the situation and is able to direct its behaviour to achieve the optimal effect within that situation.

In other words, the individual's inclination to do this or that in a particular situation must be explained in terms of its active effort to attune and optimise its behaviour according to its present state, its capacities, and the demands of the situation itself. The behaviour it actually displays is thus explained by principles relating to each individual's active organization of its own functions: that is, by principles of intentionality – for self-activated behaviour is intentional behaviour. Let us take a closer look at the kinds of self-activated behaviour that cannot be explained purely in terms of their functionality.

The transition from functionality to intentionality

The manifestation of intentional behaviour on the part of animals marks a significant transition to a new and higher level of existence which demands a form of explanation quite different from the simple, linear, causal and functional explanations appropriate to plants or inanimate matter. Engelsted (see Engelsted 1999) characterises this kind of behaviour – this way of connecting with the world – by adopting the concepts of interface and interspace. A plant exists by virtue of its metabolism, meaning the various internal biochemical structures and processes that depend on external input, primarily in the form of sunlight and various nutritious substances. This input occurs via the plant's interface with its surroundings

– that is to say, through the points at which it comes into contact with the surrounding world. The plant has cells which can make use of sunlight through photosynthesis, and others which can absorb the elementary substances required for this and other processes, and these cells represent the plant's interface with the world: the only surface on which the world can, so to speak, make an 'impression' and hence 'impress' the plant. We are not, of course, speaking of 'impressing' here in the psychic sense of the word. The plant has no mind, no psyche, no ideas of its surroundings – the biochemical changes involved take place only on its interface (the amount of light and/or nutrition the plant receives will affect the biochemical states and processes on its interface, and hence the life of the plant as a whole).

The essential and fundamental difference between plants and animals, Engelsted shows, is that for animals, unlike plants, this kind of interface, which is constructed for the passive reception of essential forms of energy and nutrition, is not sufficient to sustain life. Placed in a sunny spot, the plant is able passively to absorb the nutrition it needs – whereas the animal is incapable of doing so. Ultimately, the animal's biochemical constitution is similar to that of the plant, but (in the case of herbivores) the animal's need for energy and nutrition must be covered by eating plants that have already made use of solar energy and nutritious substances and have synthesized these into plant tissue which the animal's digestive system can then absorb. Alternatively, if the animal is a carnivore, it can absorb this basic energy and elementary matter by eating other animals that have eaten plants. The decisive difference between plants and animals is that the animal, in order to get its supply of useful energy, must move to the plant or animal it wants to eat. To use Engelsted's terminology, it must move in interspace. At the same time, and because of this, another decisive difference appears. There is no such thing as 'out there' to the plant – all that exists for it are the changing states on its interface. To the animal, by contrast, objects exist 'out there', including edible objects to which it must move if it is to eat them. The object is separated from the animal by a greater or lesser distance in space, and must be hunted, or, if it is hidden, tracked down along more or less winding routes. The animal may have to overcome various obstacles in pursuit of the object, which may be elusive and may even sting or bite. Moreover, it may be removed in time as well as space: available at some time in the near future, but not immediately – and so on. Engelsted points out that, in pursuing its object through interspace, the animal must go through four different stages. The ultimate stage is consumption, but prior to consuming the object the animal will in various ways have manipulated it (caught it, killed it, chewed it, and so on); prior to this it will have had contact with the object (heard it, observed it, felt it, smelled it and hence managed to place it in time and space), and, prior to all these stages, the animal must have been impelled by hunger to move: to embark, in other words, on its search in interspace for a suitable object.

Levels of Connectedness of the Psyche

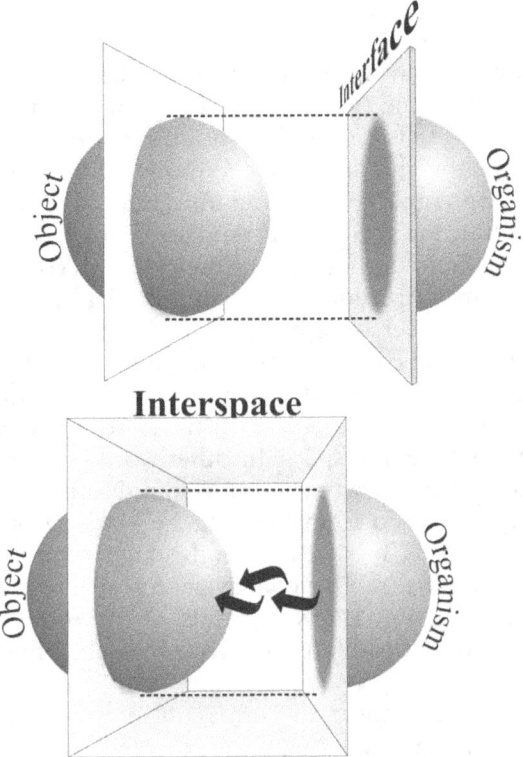

Figure 4.1 *shows the two ways in which living organisms may be connected. (1) Via an interface – here we see how the object, so to speak, makes an impression on the interface of the organism. (2) Via interspace – here we see how the organism must move into interspace and seize the object (or move towards it). In this way, the object makes an impression on the organism.*

It is precisely through their being in an 'interspace relation', rather than an 'interface relation', with the outside world that a new kind of connectedness emerges in animals. The entire state of the animal is attuned to something outside itself, an object that is separated from it in time and space. This state of connectedness – the attunement of the animal's entire organism to an active search for, and consumption of, an object – is precisely what distinguishes the animal from the plant. The animal's entire being is directed at this object – and to be directed at something is by definition to be intentionally connected to it. Plants are only functionally connected to the world via their interface with it. The animal's organism also consists of these basic, functional interfaces – for example, the cells of the animal's intestinal wall function as interfaces in so far as they alter their state according to the kind of absorbable matter being transported through the intestines. But in addition, the animal's organism is such that it is intentionally connected with the outside world through interspace.

Engelsted identifies the two different kinds of intentionality. The first, and most basic kind, is intentionality about an object. At the most fundamental level, the animal is impelled to move by its perception of, or concern with, a given object. When a rabbit is hungry, for instance, its entire being and attention are focused on the carrot nearby: whatever move it makes in this state is accordingly about the carrot. In contrast to plants, all self-propelling animals, including the most primitive organisms that consist of just a few cells, possess this basic form of 'aboutness' intentionality. However, only the more complex animal organisms can be seen to possess the higher cognitive and motivational capacities to form internal, mental ideas (however primitive) of an object which is not yet present, or cannot be seized, in its immediate interspace. In other words, only the more highly developed animals can move beyond the 'about' form of intentionality to form intentions: that is, to form ideas of the kinds of object that would cover their present needs. It is only when this higher form of intentionality is present that the animal can begin actively to search with the intention of finding the object that will satisfy its wants. This form of intentionality is thus a more highly developed form of directedness than the 'about' form on which it is based.

The need for explanation in terms of intentionality, rather than functionality alone, begins then with the emergence of organisms that are intentionally connected with the outside world through interspace, rather than functionally connected to it through an interface. This basic model has been further elaborated by Mammen (1999), who distinguishes between what he calls sensory categories and choice categories. Mammen (1983) bases this distinction on mathematical set theory. Here we will content ourselves with illustrating the distinction in terms of the ways in which living organisms connect with their surroundings.

As we have seen, when a living organism connects to the surrounding world, the world in turn can be said to 'make an impression on' the organism. It may, for example, leave traces on the interface of the plant, in the form of sunlight or other forms of nutrition which the plant is able to absorb, or it may make an impact on, for example, the sensory or intestinal cells of animals. A vast array of other physical or chemical processes may be going on around the plant, but if these do not 'match' the plant's interface, they will leave no significant biological trace (to use a completely misplaced mentalist expression, one might say that such processes go right over the plant's head). For instance, the chlorophyll granules of plants are light-sensitive, and sunlight therefore makes an impression on them. At the same time, these granules are exposed to a variety of other phenomena, such as smells and sounds, which leave no significant biological trace on them at all. Together with an endless variety of other phenomena, these smells and sounds simply make no impression on the plant. Those impressions of the world which the organism does receive through the structure of its interface, however, will be categorised by the organism in sensory terms. These are what Mammen refers to as sensory categories.

Sensory categorization represents an algorithmic way of connecting and relating to the surrounding world: in other words, the impressions which the surrounding world makes on the interface, and the ways in which these impressions are categorized (for example into different kinds of light and substance) are governed by certain specifiable rules and criteria derivable from the structure of the interface itself. By analysing this structure we can determine which phenomena make an impression on it and which do not, much as we may determine the exact shape of the key required to fit a particular lock by analysing the interface of the lock itself. There is, in this sense, nothing new or surprising about sensory categorization, for in principle we can work out in advance what aspects of the world a certain organism can register through its interface. A plant's relationship with the surrounding world in this sense can hold no surprises.

By contrast, choice categorization is in principle non-algorithmic: there are no rules or criteria for determining, beforehand, how a given connection with the world will be made. This can be illustrated by considering how one would choose a random series of numbers from the (endless) sequence of natural numbers. The choice can be made in an infinite variety of ways. We may, of course, choose a series according to rules given in advance: for instance, our series may consist of even numbers only, of every fifth number or of every tenth number which is not divisible by 117, and so on.

But we may also choose a random series from the entire sequence of numbers: random in the sense that is not based on any system or set of criteria known in advance, even if we can subsequently detect a pattern within the chosen series which could then, in principle, be infinitely extended on the basis of now established rules. But on the first occasion that this particular series was chosen, the rules governing the pattern of numbers was unknown to us and the series was entirely new, unpredictable, and perhaps surprising. The particular series was created in the very act of choosing, and in this sense the choice itself could be said to represent a tiny piece of true history – understood in the sense discussed in Chapter 2, where history is seen as an ongoing process in which genuinely new phenomena emerge in an unpredictable way.

This is the key difference between an algorithmic, criterion- and rule-based form of categorizing the impressions made by the surrounding world, and a non-algorithmic choice of how the world may make an impression. It is only through the exercise of choice that something new and surprising may emerge – and as we shall see further on in the present chapter, and in those that follow, this applies all the way through to the personal and social actions of individual human beings and their existential choices in life.

This distinction can now be used to characterize in detail the difference between the connections established by animals on the basis of choice, and those established by plants (or by the functional cells of animals). The difference is precisely that the animal needs to move into interspace in order to search for, make contact with, and manipulate another (moving) object.

A fox, for example, moves in search of food. It scents a rabbit and initiates the process of the hunt. But the details of this particular hunt, and the course it will take, are quite unpredictable. The rabbit will rush along in unpredictable ways, changing direction from right to left, in part due to the various unforeseeable features of the landscape it runs through (bushes, streams, various kinds of obstacles). The fox will rush off, catch up with the rabbit, then choose to move first to the right, then a little to the left of it in order to knock it off its feet or sink its teeth into it. The particular course of the hunt thus emerges gradually and unpredictably. As the hunt proceeds, the fox continuously receives new impressions, which in turn prompt it to find new ways of pursuing its goal.

Because the fox is moving in interspace, it needs to possess more than the ability to register algorithmic patterns given in advance. It must also be able, often very rapidly, to develop its pattern recognition in response to a particular situation. It must be able to learn from the development of the situation and, on this basis, to evaluate it anew and act accordingly in the next move it makes. To put it in more abstract terms: the impressions of the world that the fox must be able to receive cannot be determined in advance, but are constantly created anew. In this sense, the fox must be creative in forming its tactics. One might contrast its behaviour with that of a heat-seeking missile, which would respond only to the infrared radiation of the rabbit and, via sensors and negative feedback, constantly correct its course as the rabbit changed direction. The fox, by contrast, will try now this move, now that in its attempt to beat the rabbit, and this trial-and-error method leads it to weave a complex and unpredictable course. There are, of course, certain constant factors at play: rabbits will always provoke a chase-reaction in the fox, and this particular rabbit is bound, like every other, to behave in a 'rabbit-like' way: it will run as fast as it can and jump alternately to right and left, or it will take cover if it has gained a sufficient lead. Nevertheless, the details of a particular rabbit's behaviour in flight are unpredictable, as are the specific actions of the pursuing fox who, constantly under the impact of new impressions, continuously reviews its situation and makes fresh choices on the basis of it.

In other words, the very fact that, unlike plants, animals and human beings move into interspace, means that they develop a non-algorithmic, intentional form of connection with the world, which (1) makes an impression: in this sense the animal's intentionality is about something in the world, and (2) triggers expression in the form of an active effort to search for, make contact with, and manipulate objects in the world: in this sense, the animal's intentionality is also characterized by purpose.

Intentionality, behaviour, and action

As we have seen, functional explanations are inadequate to explain the behaviour of animals, whose defining characteristic is that they establish an active and intentional connection with the world by moving in interspace. To say that a form of connectedness is intentional is to say that it is always directed at something in the surroundings. From the 'inside-out' ($\Rightarrow$) perspective of the organism – the animal or the person – this intentional connectedness will take the form of an active search, on the part of the subject (S), for a certain object, and a reaching out at that object. This aspect of intentional connectedness – the subject's directedness as viewed from the inside – can be called the *intentio aspect* (S$\Rightarrow$). Intentio is the subject's directedness, or behaviour, seen from his/her point of view, i.e., from the inside out.

To say that any form of behaviour is intentional, however, is also to say that it is directed by something. The rabbit may be hungry and will therefore direct its search activity at the food on offer in the surrounding environment. However, the rabbit's behaviour is just as attuned to, and determined by, the nature of those surroundings as it is by its own present state. If there is a fox nearby, the need for food will take second place to the need for safety, and the rabbit will go into flight. But if all is peace and quiet, and there is sufficient food on offer nearby, the rabbit will start to eat. Thus its behaviour is not only directed at the surroundings, but by the surroundings. So, if we take the opposite, outside-in ($\Leftarrow$) perspective, looking at the rabbit's behaviour from the point of view of the surroundings, the rabbit's directedness will be seen to be directed by something (O). This 'something' is just as much the reason why the subject directs its behaviour in a certain way as is the rabbit's own condition (for example, its hunger, anxiety or desire to mate) and its various capacities. This aspect of directedness, where the behaviour of the subject is directed by something in the surroundings, may here be called the intentum aspect ($\Leftarrow$O). Intentum is the subject's directedness, or behaviour, seen from the outside in.

Thus the behavioural or action-based connectedness of a self-activating organism cannot only be defined from 'inside' or from 'outside'. Because of the dual nature of intentionality, our reasons for action will always have both an outside-in aspect (intentum) and an inside-out aspect (intentio). A self-activating organism is always directed both at something and by something. Any intentional behaviour contains both an intentio and an intentum (S⇒⇐O). (See also the previous chapter).

As we have seen, functional explanations are inadequate to deal with the self-activating, intentional behaviour of both animals and humans. But they also run into a specific difficulty as far as human activity is concerned.

As biological, evolutionarily developed beings, we are, of course, able to display the kind of functionally optimal behavioural connectedness previously described. Behaviour should be understood as goal-directed activity on the part of a living organism (that is, as activity designed to connect the organism in a certain way with its surroundings). This general definition allows for the manifestation of behaviour on the part of even the most simple single-cell organisms. They too are able to activate themselves to move in the direction of food or away from poisonous or otherwise unfavourable milieus. But obviously, the forms of such behaviour become gradually more complex and advanced as we move up through the more developed species.

By means of its behaviour, the animal is able to move into interspace and to facilitate its own activity (see also Engelsted 1989, 1994; Katzenelson 1996). Plants cannot display this kind of self-activating goal-directed behaviour. The gradual extension of a plant's roots further out or further down, for instance, is a purely functional process that serves an evolutionary purpose, rather than a form of goal-directed behaviour. As a rule, self-activated goal-directed behaviour is exhibited only by animals. The transition from plant to animal life is thus a transition from organisms displaying purely functional processes to organisms displaying actual behaviour.

Moreover, it is only when an organism exhibits behaviour as such that one may begin to speak of its psychic qualities – that is, of a form of organization by the organism itself of its own constitutive functions. The purely functional processes are not psychic processes, but proto-psychic forms of connectednesses, which represent the basic, constitutive elements of genuinely psychic states or events.

In the case of human beings, however, we find not only behaviour but a more developed form of activity that may be designated as 'action'. As a form of connection with the outside world, actions cannot be explained in the same terms as behaviour. The form of connectedness which actions produce, and the reasons that direct them, depend on principles that go beyond mere behavioural explanation. Our reasons for action stem from our values, our dreams and desires, our sense of what is right, our engagement in life, our empathy for other people or, conversely, our irritation with them and condemnation of their actions, and so on. As will be apparent from our account of the evolutionary development of the distinctively human traits (in the previous chapter), behaviour is found first and foremost at the centred and decentred levels, and may be characterized

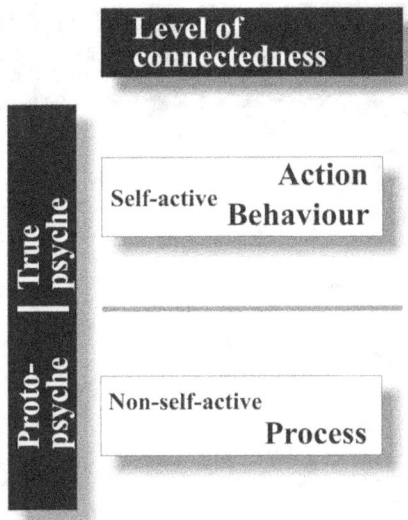

Figure 4.2 *illustrates the distinction between non self-activated processes in nature and true self-activated behaviour. Psychic phenomena emerge with the emergence of behaviour.*

by individual inclinations and preferences. But it is only at the individuated level that we find genuine actions, that is, forms of activity that are self-consciously undertaken, of the individual's own free will, on the basis of his/her professed beliefs or – in the most modern human societies – on the basis of his/her search for authenticity.

In order to distinguish more clearly between intentional behaviour and intentional action, we may follow Katzenelson's taxonomy (1996), designating behavioural connectedness as intentional, and action-based connectedness as intentioned. Both forms of activity are distinct from the kinds of processes that can be explained in purely functional terms, but whereas intention*al* explanations are concerned with self-activated behaviour, intention*ed* explanations are concerned with self-initiated actions.

Organization and constitution

Organization and constitution from an epistemological and an ontological perspective

We have now seen how different levels of reality (from an ontological perspective) correspond to different levels of theoretical explanation (from an epistemological perspective). This is illustrated in Figure 4.3.

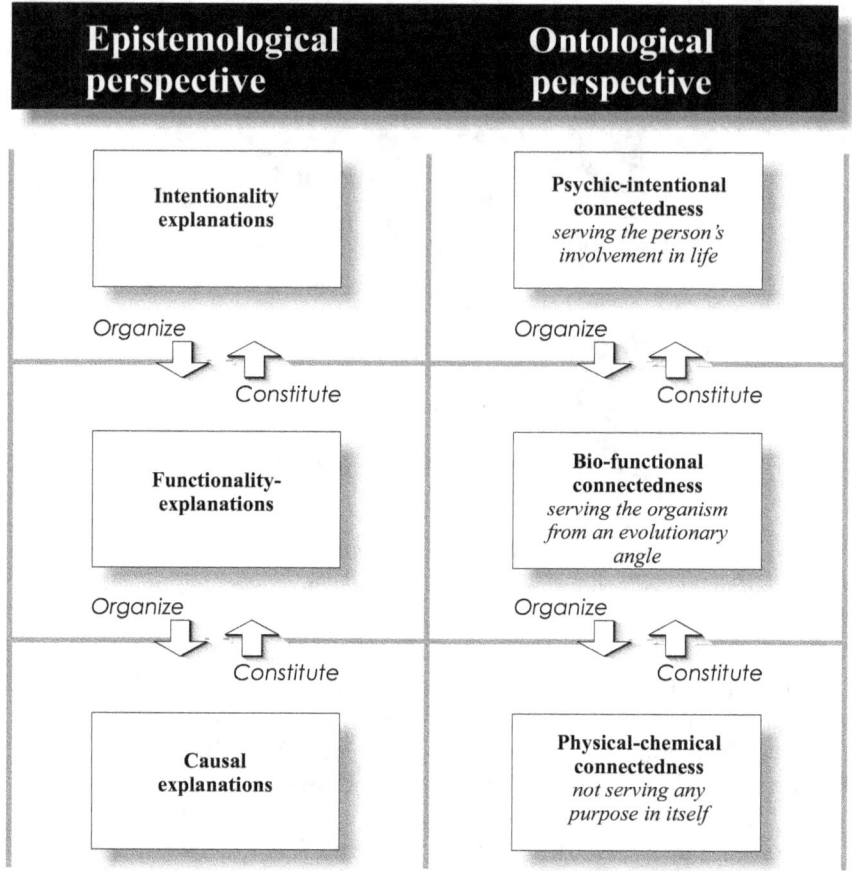

Figure 4.3 *Schematic representation of the relation between explanatory levels and levels of reality.*

Moreover, we have looked at the mutual relation between organization and constitution, in which the lower levels form the basis for, or constitute, the higher levels, which in turn rise above these lower levels by organizing their constitutive elements in a particular way. Thus, for example, self-activating behaviour is both constituted by purely functional, non-self-activating processes and, at the same time, becomes superior to these processes by organizing them.

Thus any explanation based on intentionality, of the kind that we must use, in general psychology, to explain the nature of the psyche and, in anthropological psychology, to explain the distinctive features of the human psyche, must be based on an understanding of this 'downward' hierarchy, in which the lower levels are organized by the higher ones.

Downward causality and the dynamics of organization

To reach a more precise understanding of this kind of downward organization, we may use the concept of *downward causality* or of downward cause-and-effect between the different levels.

Viewed from the bottom up, functional explanations are quite simply built on, or constituted by, causal explanations. That is to say: 'Function B is due to preceding cause A'. Viewed from the top down, the constitutive elements of causal explanations are organized by higher-level evolutionary principles. Thus: 'Function B is due to preceding cause A according to the higher evolutionary principles'.

Likewise, functional explanations, when viewed from the bottom up, represent the constitutive elements of higher-level intentional explanations, which, when viewed from the top down, can be seen in turn to organize these functional elements.

Within this kind of explanatory hierarchy, cause and effect operate in two directions. On the one hand, we have (1) what may be called constituting upward causality: by becoming a constituent within the overall organizational pattern at the higher level, a cause is transformed into an effect. On the other hand, we have (2) what may be called organizing downward causality: by organizing the constitutive elements according to certain well-defined principles, a cause operates 'downward', determining the way in which the basic elements – the basic causes – interact and hence become constituents at the higher level. The existence of an 'upward' causality, in which the lower elements make up the constitutive basis for existence at the higher levels, seems intuitively obvious: 'Of course one must have a brain in order to have a psyche, and of course the brain processes fundamentally influence what we experience and identify as psychic processes'. 'Downward' causality, by contrast, may seem counter-intuitive. In fact, there is nothing mysterious about it. It is quite simply causality operating in a particular direction. Thus the question as to what we mean precisely by downward causality is misplaced. After all, we do not question 'ordinary' causality. When explaining phenomenon B by its preceding cause A, we do not go on to ask: 'OK, but what exactly do you mean by A causing B?' The explanation is sufficient in itself. Causality is the basic building block of all forms of explanation – and a very effective one at that! Downward causality is nothing but ordinary causality embedded in and directed by principles of organization, so there is no purpose in enquiring further what it actually is. If we were obliged to legitimate any scientific explanation involving ordinary causality by explaining on each occasion what we meant by causality, our efforts at scientific explanation would collapse, for causality is the very premise on which they are built. This applies equally to explanations involving 'downward' causality. We must thus accept this form of causality as a basic epistemological element that corresponds to basic ontological facts: the world is organized, and as such must be explained in terms of downward causality.

Although the existence of downward causality is an essential premise in the explanation of any organized structure, and cannot thus be questioned without questioning the validity of scientific explanation as such, varying accounts may be offered of the relationship between upward and downward causality. Here, we will identify three different versions of downward causality ('strong', 'weak' and 'medium') (Emmeche, Köppe and Stjernfelt 1997, 1998; see Figure 4.4).

Strong downward causality means that entities and processes at a higher level can cause changes in entities and processes at a lower level. At its most fundamental, this version of downward causality suggests that higher-level phenomena can actually alter the fundamental laws of nature. As such it belongs outside the domain of science, which operates on the assumption that the laws of nature are by definition fundamental and unalterable. Modern scientific theory has consigned this kind of notion, involving supernatural phenomena, divine intervention, or indeed the belief in any almighty deity, to the realm of non-science, miracles and superstition.

Weak downward causality does not allow for the possibility that the fundamental laws and phenomena of nature can be changed, and in fact goes further in denying that anything new can emerge in the world at all. True, this weak version of downward causality recognizes, for example, that new species may emerge in the process of evolution. But the nature of any

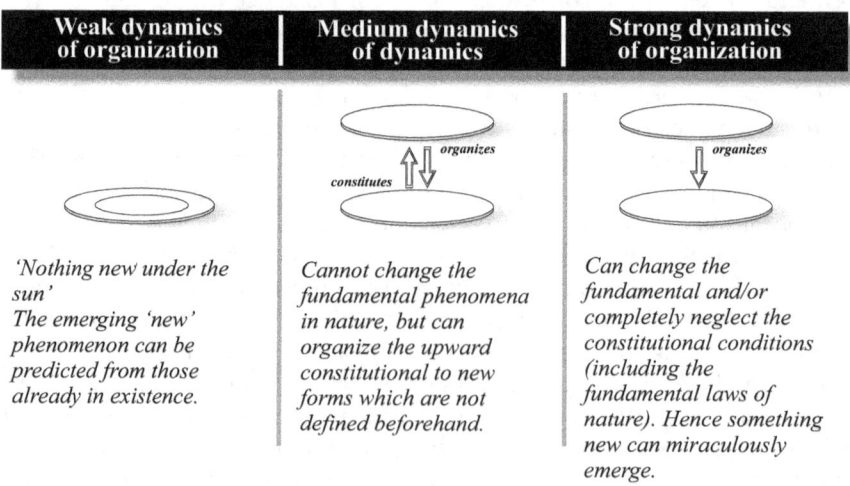

Figure 4.4 *shows the difference between three views of the dynamics of organization, of downward causality, and of the possibility or otherwise that genuinely new phenomena may emerge.*

new species, according to this version, will necessarily be determined by functional, evolutionary principles that always favour those with the optimal chance of survival and reproduction. These principles are universal and unchanging, which means that, in principle, all the new species that have ever developed (or that may develop), together with their forms of behaviour, could have been predicted from the dawn of time. Thus in reality there is indeed 'nothing new under the sun'.

According to this weak version, moreover, any new phenomena that have emerged have done so on the basis of algorithmic principles, since the appearance of any 'new' phenomenon was 'calculated' by the evolutionary process according to established rules laid down in advance. In this sense the 'weak' version does not really allow for downward causality at all, since it does not recognise the possibility of new higher-level phenomena that may establish new ways of organizing existing elements and processes.

Medium downward causality (which we will elaborate further in what follows) differs from the strong version in that it denies the possibility that the fundamental laws of nature can be changed: it does not, in other words, allow for miracles. However, a basic ontological premise of this version is that the nature of upward causality (in which phenomena at a higher level are constituted, and hence caused, by phenomena at a lower level) is such as to permit the unpredictable organization of these constitutive elements by the higher-level phenomena: in other words, to permit downward causality as such. This downward causality is necessarily non-algorithmic in the sense that it is not possible to 'calculate' in advance. We cannot predict, on the basis of the constitutive elements, what the new forms of organization will be like. The new 'rules' or principles behind these forms of organization have yet to emerge (see above). Piet Hein has expressed the nature of non-algorithmic processes in terms of artistic creation: 'Art is the solution to problems which cannot be clearly formulated until they are solved' (see our discussion above concerning the distinction between interface/sensory categories and interspace/choice categories).

This brings us back to the topic of Chapter 2: the centrality of the historical approach, and the historical form of explanation, to our understanding of anthropological psychology. It is only by taking a historical perspective that we can follow the real genesis of a phenomenon (be it organic, cultural or intellectual). The reality of its final form or outcome is not given: it cannot be calculated in advance on the basis of known principles (see the section above on the 'transition from functionality to intentionality').

So the medium version of downward causality, unlike the weak version, allows for the emergence of genuinely new phenomena, but, in contrast to the strong version, denies the possibility of miracles by assuming that the fundamental laws of nature are unalterable. Viewed from the bottom up, higher-level phenomena are always constituted by lower-level elements.

From this perspective, it might seem that there are virtually unlimited ways in which these elements could be organized. In fact, however, there are limits to this freedom of organization, and there is a finite number of possible forms it could take.

The medium version of downward causality differs from the strong version in recognising these limits. To illustrate this principle, take the example of a pile of Lego bricks, which may be assembled in a variety of different structures. One might say that one 'degree' of freedom exists for every different possible structure that could be made from these constituents. At this lower level, then, a great many degrees of constitutive freedom exist. If we move from Lego bricks to the fundamental chemical components of the DNA molecule, the number of such degrees becomes absolutely vast, for these basic components can be put together in a multitude of different sequences, each setting in train different biological processes and containing directions for the creation of different species. But while the degrees of constitutive freedom appear, at the lower level, to be almost endless, the higher levels impose certain limits to this freedom. Just as only some of the possible arrangements of Lego bricks will create a solid structure, so only certain arrangements of the basic elements of DNA will lead to biologically functional and viable organisms. (See also Polanyi 1969). If we count one degree of organizational freedom for every viable organism resulting from the constituent elements, we can see that there are now considerably fewer degrees of freedom than appeared at the constitutive level. In other words, the scope for the creation of new and viable organisms is defined not only by the number of constituent elements but by higher-level principles of organization.

The levels of psychology (and a definition of psyche)

A fundamental, theoretical model of the levels of psychology

It is now possible to make an overall theoretical model of the psyche involving different levels, which in turn require different levels of explanation

Low-level psychology bases its theories on elementary causal and functional explanations, and is concerned with the fundamental forms of connection between a living organism and its surroundings at the level of its biological, biochemical, and physical constituents. Disciplines such as neuropsychology and neuro-endocrinology belong to this low-level psychology.

Some theoreticians argue that psychology should never deal with anything but these low-level processes. By the same token, they would defend 'the astonishing hypothesis' (Crick 1994) that what we know as the psyche consists of nothing but neural mechanisms and brain processes, which operate completely independently of any non-physical, volitional and self-conscious 'I'. According to these theorists, these mechanisms and processes are not controlled by any higher principle. The brain works the way it does whether we want it to or not – it is quite simply not up to us to decide its functioning. This point of view corresponds to what we referred to above as 'weak downward causality', according to which it is impossible, in principle, for new or higher forms of organization to be created (see again Figure 4.4). The obvious objection to this argument is, of course, that while low-level psychology, in offering causal explanations for the activity of neurons, is an essential part of the overall endeavour to provide an explanation of our psyches, there is more to neurons than their simple chemical mechanisms, and this more consists in their organization. Neurons, and the constitutive low-level psyche, work in a highly organized way. A complete model of the psyche must therefore include higher-level forms of explanation for this complex organization.

Medium-level psychology goes beyond offering causal and evolutionary/functionalist explanations for the ways in which an organism connects at the basic level with its environment, to explaining the higher forms of connectedness – namely, behaviour and action – in terms of intention (see Figure 4.3).

As previously discussed (see Figure 4.2), we can differentiate between two levels of connectedness: the level of passive or structural connectedness and the level of self-activated connectedness. This distinction corresponds to the distinction between non-psychic or protopsychic connectedness and genuine psychic connectedness. It follows that we can define psychic activities as the activity of a medium-level or high-level organism which in a goal directed way is directed at the surroundings. This definition grants the existence of a psyche not only to the higher animal species but also (albeit in an extremely elementary form) to the simplest organisms, in so far as they too are able in a self organizing way actively to direct their behaviour at, and be directed by their surrounding environment.

At this medium level, where psychic activity is defined in terms of active, goal-directed connectedness, we may further distinguish between two forms of goal-directedness: one relating to meaning and the other to sense, to use Frege's classic distinction (Frege 1975). A rabbit's goal-directed search for food, for instance, is based on elementary biological processes (a drop in its blood sugar level, for instance). However, as a self-activating being the rabbit is not obliged passively to wait for food to turn up in its immediate surroundings, nor is it left to run about blindly, just occasionally stumbling on something edible. With its psyche, the rabbit is directed at/by whatever has biological meaning for it. It will ignore virtually everything that has no meaning for it (including those things that may be biologically meaningful to another species, as for example a worm is to a mole). Only those things that serve the rabbit's goal of survival and reproduction (or, on the contrary, pose a threat to its existence) have meaning for the rabbit, and these things are organized by the rabbit's psyche as meaningful goals at and by which it directs its behaviour (or, on the contrary, as potential threats which it seeks to avoid).

These things have meaning to the rabbit because it is connected to them at a basic level; in this sense it is not up to the rabbit to decide what is meaningful to it. On the other hand the rabbit is free to choose its own methods of pursuing its goal and in this way to establish its own form of behaviour, since there are many different ways to get at the same meaningful kinds of food. To borrow an example from Engelsted (1994): the rabbit may slip under the fence to reach the carrots, or it may run round the fence to get them. In either case, regardless of the kind of behaviour the rabbit uses to connect with them, the carrots represent the same meaning. However, the *sense* of the carrots changes according to the rabbit's method of reaching them. Depending on the method chosen, the carrots may either carry the sense of 'the-ones-you-get-at-through-the-hole-in-the-fence' or that of 'the-ones-you-get-by-running-around-the-fence'. Thus the carrot's meaning for the rabbit is given by its constitutive value and is not a matter of choice. The sense of the carrot, however, depends on the choice or choices that the rabbit makes in reaching it, and in this sense the rabbit enjoys a certain degree of freedom in determining the particular significance of the objects it connects with.

Any self-activating organism endowed with this kind of psyche enjoys this freedom in some degree. Of course, when it comes to the activity of single-cell organisms as they propel themselves towards food or away from dangerous surroundings, the degree of freedom is very elementary and limited, and the behavioural freedom exercised even by the rabbit is still very far from the human form of action-based free will. Nevertheless, a degree of freedom exists wherever there is a medium-level organization of an organism's functional forms of connection with the surrounding world, or, in other words, a psyche, in however elementary a form.

High-level psychology – at this level we move from the explanations of intention*al* behaviour at the medium level, to explanations of intention*ed* action at the high level. All animals, including man, connect with the surrounding world in functional and goal-directed ways that belong to the low-level psyche (or proto psyche). As we have stressed, these forms of connection are not a matter of choice. Similarly, all animals, including man, make behavioural, goal-directed connections through the medium-level psyche, and at this level enjoy varying degrees of behavioural freedom. If we remain at the level of explanation appropriate to the medium-level psyche, however, our view of man (and probably, indeed, our view of higher animal species such as bonobos and chimpanzees) will be reductive and naturalistic.

Reductive naturalism provides us with an essentialist picture of a static psyche, that is, a picture of unchanging behavioural connections between, on the one hand, a given organism with a given behavioural repertoire (from which it may, with some degree of freedom, pick and choose according to inclination) and, on the other, an equally given, though meaningful, surrounding world.

Real freedom, however, consists not just in the freedom to choose one or other means of connection from a given behavioural repertoire, but in the production of genuinely new forms of connection through new, and more highly-developed, ways of organizing the behavioural and functional elements of the medium-level and low-level psyche. Only beings endowed with a high-level psyche, capable not merely of exercising some degree of choice in behaviour, but of self-consciously initiating actions on the basis of their own free will, enjoy this real freedom. At this level, the constitutive functional and behavioural elements are organized as actions through which the individual human being forms his/her life – not, of course, with infinite freedom, but self-consciously and volitionally. It is only at this level that we move beyond variations in the form merely of behavioural inclinations and preferences, to differences based on professions of belief concerning what is valuable in life, and on endeavours to achieve authenticity.

In the following chapters concerning free will, consciousness and the self, this high-level psyche and its organizational principles will be discussed in detail. Here we will conclude by summarising the overall model of the psyche that we have presented so far.

An overall model for the levels of the psyche and psychology

Thus far we have put forward three models of the psyche that describe its layers in various different terms: (1) a model in which the different layers are identified as centred, decentred and *individuated* (see Figure 3.8), (2) a model in which the different layers are described respectively as low-level, medium-level and high-level and (3) a model in which the different layers are distinguished in terms of the types of explanation appropriate to each. We can now bring these three models together in an overall taxonomy of the human psyche, as illustrated in Figure 4.5.

Psychology is concerned with all levels of the psyche. Nevertheless, one frequently comes across claims that only one given level of the psyche constitutes the proper domain of the discipline. It may be said, for instance, that psychology should deal only with the low-level neurophysiological processes, or that it should concern itself only with functional behavioural processes, cognitive processes, and so on at the medium level, or that it should properly address itself only to the discursive, socio-cultural self-understanding of human beings at the highest level. However, claims of this kind result from confusing general psychology with some particular branch of the discipline, and risk confining the overall science of psychology to much too narrow a domain. For the sake of clarity, each of the individual disciplines not only can, but must focus on a particular level and model of the psyche, conceptualising specific aspects of it from the particular perspective of that discipline. But general psychology, with its interdisciplinary perspective, must necessarily be able to embrace the whole – from the lowest to the highest level.

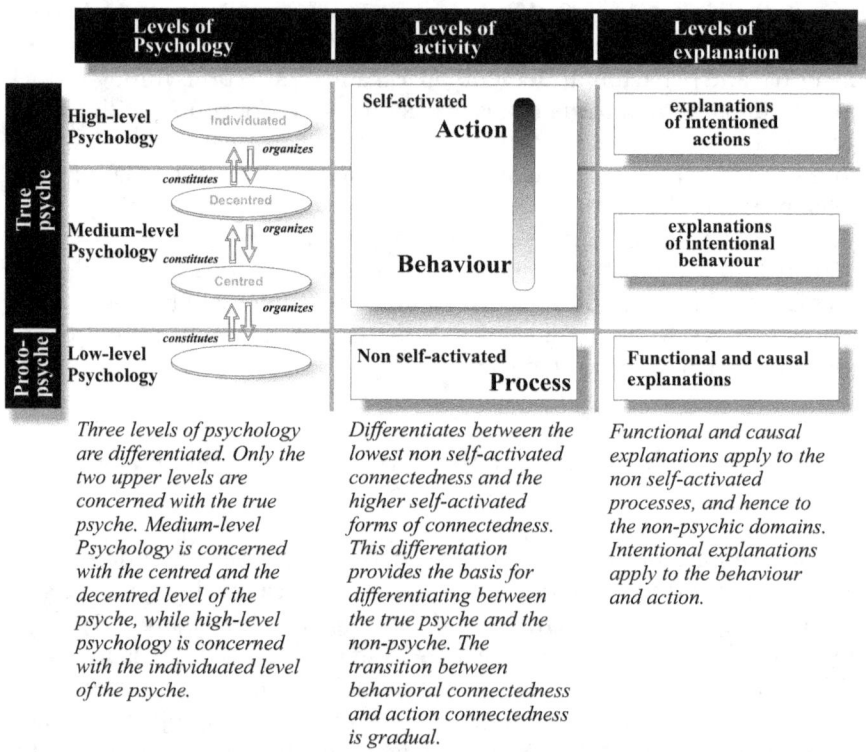

Three levels of psychology are differentiated. Only the two upper levels are concerned with the true psyche. Medium-level Psychology is concerned with the centred and the decentred level of the psyche, while high-level psychology is concerned with the individuated level of the psyche.

Differentiates between the lowest non self-activated connectedness and the higher self-activated forms of connectedness. This differentation provides the basis for differentiating between the true psyche and the non-psyche. The transition between behavioral connectedness and action connectedness is gradual.

Functional and causal explanations apply to the non self-activated processes, and hence to the non-psychic domains. Intentional explanations apply to the behaviour and action.

Figure 4.5 illustrates how the various levels of psychology, the levels of activity, and the levels of explanation belong together taxonomically. Actions are explained as intentioned and are found at the highest, individuated level. Behaviour is explained as intentional and can be found at the medium, decentred, and centred levels of psychology. The non self-activated processes, by contrast, do not belong to the domain of the true psyche, but represent proto-psychic phenomena requiring only functional and causal explanations.

Chapter 5

The Free Will

The free ...

In this and the following two chapters we will return to the principles of high-level psychology, hence taking the step from general to anthropological psychology. We will begin in this chapter by looking at free will as a characteristic of the individuated high-level psyche.

The precondition for holding a person responsible for his/her own actions is that the person could have acted otherwise. If he/she could not have acted otherwise, because of some external or internal compulsion, there is no point in demanding that he/she should have done so. We will not, for instance, convict a person of a crime committed in the face of threats to his/her life, nor will we hold him/her responsible for an act committed in a state of insanity. From a moral as well as a judicial point of view, the precondition for holding a person responsible for his/her own actions is that the person in question had both the freedom and the will – free will – to be capable of acting otherwise, had he/she wanted to. Similarly, there is no point in demanding in a therapeutic interview that the client take responsibility for his/her own life if, fundamentally, the person in question does not have the free will to do so.

It would seem that in order for us to think, feel, judge and act freely, we must be free from external compulsion. However, it is somewhat more complicated than this. A pilot who, when a gun is pointed at his neck, carries out the orders of a hijacker, may be said to be acting of his own free will, so long as his reasoning tells him that this is the proper thing to do under the circumstances; whereas a pilot who, in a state of panic, attempts unreasonably to resist the hijacker, could not be said to have acted freely. His action, we would argue, was prompted by an inner compulsion of insanity. Thus the existence of some external compulsion does not, in itself, deprive the agent of free will, provided that some inner compulsion – such as insanity or incapacity (for example, brain damage) – does not deprive him of his capacity to reason.

But what if our nature – indeed, the nature of our reality – is such that free will cannot exist at all? Perhaps free will is just an illusion? And perhaps this illusion is only the conscious expression of a purely functional brain programme designed to ensure our optimal effectiveness as agents? The question, then, is whether we are capable of possessing free will, and if so, what is the nature of that free will? In the present chapter, this question will be approached in two steps. We will look first at the meaning of 'freedom' in the term, and secondly at the meaning of 'will'.

Is the assumption of free will compatible with science?

Traditionally, the argument for free will is contrasted with determinism. Classical determinism is the view that whatever happened in a given situation necessarily had to happen according to the laws pertaining to that situation. As we saw in the previous chapter, these deterministic principles can be found at different ontological levels: when pushed by another ball, a billiard ball is bound to move. The principles of evolution are such that a particular species of animal was doomed to extinction. A given person, in a given situation, was bound to display a certain kind of behaviour, and could not have acted, thought or felt otherwise than he/she did, because of the innumerable, interwoven chains of causes and effects in which he/she was entangled.

Broadly speaking, three different positions may be taken on the question of determinism versus free will: (1) Science and scientific explanations are based on deterministic principles, and as such necessarily exclude free will – science and free will are simply not compatible. (2) Free will and science are not compatible, but since free will exists, it must belong to that part of reality which is not susceptible to scientific explanation. This viewpoint is known as 'libertarianism.' (3) The existence of free will is compatible with science and can be scientifically explained. These three positions are illustrated in Figure 5.1.

The third position, compatibilism, can be approached in two ways: respectively from a libertarian and a deterministic perspective. Each approach in fact involves a range of positions, graduating from 'hard' versions of libertarianism and determinism, respectively, to 'soft' versions, which can in fact be combined in a compatibilism that is at once scientific and able to accommodate the phenomenon of free will. 'Hard' determinism uncompromisingly insists on incompatibility: scientific principles of explanation are such that they necessarily exclude free will. 'Soft' determinism, by contrast, claims that there exist scientific principles of explanation that do *not* exclude free will. 'Hard' libertarianism maintains

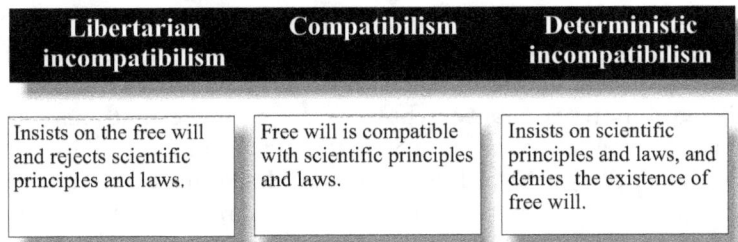

Figure 5.1 *illustrates the three main positions regarding the relationship between free will and scientific principles.*

that one can defend free will only by abandoning the rules and principles that govern science, whereas 'soft' libertarianism recognizes that our conception of free will must be based on scientific principles.

In the section that follows, we will see that the 'hard' versions of determinism and libertarianism, respectively, are invalid and degenerated versions of these theses. Further, we will argue that the solution to the problem of free will lies in a genuine compatibilism that combines the 'soft' versions of both libertarianism and determinism.

Degeneration into hard determinism and a return to soft determinism

Hard determinism bases its refusal to recognize the existence of free will on the following considerations: (1) From the moment he/she is born, and throughout his/her psychological development, an individual human being is subject to developmental forces and influences (stemming both from heredity and environment) that do not originate from him/herself. Indeed, each person is simply an effect of innumerable causal chains in nature. Hence the individual is not responsible for being the person he/she is or for acting in the way he/she does: each of us acts the way we do because of being the persons we are. (2) To say that one possesses free will and is able to act freely implies that one is oneself responsible for having become the person one is. However, if one has developed into that person on the basis of hereditary and environmental factors over which one has had no influence, one cannot be held responsible for being the person one has become. (3) Only if it were possible, so to speak, to skip one's own development and jump fully fledged into life as oneself could one arguably claim to possess free will. (4) But this is an impossibility: it would amount to saying that, instead of developing as an effect of innumerable causal chains, one was one's own first cause (as a self-creating god must be). The very idea of a first cause is counter intuitive: any phenomenon must have a prior cause. Therefore, hard determinists maintain there can be no such thing as free will.

From the viewpoint of soft determinism, this argument is naive. As we saw in our discussion of functional and intentional forms of explanation (see Figure 4.3), nature has produced organisms that are not obliged merely to await developments passively, but possess a psyche that enables them actively to pursue goals, connecting with the surrounding world in ways that optimise their chances. According to this soft determinist view, this kind of self-activating psyche is indeed part of an infinite number of causal chains: not only as an effect, however, but as a cause that plays a decisive role in determining a given subject's action.

Thus, although the self is seen from this perspective as the result, or effect, of impulses within a functionally optimising apparatus, it nevertheless makes a difference, according to this view, that the point at which all the causal chains converge is precisely the person, or subject, who as such plays a decisive role in determining the future course of his/her own life. From this point onwards the optimised and functional life that unfolds is precisely the life of that person, that 'self'. *The self* is the point from which life unfolds as a specific and unique personal life.

For the behaviour of a subject to be considered the product of free will, therefore, it is sufficient, according to soft determinism, that the subject's entire functional apparatus, including the psyche, has not been thwarted by any external or internal forces in performing its function: namely, to behave in the way that is optimal for that subject in a given situation. (see the pilot example above). Further, soft determinism would argue that the possible ways in which this optimising apparatus may display behaviour are so numerous that in practice it is impossible to distinguish between functional optimization and the unhampered exercise of free will – in both cases the outcome will be the choice of the optimal behaviour from among myriad possibilities. In this sense, so the argument goes, the question as to whether or not free will exists is trivial. The way in which we function is in any case so complex that we will never be able to discover whether we are only carrying out (or indeed, whether we merely consist of) functional routines which it is not up to us to choose.

Thus, soft determinism states that one is exercising free will when one can do what one wills to do – and then it does not matter whether one wills what one wills as the result of certain determining forces. Provided that one's will originates from 'the place' which is oneself, which functions as the 'I' and is conceived by the 'I' – then it is *I*, who will. The point being, that all these determining forces have converged at that point in the world which is *me!* According to this view, it does not matter that one may be forced into certain actions by outer circumstances (like the pilot with a gun pointed at his neck), provided that the self is free to will what is reasonable within that situation. In other words, a person can still act of his/her own free will so long as the 'I' is not rendered incapable by inner circumstances (mental incapacity, psychic problems, ideological brainwashing and so on), which are not themselves a part of the self or 'I'. (As will become clear further on in this chapter and in Chapter 7, this attempt to 'save' free will is doomed to fail.)

Degeneration into hard libertarianism and a return to soft libertarianism

This kind of soft determinism is sometimes presented as a compatibilism that combines the concept of free will with scientific principles. But, as libertarians have argued, this version of soft determinism does not allow for genuine free will. For free will to exist, or to operate, it is not sufficient that there be innumerable different life opportunities and that the agent not be deprived of his capacity to will, or to choose, by various external or internal forces. According to the libertarians, the problem with the soft determinist view is that it fails to capture the essence of a subject, a self, which, by virtue of its own inner dynamics, develops its own reasons for action and its own life projects. In other words, soft determinism misses the point of the self's endeavour to achieve authenticity (see the section on authenticity in the previous chapter). It will not suffice to emphasize that, for example, outer socialising forces and life-historical events are assimilated by the individual as part of his/her functional apparatus.

However, libertarianism, too, has issued in degenerate 'hard' versions, such as the radical existentialism expounded by Sartre. According to the radical existentialists, each individual single-handedly, so to speak, creates the person he/she would like to be, or believes he/she ought to be. To put it another way, a human being is defined by the fact that he/she has his/her own personality and developmental task in life. The choice of personality and life is thus a radical choice, not one imposed by any form of rule-bound necessity nor defined by the individual's fundamental constitution as a biological and social being. In Sartre's words: we are doomed to freedom. Our existence precedes our essence: that is to say, our experience, and our choice of life, determines our nature – not vice versa.

The obvious objection to this radical position is that true choices are not simply random jumps in one direction or another. If our choices were entirely random, they would not be real choices, but merely random movements or fluctuations in our lives. Taylor (1982), and others, have emphasized that true choices can only exist on the basis of values. A more precise way of putting this would be to say that true choice exists only where it is made necessary by mutually conflicting values (see also Midgley 1994). Or to paraphrase Taylor: it is true that we may choose between values, and indeed such choices are truly radical, in the sense that they are unforced and not bound by rules given beforehand (in other words, true choice is a non-algorithmic phenomenon, as discussed in the previous section). But we cannot choose whether or not we have values, or whether the existence of mutually-conflicting values requires us to make a choice. Without values, nothing would matter at all.

This brings us back to the soft version of libertarianism, which recognizes that we are constrained as free-willed beings by our constitutions and certain frame conditions, including our necessarily value-directed involvement in life. However, although libertarians recognize in principle that the psyche is constituted by certain basic, social, cultural and biological conditions, the implications of this for our understanding of the self are seldom made explicit, or discussed systematically, in libertarianist theory. The actions and life project of a person are understood primarily in terms of the activities of the self.

Genuine compatibilism and a genuine concept of free will

Despite the drawbacks of each theory individually, the soft versions of determinism and libertarianism respectively can be combined to form a genuine compatibilism: one that operates with a genuine concept of the free will, arguing that the experience of free will is not only a smart conjuring trick on the part of our functional apparatus, but that nature may be ontologically constituted in such a way as to make free will possible. In so far as this is the case, moreover, free will must be susceptible to scientific explanation.

This genuine compatibilism is in fact implicit in the hierarchical models which we presented in the previous chapter. In terms of these models, we may say that whereas soft determinism assumes an upward perspective, soft libertarianism assumes a *downward* perspective. They are compatible because they represent different perspectives within the same hierarchical model (see Figure 5.2).

Soft determinism emphasizes the constitutional elements of an event (in the form of behaviour, action, thought, feeling or will), explaining the event in terms of its constitution. By contrast, soft libertarianism argues that an event can be explained by the way in which these constituent elements are organized.

Genuine compatibilism, combining these insights, takes the view that free will, or the phenomena resulting from the exercise of free will, must be explained both from the bottom-up perspective – in terms of their constitutents – and from the top-down perspective – in terms of their organization.

This genuine compatibilist model succeeds in dissolving a number of the determinist objections against free will. As we recall, the soft version of determinism argues that one cannot in practice differentiate between the complex functioning of a deterministic system, which is able to generate innumerable different forms of behaviour, and the activities of a self,

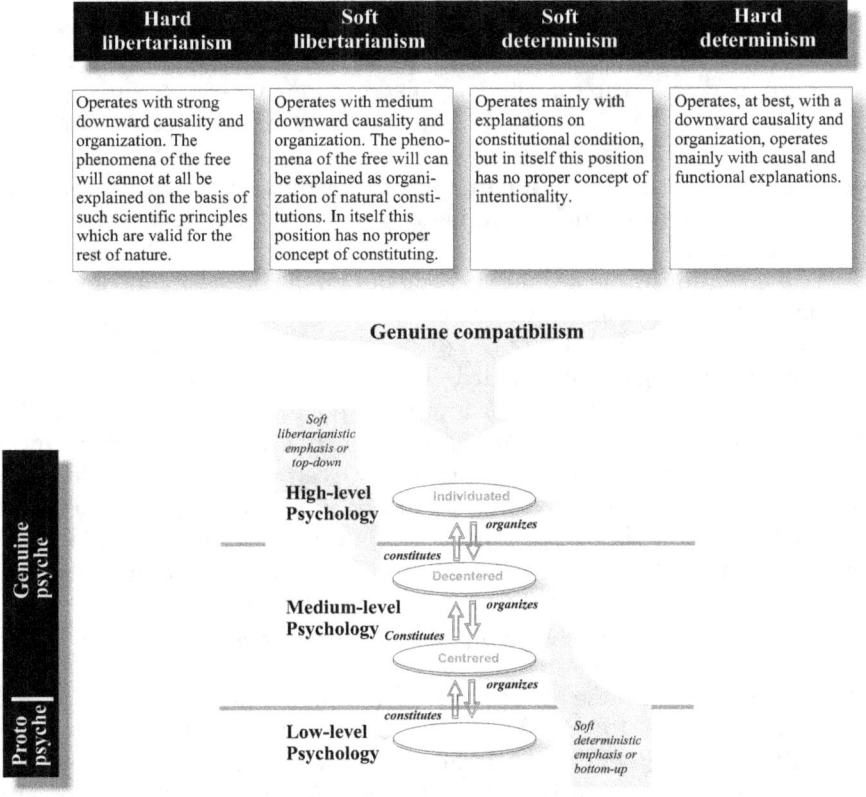

Figure 5.2 *illustrates the conception of free will from the perspective of genuine compatibilism.*

operating with genuine free will. Thus the question as to whether or not we have free will is, to all intents and purposes, trivial. An answer to this objection, however, can be found in the hierarchical model of the self and the concept of two different kinds of freedom introduced in the previous chapter. Thus, the type of 'freedom' acknowledged by soft determinism corresponds to what we referred to in Chapter 4 as *constitutional freedom*. As we saw in Chapter 4, the greater the number of constituent elements involved, the greater the constitutional freedom those elements allow. Similarly, the more complex the psychic apparatus of a given organism, the greater the potential variety of its behaviour. From this bottom-up perspective, it is indeed true that one cannot distinguish between genuine free will and the soft deterministic version of it.

Genuine free will can only be identified in so far as we have a model that allows us to assume a downward perspective and hence to consider organizational freedom. The soft determinists' insistence that the workings of an advanced functional apparatus are indistinguishable from those of free will results from their blindness to the downward perspective and downward causality.

Hard determinism, as we have seen, argues for the impossibility of free will on the basis that its existence would presuppose a denial of the basic principles of causality and the assumption of a miraculous first cause. No such irrationality or 'magic' is demanded, however, if we recognize that causality operates downwards as well as upwards, and that we need to consider organizational as well as constitutional freedom. In the light of the hierarchical model proposed by genuine compatibilism, we can see that free will does not imply that we create our own constitutions, only that, as the concept of downward causality implies, we possess, to varying degrees, the freedom to organize and to connect, in a variety of ways, our given, constitutive elements.

Libet's experiments and the free will

Determinist sceptics often refer to a series of experiments conducted by Libet (see e.g., Libet et al. 1999), which, it is claimed, prove that we do not have free will. However, there are a number of problems with these experiments. In one case, subjects were asked to state the moment at which they made a decision, for example, to lift a finger. The results allegedly demonstrate that cerebral neural activities (readiness potential) take place at least 350 milliseconds prior to the subject's awareness of his/her intention or wish to act. The aim of the experiment was to demonstrate that the neural initiation of an action appears prior to the formation of a conscious plan to act (for example, to move a finger); hence the action is initiated by something other than the person's free will. However, this experiment is based on a number of assumptions which in my view are invalid. I present two of these below.

(1) The experiment assumes that it is possible to measure exactly when a subject mentally decides to do something, based on his/her verbal, introspective report on the matter ('now I intend to lift my finger'). This is not in fact possible.
(2) The experiment assumes that a willed decision is an act that takes place at a particular point of time. In fact, a decision is a process which occurs over a period of time and is composed of sequences which can be registered as brain activity at different times during the process. Early sequences within the process may therefore be incorrectly interpreted as

physiological processes, which appear prior to the point of the 'decision itself'. As stated, however, a decision is a process consisting of a number of components which temporally succeed each other (A ⇒ B ⇒ C ⇒ D, etc.) but which, at the same time, are organized by the decision. The fact that it is possible to register certain sequences (A, B and C) prior to the final sequence D, does not necessarily mean that D is determined by A (or that D constitutes the decision, or intention, itself). On the contrary, it is the whole sequence A ⇒ B ⇒ C ⇒ D that constitutes the intention.

Libet recognizes the existence of free-willed control, acknowledging that after the unconscious, functionally-determined inclination to act has been measured in the brain, the subject will still have about 100–200 milliseconds, prior to carrying out the motoric action such as lifting a finger, to suppress or veto this unconsciously initiated process (that is, not to raise the finger after all).

The crucial question to ask, however, is at what level of the psyche, this kind of conscious suppression takes place, and what kind of freedom it implies? What is the reason for the suppression? Libet's experiments are unable to shed any light on this point – yet this is precisely what is at issue in the question of free will. There is a fundamental paradox in stating, as Libet appears to do, that the consciousness controls by means of prohibition rather than command. To say that our consciousness is able to order anything, be it a command or a prohibition, is to say that it is able to form intentions. If the process of inhibiting an action is purely functional – if it is not up to *us* to prohibit an action – then even Libet's measure of free will is denied. If, however, we acknowledge – as Libet does – that we are able freely and consciously to inhibit an already initiated action, it follows that we must also be able to formulate an intention, that is, consciously and creatively to make a choice. Libet appears to have drawn the wrong conclusions from his own empirical work, or to have failed to have followed it up with the proper theoretical explanation.

... will

Thus far we have looked at the meaning of 'freedom' in the term free will, and have demonstrated that freedom is an ontological possibility within the explanatory domain of science. We will now take a closer look at the meaning of 'will'.

The cultural history of the will and God as transitional object

The will as a distinct psychic component in a self-organizing or individuated discourse crystallized around the fourth century, most notably in the thinking of St Augustine. It is only now that the third of the three great aspects of the psyche, the conation (or will to something), makes its appearance in an explicitly formulated discourse. It is from this period that we can date the modern model of the psyche, containing the complete trinity of cognition, emotion and conation, and, with it, the emergence of a common, acquirable, individuated discourse concerning the self. A new awareness of the tripartite nature of the self made possible, in turn, the organizational dynamics by which a human being could, in the proper sense of the word, will something for him/herself or for him/herself in conjunction with others. This historical development has been described in detail by Bertelsen (2002); here, we will review only the main points of the argument.

It has often been observed that ancient Greek thought did not include a concept of the will, and that the Greeks spoke only of reason. However, this is only partially true. To be sure, the Greeks, had no distinct concept of the will, and hence it was not possible to state or think of a person that he had done something at will, or that will was required in order to realize a life project. Nevertheless, a concept of will existed, in embryonic form, as an implicit element of ancient thinking, although it would only be fully formulated by Augustine.

In its implicit form, the concept of will can be found in the doctrine of eros put forward by Plato. Eros is the innate urge present in all things to move towards a state of completion (as, for example, a seed grows towards completion as a flower). In the human being, eros is felt as an inner unrest, a refusal to be content with the incomplete, the mediocre, the not completely human. To the human being, the highest stage of life is represented by the highest form of reason, as possessed by the philosopher or the wise man. Proper human development thus consists in letting the eros flow freely: in following the course of reason to become ever wiser and more reasonable, and to gain ever greater insight. Not insight into the deceptive and transient forms of the world (even the best drawn triangle will never be completely mathematically correct), but insight into the underlying scheme, the ideas of things (such as the ideal triangle within geometry). Even the most flawless horse represents only a rough version of the essential idea of a horse. Since everything that exists in the world is by definition only a rough version of an underlying idea, it follows that ideas themselves cannot be of this world, but must belong to another – the realm of ideas. The human being, as we have said, experiences eros as a state of unrest, and it is only through exercising reason, by gaining insight into the idea of all things, the idea of the world, the idea of life, that the soul can achieve a sense of completion and arrive at a state of rest.

A more materialist thinker than Plato, Aristotle saw the anonymous dynamics of things (anonymous in the sense of unwilled by any particular someone) in terms of their striving for their own true resting-place in the world order. Thrown into the air, a stone is in a state of dynamic unrest, and will immediately seek to return to its true place on earth – the resting-place where its dynamic unrest will vanish. Similarly, flames are compelled to strive upwards, the resting-place of an acorn can be found in its unfolding as an oak tree, and so on. The human soul, too, is bound to seek its resting place – in this case in a state of completed reason: its completed philosophical and scientific insight into the natural world order.

As we have indicated, however, classic Greek philosophy treats this human striving as part of a universal, and anonymous dynamic, rather than as subjective will to develop as an individual. It was Augustine who took this discourse further by presenting the idea that each individual wills what to do with his/her life; each, in other words, choosing a 'life project' of his/her own free will.

Judaism formed another strong current in St Augustine's thinking. For the Greeks, even the gods are subject to an anonymous world order. The gods did not create the world and cannot challenge the fundamental laws of nature. In Judaism, by contrast, we find a creating god: one who is thus not bound by his own creation, but can freely dispose of it and change it at his own convenience. According to the Jews, God meets us with commandments and orders which he reveals to us. Through these revelations, we may get some partial inkling of God's plan for the world and for us, but we are incapable, even through the utmost cognitive effort or learned insight, of comprehending the plan as a whole. We can conceive only that corner of God's plan which he chooses to reveal to us in the organization of the world, in the feelings of the heart, and in the words in holy texts.

In this sense, neither reason nor will are important in Jewish discourse. In common with a discourse prevalent throughout the Middle East, to lead the good life means simply to obey the commandments and orders which God chooses to reveal to us. God is almighty and requires our unreserved obedience – a conception that also has considerable weight in Augustine's thinking. This concept of God adds a decisive element to the discourse: the idea that it is not only the anonymous forces of nature that form the dynamic basis for human (and other forms of) life; on the contrary, the dynamic force that moves our lives is the will of a personified God.

A third current in Augustinian thinking originates from the Fathers of the earliest Christian church during the first decades AD. Common to them all is that, in a continuation of Jewish and fundamentalist thinking, they take their point of departure in a set of revealed truths. Within this discourse, there is no place for intellectual dispute or scepticism. Nor are we granted the possibility of knowing anything of God's plan as a whole, not to mention of God. Prominent early Christians such as Clement of Alexandria (150–215 AD), Origen (185–253 AD) and Gregory (330–395 AD), who all belonged to the Greek Christian church and whose thinking was thus anchored in Greek philosophy and natural science, agreed moreover that because we cannot know anything about God, it is also beyond our capacities and scope to know anything about our own human soul. Within this discourse, then, the self is rendered impotent as the organizer of his/her individual destiny. Indeed, the line of thinking in which the direction, organization and development of the soul is seen as a province of individual will, is simply inadmissible. At the same time, the fact that we are creations of God means that God is present at the core of our souls. Ultimately, then, at our souls' centre, we are related to God. And it is this relationship that determines the course of our life projects: an anonymous course, in the sense that it is independent of our will and insight, yet one that is guaranteed to be right and true. God is indeed the determining force or dynamic within our soul: it is God who decides on the nature of our lives and the direction they are to take. All we are required to do is fully, wholeheartedly and humbly to submit ourselves to God's will, and everything will work out by itself.

From this perspective, then, the project of becoming oneself, as an individual, must necessarily occur through an abdication of will. One can become oneself only by, so to speak, letting go. On this point the ancient Greek philosophers, the Jewish thinkers and the fathers of the early Christian church all agree (along with many modern therapists).

The idea that God was contained within us at the core of our souls was also shared by St. Augustine. However, the radical step in Augustine's anthropology was to raise psychological questions concerning the very nature of the soul. What kind of psyche, he asked, would enable us in the first place to open up to and submit to God, to let him flow through our souls and direct our life project to completion?

Fundamentally, Augustine's world picture is modelled on that of the Greeks (in particular Plotinus), with God at the top of the hierarchy and then, in descending order, the soul of man, his body, the animals and other forms of life, inanimate matter, and finally nothingness. Anything that exists in the world is God's creation and is there in precise accordance with God's plan, and anything that happens in the world is ultimately an expression of God's will. The Augustinian notion of morality, or the moral world, also accords with ancient thinking. All that exists is good because it was created by God; only nothingness, non-being, non-creation is evil. The higher we move in the hierarchy towards God, the greater the proportion of good. Conversely, the further down we move in the hierarchy, the more we descend into moral decay and the realm of the physical, of base needs, sexuality and sensual enjoyment, finally dissolving into the absolute evil of nothingness.

How, then, do we achieve our goal as human beings and ensure our upward ascent to the higher things? Again, the answer is at first in complete accordance with ancient Greek/Platonic thinking. We do so by means of reason. Here, Augustine differentiates between the form of reason to be found in wisdom and that to be found in science. Science involves an understanding of things in their earthly forms, a knowledge of their true resting-place in the world order and of the material ways in which they move towards that resting place. This kind of science is of no particular interest to Augustine. What concerns him above all is wisdom, the sense of the sacredness of all things, of their connection with and ineluctable movement towards God, and in particular of God as the resting-place or ultimate goal of the human soul.

In achieving this goal, according to Augustine, reason alone will not suffice. The will – the genuine will – is decisive. We live in a universe which is full of dynamic unrest because the things within it have not found their true resting-place. In the case of human beings, this dynamic is to be found precisely in the will, in what the individual wills and, crucially, the willed goal of the human being, unlike the goals of other creatures or things, cannot be determined a priori – it is not fixed in advance. Stones, plants and animals move along one, and only one, preordained path. The path taken by each human being, by contrast, is up to him/her to decide. Still, there are, broadly speaking, only two main directions to be taken: up or down. Either one wills the good, or one wills evil. Any kind of dynamic is innate – the dynamics of the stone come from its gravity, which will inevitably lead it downwards. Likewise, the 'gravity' of the soul is something innate; in this sense, the will of the individual is not merely a reaction to some external force. In Augustine's words: one may force people to do this or that; but one cannot force them to will to do it. People have to decide for themselves.

To be sure, the direction of the will in each case will be affected by external circumstances. Most of us are susceptible to fascination by material things and superficial appearances. Habits, too, will tend to turn our will in the wrong direction. Most of us are afraid of breaking with habit, fearing that our lives will become empty and sterile, and that we will lose our sense of identity, without our habitual activities and ways of making life meaningful.

So, in this phase of his thinking, Augustine argued that one can become oneself only by an effort of will, and that individuation consists precisely in holding on to (as opposed to letting go of) one's individuated life project. Subsequently, however, Augustine abandoned this conception, replacing it with a philosophy based on the Christian doctrine of original sin and the grace of God. This philosophy was to have dire consequences in the history of European thought – consequences which are still present with us today; but that is another story (see Bertelsen 2002).

Different forms of will and different conceptions of will

As will be evident from the foregoing, the key issue at the centre of these discourses lies in whether the will is reasonable or contrary to reason.

According to Kant, our will is synonymous with rational endeavour. It consists of what we intend to carry out after carefully considering and weighing up the options, and making a decision on that basis. The will, in this sense, is seen as subordinate to reason. Schopenhauer took the opposite view, arguing that reason is subordinate to will. Our will is expressed in our immediate endeavours, in that which we want, regardless of whether or not it is reasonable. In Schopenhauer's view, then, the will is a blind force, while Kant saw it as clear-sighted. Indeed, our will is free, in Kant's view, only in so far as it is subordinate to reason: more precisely to what he called our practical or moral reasoning. Or rather, freedom is attainable in different degrees: the more the will is susceptible to inclination, the less free it is; conversely, the more the will was governed by reason – the more it is rationally organized according to moral principles – the freer it will be. Schopenhauer found this conception naïve. That which we will has nothing to do with reason; rather, our will is the expression of the deepest, untamed forces within us and of our amoral zest for life.

In both cases, the will is seen as concerned with realizing action; the essential difference between these two conceptions, however, will become clear when we incorporate them into our hierarchical model of the free will (see Figure 5.2). Kant's conception of the will corresponds clearly to what we have called the libertarian, 'top-down' view, which may be expressed as follows: the degree of freedom of the will increases to the extent that our immediate endeavours are organized. Schopenhauer's concept of the will, on the other hand, corresponds to what we have called the soft deterministic view: here the will is seen from a 'bottom-up' perspective as the expression of our behavioural and action-based constitution. Although our reason remains intact, enabling us to judge what is good and right even when this does not coincide with our desires, our basic will – representing these fundamental needs or desires – will not leave us in peace. And in so far as our reason opposes, or suppresses, this basic will, the latter will continue to torture us, 'demanding' to be realized with ever greater force (this conception of the will would later inspire Freud).

Clearly, in considering these differing perspectives, we have touched upon two different aspects of the will: the will as power and the will as organization and constitution. An overview of these combined aspects is presented in Figure 5.3.

Will as downward organization

The next question that arises is how more precisely to understand the will in terms of downward organization. As we have seen, there are, broadly speaking, three versions of downward causality/organization (see Figure 4.4), which we have respectively dubbed 'strong', 'medium' and 'weak'.

Will as power	Will as directedness
Willpower That a person wants something out of a strong or weak force, e.g. ranging from *lack of willpower* or *inhibition* (not having any energy, or revolving and constantly reflecting without getting anywhere) via large or small *acts of will* (to realize a decision) to a *'hyper will'* (compulsory and narrowminded ways of concentrating on certain actions or projects). *'The will as impact'*. Intensifying the will in order to direct *'in an instant'* at/by something specific. *'The resiliency of the will'*. The intensity of the will in order to be persistant in one's directedness - over time and contrary to resistance. *'The will as inhibition'*. The intensity of the will in order to restrain.	**Organizing (soft libertarianistic)** **The 'seeing' will (Kant).** At two levels: *High-level psychology:* *'The will as commander'*: goal directed, defined by finality. The commander will shape his own course for life and ethics in an authenticity-endeavouring way. *Medium-level psychology:* *'The will as a switch'*: In this understanding, the will has no force and actually no possibility for laying down rails either. Only able to change in an optimizing way between given rails. The will is tracked on the rails of reasoning. **Constitution (soft deterministic)** **The 'blind will' (Schopenhauer):** *'The will as a wild horseride'*. Hardly a rational optimization as compared to the metaphor of changing points. The horse/unconsciousness goes whereever it wants to go. The will staggers along, blindly and unreasonably.

Figure 5.3 *lists the most important characteristics of the will, respectively as power and as organization/constitution, and presents Kant's and Schopenhauer's views in relation to each other. The metaphorical expressions of the will ('the will as ...') are borrowed from Weinert 1987.*

In the weak version, no role at all is allotted to our will. Our life and our actions are seen, fatalistically, to be determined entirely by outside forces, which no acts of will can change. To be sure, this weak version allows that our behaviour may follow now this, now that impulse, inclination or preference, without, however, being governed by any overall, individuated organizing perspective, profession of belief or endeavour to achieve authenticity.

The strong version offers what might be called a Victorian conception of the will. Here, the will is seen to be in total control; no action of ours can occur without our actively willing it to happen. According to this view, both our selves, and our surroundings, are objects to be directed and manipulated, without inhibition, by our will; no attention need be paid to the body or to those deep-seated inclinations that are part of our basic constitution. In this Victorian conception of the self, an absolute distinction is made between desire and inclinations on the one hand, and will and reason on the other.

The medium version, by contrast, recognizes the fact that we remain constituted, as human beings, both by our biological make-up and by older, more basic forms of behavioural connection with the surrounding world. In organizing these basic constituents of our being, our reason and our will do not have absolute freedom; but must work with the more basic forms of connectedness which we have established in relation to the world. We are not just individuated beings, but also, fundamentally, socially centred beings (see Figure 3.8).

It will be evident from the argument throughout this chapter, and the foregoing ones, that the position followed here is that of the medium version: namely, that our will consists both of those elements that constitute, and those that organize, our way of connecting to the surrounding world. The will is the strength and the organization by which we are directed at/by something.

The basis of the will

To will something is to organize oneself, and one's constitutive elements, in a way that expresses one's strength and directedness in realizing a certain goal. A person who wills a certain end is said, expressively, to 'pull himself together' – organizing and focusing his various capacities in an effort to reach that particular goal.

The exercise of will in the realization of a goal thus crucially involves these underlying, constitutive elements of the self. In the first place, these underlying elements may contribute to, or determine, the goal itself. In some cases, the goal may be articulated: that is, clearly and consciously formulated to the self as a goal. But, equally, such goals may be tacit and unconscious, manifesting themselves only in the actual course that a person's life takes. In other words, the less conscious, more 'primitive' elements of the self may tacitly direct the way in which one lives one's life from day to day.

Second, the will involves our constitutive/organizing capacities to realize our goals. One's power to do something is conditional, in part, on one's capacity to do it.

Third, the scope of the will is circumscribed by external conditions and limitations imposed by nature, culture and society. To will something is thus to strive to achieve a goal under given internal and external conditions.

The basis of the will can thus be explained in terms of the more or less tacit formulation of goals, and the more or less thorough weighing up of these goals in the light of internal and external conditions: are the goals in question realisable, given the limitations imposed by one's own potential and the conditions laid down by the outside world? (See also Wackerhausen 1994, who has inspired the following considerations on this process of 'weighing up', although they are not identical with his).

This process of weighing up consists of considering, in turn, whether a given goal is genuine, realistic, rational and ethically justifiable. To ask whether the goal is genuine is to ask whether it is one's own goal or one that has been imposed. This is not always simple to determine. Let us remember the pilot with a gun pointed at his neck: although his goal, in acting as he does, may appear, at first sight, to be forced, it may be quite genuine, given the limitations imposed on him. If, on the other hand, he has suffered a

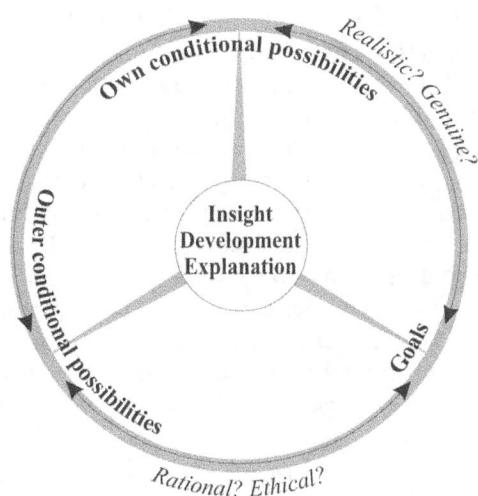

Figure 5.4 *illustrates how the basis of the will consists of the weighing up of goals against internal and external conditions, with regard to the realism, genuineness, rationality and morality of the goals.*

personal breakdown, so that he is not in a condition to organize himself properly, to concentrate and to weigh up his possible options, then whatever goal he formulates will not be genuine. Likewise, one might imagine that the hijacker holding the gun to the pilot's head is a mere boy whose present goal is the result of ideological indoctrination, rather than a consciously-acquired philosophy of life or an expression of his real personality and desires in life. In this case, too, the goal cannot be said to be genuine, although the hijacker is not apparently acting under compulsion from any external or internal force. In order to be genuine, the goal must be formulated by the individual when working at his/her maximum organizational capacity as a result of strong evaluations, as Taylor would say (see Chapter 3), on whatever level that may be (animals with a relatively low level of autonomy, such as bonobos or dogs, are also capable of having goals).

Second, one must determine whether the goal is personally realistic, that is, whether it is achievable, given the agent's internal possibilities. There is no point in setting out to do something if one is guaranteed to fail. This also means that, in order to be realistic, one's goals in life may have to change in the light of changes in one's own internal capacities. As one grows older one may not be able to perform the same physical feats that one used to be capable of. Likewise, a serious illness may force one to adjust one's life project and to formulate new goals to fit the new limitations imposed by one's circumstances. Conversely, new insights gained from greater experience of life, or from investigating, through therapy, the limitations imposed by one's own life history, may lead one to dare to try out new ventures or to open up to the world in a way one has never done before, setting goals that used to be unrealistic but are now achievable.

Finally, the question can be raised as to whether the goal is attuned to external possibilities. On the one hand, this is to ask whether the goal is rational, that is, whether it can be realized at all under the given external conditions. To dive more than forty metres into the ocean with only ordinary atmospheric air in one's tank will enormously increase the risk of various physical complications, and may ultimately lead to death; in this sense (assuming the diver wants to survive) it is irrational to pursue such a goal. On the other, to ask whether a given goal is attuned to external reality is to ask whether it is ethical and/or culturally acceptable: whether, in other words, it accords with the cultural and social norms governing our lives. Would our realization of this goal be ethically justifiable to other people?

The will as a process

Whether or not an act of will is characterized by a sudden 'push' or by a persistent and long-lasting effort, it may be seen as a *process* which can be divided into two main phases (see also Heckhausen 1987).

The first phase may be termed the intentionalization phase. In this phase, the agent is directed at, and by, some specific object, actively concentrating his/her will or force on achieving it. This intentional phase ranges from a state of open weighing up (where the agent has not yet considered whether the goal in question is genuine, realistic, rational or ethical) to a state in which this process of weighing up is more or less complete, and in which the intentionality is unified and directed with a certain force. The schematic illustration in Figure 5.5 shows that this intentionalization phase is characterized by a gradual narrowing down of the field under consideration. The goals become clearer and have been more thoroughly weighed up in relation to external and internal possibilities; and the act of weighing up will become gradually more focused as a great many possibilities are eliminated. In this way, through the gradual narrowing of the field of possibilities, we move from the phase of intention to that of decision. This is what one wills. One has this directedness and this willpower.

The second phase in the process of willing includes its realization. This phase ranges from the state of decision, reached in the previous phase, which can be seen as the initiating force behind a given course of behaviour or action, to a state of goal achievement, marking the temporary closure of this particular

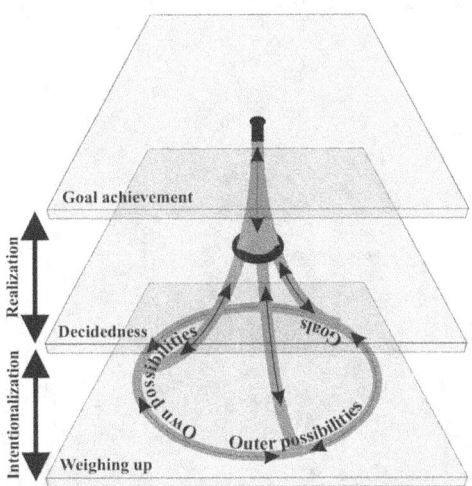

Figure 5.5 *The figure shows the process of willing and the different states that the agent may find him/herself in within that process. (1) In the weighing-up phases, the various elements to be weighed are clearly differentiated. (2) During the intentionalization phase, these components have been compressed in a general state of decidedness (decision) and intention to act. (3) Finally, the components of the state of achievement have been compressed to a sheer point: what might be called punctiform intentum.*

course. It is only at this point, when the intentionalization is transformed to realization that one may speak of a willed behaviour or action. The previous phase in the process of willing includes only the intention, the will to move towards a decision without necessarily reaching a state of decision, let alone realizing that decision through a specific act or form of behaviour.

Elaborating on our previous model of the will and its components as depicted in Figure 5.4, Figure 5.5 illustrates the process of willing described above.

It is important to read Figure 5.5 correctly. (1) It is not a picture of an intentioned connection between a subject and an object. (2) Nor is it a picture of a process that will necessarily range, temporally, from the most open kind of weighing up (to the 'left' of the figure) to the 'closed' state of goal realization (to the 'right' of the figure). (3) The model presented does not imply, moreover, that action is initiated 'from within'; in other words, that internal consideration necessarily precedes action; or that the psyche lies 'within the individual' and from there pulls the strings of action outside the individual. On the contrary, the figure shows that the psychic is implied by the very process of willing an action, in the very fact of action itself, whether that action is first and foremost found in the phase of intention or in the phase of realization (see also Taylor 1983).

The following figures show some of the main states in the willing process.

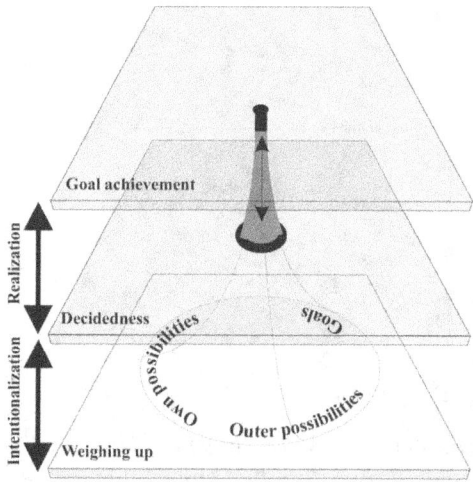

Figure 5.6 *shows how the realization phase is in the foreground. It is also possible to read the figure as follows: here the will is implied by the very behaviour/action defined as willpower directed at/by a goal. Hence the weighing-up phase is also implied in the very direction of the action. This model accords with Taylor's (1983) qualitative theory of action.*

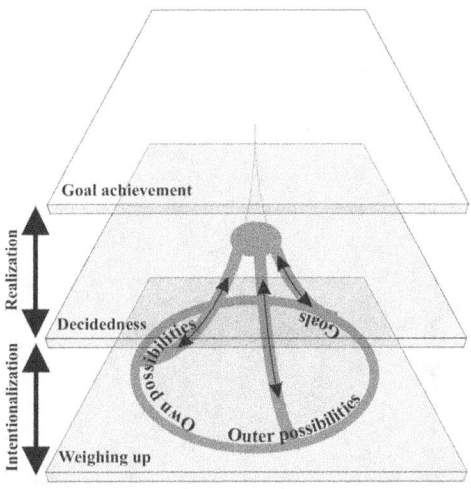

Figure 5.7 *shows that the will is primarily expressed through intention. At this stage, one may either be in a state of will or somewhere along the line from open weighing up to determination. Or one may be in the position of revolving between a first decision, which one may abandon in favour of a renewed (and indeterminate) weighing up, and a second decision which may again be abandoned, etc.*

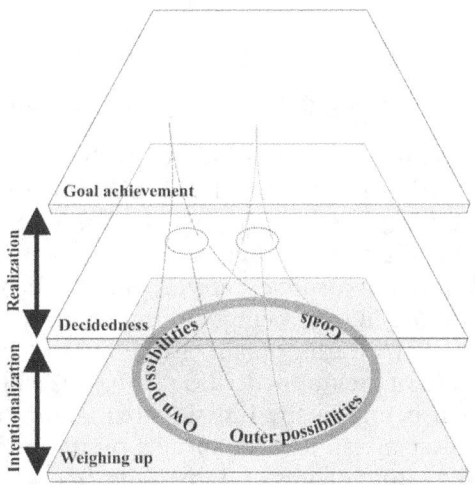

Figure 5.8 *shows that the person is in a state of open weighing up. The figure attempts to illustrate how the weighing up may lead to one decision or the other, and to the achievement of one goal or another. The positive aspect of this state of open weighing up is that one will not jump to conclusions. The negative aspect is that one may remain in a state of indeterminate perplexity.*

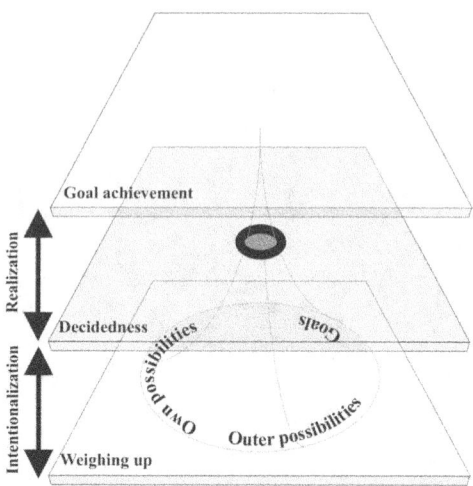

Figure 5.9 *shows, finally, that one may also be in a state of determination without actually realizing one's goal. One has decided. One knows what the right thing to do is. One has a clear intention which has not (yet) turned into any form of willed behaviour or action. In positive terms: one's attitude towards a particular case or action is clear; no further weighing up is necessary. In negative terms: the realization of one's decision, which one may perhaps 'owe' to oneself, to others, or to the situation, has not yet occurred – it may remain 'a pious hope'.*

Concluding definition of the free will

Hence the overall definition of the free will can be formulated as follows: Free will is the medium, downward organization of the constitutive elements of the self, expressed through a process that moves in various stages from intentionalization to realization.

This definition does not assume that free will is to be found only in the high-level psyche of the human being. On the contrary, by definition it is present wherever 'downward' organization by the psyche results in intentional behaviour or intentioned action. Thus free will can be found not only among human beings at the individuated, autonomy-seeking stage, but among our earliest ancestors at the socially centred and decentred stages – although, in these earlier phases of human life, free will took the form of impulses and inclinations rather than of self-conscious professions of belief or endeavours to achieve autonomy and authenticity (see Chapter 3). According to this definition, free will may also be found among higher-level animal species, such as bonobos and dogs, and indeed among the much lower species. An attempt has been made to illustrate this in Figure 5.10 by

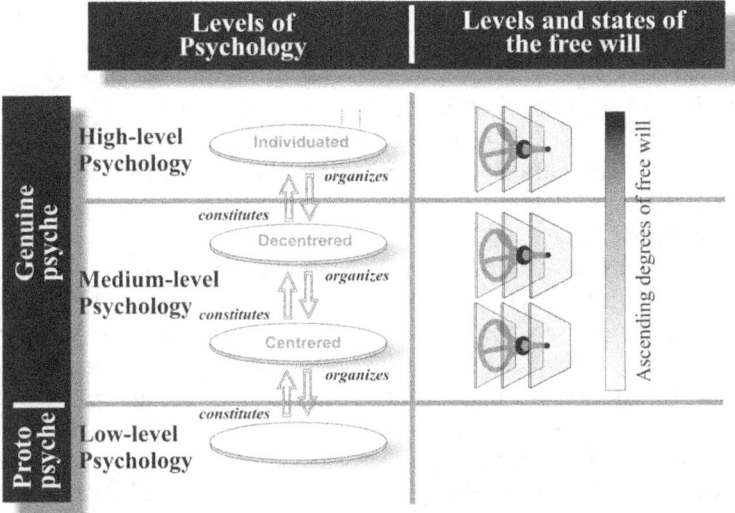

Figure 5.10 *shows the various levels of free will in relation to the distinctively human form of will/in relation to the distinctively human traits.*

placing the figure of will at all levels of the psyche. However, we cannot find free will at the level of the proto psyche, since self-activated and organized behaviour has not yet emerged at this level.

'Doomed to freedom'

We are 'doomed to freedom', Sartre said, pointing to the heavy responsibility for oneself, one's own life, the life of others and that of the community that is a consequence of our ability to decide for ourselves. However, much more meaning can be read into that sentence. Just as, through our discourse, we can work ourselves into an existential illusion of loneliness, so too can we work ourselves into despondency, or despair, at the very fact that we possess free will. We are prone to such despair, or anxiety, when we interpret the existence of free will to mean not just that we are responsible for our actions, personality and life, but for our achievements (including self-inflicted evils or the evils inflicted by one's culture). We may read into the concept of free will a demand that one must perform the optimal (indeed over-optimal) action in any situation – a demand for an (over-)optimal development of personality and for an (over-)optimal self-realization in life. This anxiety seems rife at a time when, at least in the Western world, life is no longer seen as something given, but as something one must acquire, rather as if one had entered some existential department store during the sales season, and were bound to choose from there innumerable life chances and opportunities for development. Freedom, in such a vision, is seen as a curse, not just because it imposes on us responsibility for our own choices, but because it engenders the fear that we may not have succeeded in getting the best out of our own potential and the potential of life as a whole – that we will be left behind or regarded as a loser. Under these circumstances, the 'curse' of free will can easily lead to despair (if one is the 'fighter' type) or to despondency (if one is more so-inclined). May (1977) uses the term 'existential guilt' to describe our sense that we may have failed to fulfil our own potential, or to live up to our own standards and expectations, or those instilled in us by other people (or by God). Many of us may also be troubled by guilt because we cannot or, for one reason or another, do not want to fulfil what we still perceive as our obligation to care for our next of kin. The more power we acquire, through our own consciousness, knowledge and understanding, to organize our lives and live them as we will, the more we are likely to feel this 'curse'. For the more we see ourselves as able, in principle, to master ourselves and our lives, the more troubled we are likely to be by whether we have made the right choices, and the greater the risk of our ending up in despair or despondency, if the facts of our lives do not match up to our expectations or demands for achievement.

The cure for this 'curse' lies in the development of a new kind of self-organizing and life-organizing discourse, in which the different elements that form the basis of the will – one's own inner potential, the possibilities and limitations posed by the external world, and one's own goals – are brought into harmony (see Figure 5.4). This kind of cure can be offered only by the kind of psychology which, on the one hand, does not borrow wholesale from scientific determinism, seducing us into a fatalistic or functionalistic conception of the self, but which is not, in turn, seduced by an unrealistic humanistic vision of our potential to control nature. There is a need for a psychology that bases its explanations on an understanding of the balance, and the double and mutual dynamics, between the constitutive and organizing elements of our nature: one that would help us to see more clearly the ways in which we are fundamentally constituted by our natural, cultural and life histories, while at the same time recognizing that we are, as a result of all these forces, free-willed and self-organizing beings.

Chapter 6

Consciousness

Consciousness as the formation of a phenomenological model

One of the central characteristics of the psyche, as we have seen, is free will. Another is consciousness. In the last part of this chapter, these two characteristics will be combined in a model showing their interrelation. But first we will concern ourselves with forming a model of consciousness.

The concept of consciousness is used in connection with a number of different phenomena. To be conscious may mean simply to be awake, as opposed to asleep or unconscious. It may also mean that one has gained a certain insight into something, as, for instance, in the sentence: 'During their conversation she became conscious of the fact that she had never really liked him'. Or it may mean that a person is politically or morally aware: for example, politically conscious of social conditions or morally conscious of his/her duty in a certain situation. In what follows, however, we will concern ourselves primarily with phenomenological consciousness: that is to say, consciousness in the sense of experience.

Characteristics of the phenomenological state of consciousness

As indicated above, to be conscious in the phenomenological sense means, first of all, to be awake and aware, as opposed to being in a state of complete unconsciousness, or so deeply asleep that even one's dreams (which are also phenomena of consciousness) have faded to a minimum.

To be directed at/by something. Consciousness is always 'about' something: that is to say, it is always intentionally directed at/by something. This applies even in sleep: our dreams, too, are always about something, a sensation, an image, a dramatic event, and so on.

To be absorbed in a stream of consciousness. When one is awake, consciousness also has a content. Not necessarily a content that demands one's continuous and focused attention. It may indeed consist of a free-flowing stream of thoughts, sensations or images. In certain states – for example, when one is taking a walk in the woods and letting one's thoughts wander; or when one is engaged in a monotonous, repetitive piece of work, or simply staring into space – the content continually changes, with different ideas flowing in a constant stream.

To be focused on something. Sometimes, however, our consciousness will be focused on something in particular, to which it will keep returning over a longer or shorter period of time, as, for instance, when we are preoccupied with a certain object or happening in our immediate surroundings, or when we are attempting to solve a particular problem that calls for a special kind of consideration and concentration. Two forms of attention, passive and active, can be distinguished here.

One is passively attentive to something when one's attention is drawn by something – an object or event – in one's immediate surroundings, or by a physical sensation – of desire, for example, or pain. In this case, the consciousness is first and foremost directed *by* something. No self-activity is demanded, only the ability to react (see also Figure 4.2).

To say that one is actively attentive, by contrast, implies that one is attentive to something because one has actively searched for and focused one's attention on it.

Presentative and representative consciousness. To be able consciously to behave in a certain way or to perform a certain action does not necessarily imply that one is able to *re*present that course of action to oneself. Our consciousness may simply be presentative. To be in a state of representative consciousness is more like being able linguistically to account for or state what one has in mind, rather than being able to show or illustrate it; it is more like denoting something than exemplifying it. To be in a state of presentative consciousness, on the other hand, is more like being able to show, to make clear, to carry out, to imitate, rather than being able to state, formulate, or account for something – it is more like exemplifying something than describing it (see Raffmann 1995).

To reflect on something. As we have indicated, consciousness has the structure of intentionality – it is directed at/by something. Sometimes, however, the object of one's consciousness may be oneself. One may, so to speak, take a step backwards and become conscious of what one is thinking, feeling or wanting to do, or what one could or should be thinking, feeling or wanting to do. One may, in other words, reflect on oneself. This reflexive consciousness is also directed, but in this case it is directed at/by one's own consciousness and its directedness. Reflexive consciousness is therefore a state of directedness at/by one's own directedness.

Consciousness as experience. Finally, one may distinguish between, on the one hand, the *content* of our consciousness – that is to say, our direct experience of a certain object; and, on the other, the consciousness-based structure which determines the character of that experience (which determines, for example, whether we perceive a motorbike as a noisy and dangerous machine, or as a piece of advanced technology for the optimal enjoyment of speed). It is the structure of consciousness, in other words, that ultimately determines that the content of consciousness is formed in one particular way rather than another; it is thus generic or performing, and as such is connected – as we shall see further on in this chapter – with free will and the self.

The phenomenological quality of the consciousness: Qualia and first-person perspective

Nagel (1974, 1986) formulated one of the most famous and central questions concerning consciousness: namely, what is it like to be conscious? For instance, what is it like to be conscious in the way that a bat is (see the title of Nagel's article: 'What is it like to be a bat?'). The question points to the existence of a 'someone' who is conscious in this particular way. Consciousness is not an anonymous or 'dead' process like the electric current in a circuit. There is a *someone* who is a recipient of impressions made by the world. A someone who has, or is going through, this particular experience. We must assume that even a bat is in this sense a someone – it is not just a no-subject robot or zombie.

Actually, Nagel here refers to two aspects of consciousness, although he does not take much trouble to distinguish between them. Let us look at them separately. There is, first, the content and quality of the experience itself (it smells like a rabbit, it is grey, it has soft fur). Second, there is a someone who experiences, whether this someone is a fox, bat, rabbit or human being.

Although it is less likely that a bat is able to reflect on what it is like to be a bat, it is much more likely that it may have a form of presentative consciousness: that is, that the world makes a phenomenological impression on the bat, in a way that is characteristic for bats as a species. Like other mammals (including humans), bats sense the world, seeing it with their eyes, and – in a way that is specific to bats and a few other animal species, such as marine mammals – hearing the shape and location of objects in the world, navigating among them by means of echo location. Indeed, Nagel chose bats as the subject of his article precisely because, as mammals, they are quite close to us biologically, yet, because of their echo location, the phenomenological impressions they presumably form of the world are unimaginable to us. Although we know technically how radar works and use it for purposes of navigation, this is a different matter entirely from being able to really imagine what it would be like, not just to *see* the shapes of objects in the world, but to hear them as well. Just as it is incomprehensible to us what it would be like to smell the world with the precision of a dog. We have difficulty, in other words, in reaching a thorough understanding of what it would be like to be a bat – or indeed a dog. Nevertheless it seems reasonable to assume that there is a certain way of being a bat which differs from the way of being a dog – or for that matter a human being.

Central to the particular nature of our consciousness, then, are its basic phenomenological qualities, such as the 'redness' we experience in looking at a tomato. Our experience of qualities, such as the colour red, is described by the concept of qualia. Qualia are colours, sounds, smells, tastes, or physical sensations like pain or tickling; the term refers, in other words, to the way in which something appears to us, or the phenomenological impression it makes on us. Qualia represent, so to speak, the phenomenological element of our presentative consciousness: the phenomenal qualities that absorb us when we are in a state of consciousness as opposed to unconsciousness.

The question as to what it is like to be conscious in this way – to have these qualia – also presupposes, however, that there is a conscious someone who experiences, for example, the colour red, and on whom the world makes an impression in the form of qualia. This, then, is the second quality of phenomenological consciousness: the existence of a someone whose attention is directed at/by the world in what we have referred to as the intentum aspect of intentionality (see Chapter 4). This quality of consciousness is called the first-person perspective (or, in abbreviated form, the **1pp**).

As we have noted, the fact that consciousness belongs to the first person – to a someone who is conscious – does not necessarily mean that this consciousness is reflexive – that the someone is capable of forming the self-conscious thought: 'Now *I* am conscious in this particular way'. The first-person perspective (**1pp**) is a part of any intentional consciousness (whether reflexive or not). More precisely, this first-person perspective can be seen to correspond to what we have called intentio (see Chapter 4), or an intentional connectedness viewed from the inside out. The relation between the two basic characteristics of consciousness, qualia and intentionality, may be formulated as follows: consciousness is intentional connectedness that is characterized by qualia, and illustrated in Figure 6.1.

The first-person perspective must be distinguished from the so-called third-person perspective (**3pp**). The first-person perspective refers to the subjective way in which the individual experiences the world in the form of qualia: because that individual is the particular creature he/she is, the world will impress him/her in that particular way. The third-person perspective, by contrast, is objective. From this third-person perspective, we aim to be able

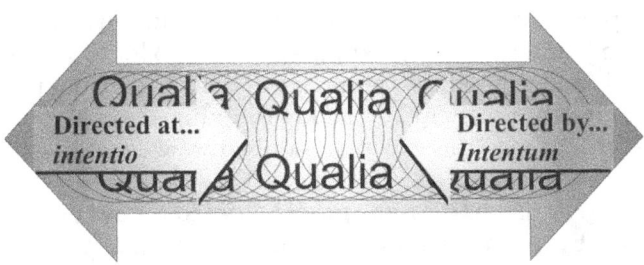

Figure 6.1 *How our intentioned connectedness is, so to speak, filled with qualia.*

to identify and characterize an object independently of the subjective way in which it makes an impression on this or that individual. We seek, in other words, to establish what it is like to anyone, irrespective of individual and subjective differences of perspective. The aim of any scientific endeavour is precisely to exclude first-person subjectivity in an effort to generate knowledge, concepts and theories that have universal validity, regardless of the perspective from which they are viewed. (Galileo was the first to clarify the difference between subjective and objective understanding, and to emphasise the necessity of abstracting the subjective element from universal scientific concepts.) In Nagel's term, the third-person perspective is the 'view from nowhere'. Thunder and lightning, for example, will obviously look and feel different from the first-person perspective of a bat than from that of a human being – because of the different ways that bats and humans connect with the surrounding world. However, science – or at least certain scientific disciplines – aims to disregard the subjective element and arrive at the essential facts about thunder and lightning: facts that hold true regardless of the viewer's perspective. Thus intelligent bats and human beings could agree on a physical theory of what produces thunder and lightning, irrespective of the dissimilar and subjective ways in which these phenomena impress themselves on their consciousness in the form of qualia.

What is it like to be a bat?

In his article of this title, Nagel proposes three central theses. First, the fact that a given organism has a consciousness means that it has a particular way of being the organism it is – thus, for example, bats have a certain way of being bats. This is what Nagel refers to as the subjective character of experience: the experience from the first-person perspective described above.

Second, the subjective character of this experience cannot be apprehended or imagined by any other kind of creature, unless that creature undergoes a fundamental change of structure. Human beings will never be able to grasp what it is like to be a bat, because although we can flap our arms like wings and draw on the knowledge of echo location developed for fishing vessels and submarines, none of this will tell us what it is like to be a bat flying through the night and taking soundings from its surroundings. We could come close to this experience only if we were to change our basic biology and turn into bats ourselves.

Nagel's third thesis concerns the problem posed for our understanding of consciousness by the fact that our scientific endeavours at explanation aim precisely to exclude every element of subjectivity – that is, to exclude the first-person perspective in favour of a third-person perspective. Science aims not only to generate concepts and theories about a given object that will be valid from any perspective, but to identify the object in objective terms. As we have seen, phenomena such as thunder and lightning will undoubtedly be experienced differently from the first-person perspective of a bat than from that of a human being; moreover, a troubled and anxious human being will no doubt experience thunder and lightning differently from one who is fascinated and excited by witnessing the magnificent play of forces across the sky. Scientists, as we have noted, aim to disregard all these subjective elements to arrive at the essential facts of thunder and lightning (or any other phenomenon) seen from the position of 'nowhere' (or 'everywhere').

In Nagel's view, this quest for objectivity poses a problem when it comes to formulating a scientific theory of consciousness. In what some may regard as a short cut to mysticism, Nagel argues that, if consciousness can only be understood as a first-person phenomenon, it cannot be grasped from the third-person perspective that science endeavours to achieve. We cannot find out scientifically what it is like to be a bat; nor, for that matter, can we apprehend scientifically what it is like to be ourselves, as the experiencing and conscious human beings we are, because, in Nagel's words, any change from a subjective first-person perspective to greater objectivity will not take us any closer to the true nature of consciousness, but further away from it. If our ambition is to formulate a scientific psychology that embraces the phenomena of consciousness, this is not a promising beginning. In so far as human beings share the same basic structure, of course, we may put ourselves in each other's place and imagine each other's first-person perspectives. So, from a subjective viewpoint, we are not unfamiliar with what it is like to be each other (and each other's other). Thus, one might argue (though Nagel does not) that our estrangement from each other's subjectivity is a matter of degree: we are much less unfamiliar with the subjectivity of other human beings than we are with that of bats, not to mention ladybirds, amoebas or some extraterrestrial creatures whose existence we do not yet know of. Nagel, however, sceptical as to whether the fact that we, as human beings, are able imaginatively at least to put ourselves in the place of other members of our own species, can be the foundation for any scientific project.

Let us discuss these hypotheses. First, consciousness has, by definition, a subjective element. This element can to be found, precisely, in the first-person perspective, and can only be recognized in so far as a similar first-person perspective exists. Thus the subjective character of consciousness can be recognized by another only if this other is able to assume a sufficiently similar perspective. In my terms, the ability to assume this perspective implies the psychic capacity for sympathy as opposed to empathy, which might be defined as the ability to put oneself in the place of the other in a hypothetical 'if-I-were-you' way. For me to empathise with you, or a bat to imagine what it would be like for me to be you or a bat, whereas to sympathise with you means to be in your place, to feel with you, *as* you, and thus to experience what it is like to be you, not simply what it would be like if I were you.

Here let us introduce the concept of perspective distance. The less one is psychologically capable of being in sympathy with another being, the greater one's distance will be from his/her subjective perspective, and the less one will be able to experience/understand his/her subjectivity. Such understanding, in other words, is a matter of degree. The distance between my perspective and that of those closest to me is relatively small, while the perspective distance between me and another human being from a culture quite different from my own is somewhat greater; that between me and a bonobo is greater still, and the distance between my perspective and that of a non-mammal – a crab, for instance – becomes almost impossible to traverse. Doubtless there is a way of being a crab, but I have no idea what it is like (except with regard to fundamental features, such as the fact that we are both subject to gravitation, and are both able to move in water as well as on land).

In short, certain aspects of the natural world – those pertaining to consciousness – are subjective in character and demand a special form of connectedness – sympathy – in order to be recognised and understood.

It follows that, if we adopt a third-person perspective on consciousness, we will automatically rule out that element of subjectivity – sympathy – without which it is impossible to 'enter another's consciousness' or to recognize and understand subjectivity. In the realm of objectivity, perspective distance is not just a matter of degree, but represents an absolute gap – one which, according to Nagel, is not bridgeable by any (known) method.

To a large extent I would agree with the view underlying Nagel's hypotheses. It is true that subjectivity, the first-person perspective, is a specific feature of consciousness. In his concept of subjectivity, Nagel has identified what one might call a 'constant factor' of consciousness – one that is common to all kinds of consciousness, irrespective of the organism involved: namely, that in each case there is a way of being that organism. In my words, the element of intentio – the **1pp**-point, so to speak, from which any form of connection with the outside world is made – will remain, regardless of the nature and level of the consciousness in question.

I differ from Nagel, however, in certain respects – and particularly with regard to his pessimism, or scepticism, concerning the possibility of developing a scientific, psychological, theory of consciousness.

First, Nagel sees subjectivity as an entirely 'inner' characteristic of the organism itself. He makes no allowance for the fact that organisms must necessarily maintain their existence through an active connectedness with their surroundings. One consequence of this condition of existence, crucially, is that the subjective experience of an organism is inextricable from its connectedness (see the argument in Chapters 3 and 4). To be precise, subjectivity can be defined as intentio – as the inside-out aspect of intentionality – which is inextricably bound up with *intentum:* intentionality seen from the outside in.

In other words, subjectivity is always embodied in, and will always be related to, the connectedness between an organism and the surrounding world.

Second, in so far as subjectivity relates to an organism's connectedness with the outside world – a connectedness that is crucial to its existence – the different forms that this connectedness takes in each species will naturally lead to different forms – and levels – of subjectivity. The fact that a bat, a bonobo and a human being connect with the outside world in ways that can be differentiated psychologically and ranked hierarchically means that their subjectivity, too, will take different forms and be on different levels. Because bonobos as a species are on a level not dissimilar to ours, for example, the 'perspective distance' to be overcome between us is relatively small: smaller, for instance, than the 'perspective distance' between ourselves and bats. Likewise, as mammals, we find it easier to sympathize with both bats and bonobos than we do with seahorses (though many people may think that seahorses are more attractive than bats). Thus there are not merely different forms of subjectivity, but different levels of it. Obviously, the existence of these different levels should not turn our heads – the fact that we are on a developmentally higher level than other species does not entitle us (as our ancestors at the time of the Renaissance believed) – to treat the world as our private playground, in a non-ecological and immoral way.

Nagel's super-abstract concept of subjectivity is silent on this matter. Like Kant, Nagel has no concept of 'care' (Heidegger's 'sorge'), of ethical demand (The Danish philosopher Løgstrup), of sympathy (Midgley 1994) or of directedness at/by, the directedness of others (as presented here). To exclude a notion of 'care' from one's concept of subjectivity is to risk proposing an inhuman form of rationality or forcibly to deny one's own conflicts of motive (Kant), or else to descend into a cynical utilitarianism, in which such conflicts of motive are settled by simple rules of calculation (Nagel).

Third, Nagel distinguishes between a first-person and a third-person perspective and argues that we can perceive or know something about the consciousness of another someone if, and only if, we are able to assume the first-person perspective that makes that other into the someone they are. In other words, a particular methodology is called for in seeking to apprehend someone else's subjective world: one that involves assuming a different perspective and placing oneself in the situation of the other. This methodology is indeed quite different from the 3pp method of science, which consists precisely in extracting any subjective 1pp – in avoiding looking at a given object or problem from one (subjective) perspective only. The key question, then, is whether we would miss any aspects of consciousness by looking at it only from a 3pp perspective (or conceptualizing it in universal epistemological terms)?

Manifestly, 3pp-methods do not provide us with an understanding of the essential element of subjectivity. Does it matter? What more do we need to know; or rather, for what purpose do we need the extra element that can only be provided by 1pp sympathy?

Can a blind person teach a course on water colour painting? Is a therapist able to do therapy? My guess is that, in certain kinds of therapeutic processes, there are long periods in which no proper sympathy between therapist and patient is evident at all; what is evident, at most, is a form of empathy which maintains (as a matter of modern therapeutic virtue) the 'perspective distance' between the two participants in the process. But again, does it matter? Even though most therapists are able, at most, to mobilize only empathy – and for much of the time hardly that – they will probably nevertheless be able to facilitate a therapeutic process. Though few practitioners of psychology would be willing to abandon their 3pp methods (which may protect them efficiently from getting into existential crises) in favour of genuine 1pp methods, they are nevertheless able, to a reasonable degree, to give their fellow human beings some help in navigating their way through life and developing their life projects. What more could one ask?

In our relationships with other human beings, then, we can manage a good deal with our 3pp knowledge. To a great extent, too, we are able to recognize and understand the subjective experience of other human beings, simply as members of our own species, even when the perspective distance between us is relatively large. It is, of course, a rare and significant experience to assume an identical – or close to identical – 1pp with another human being. Yet despite the rarity of this experience, we are neither doomed to loneliness nor to solipsism.

Fourth, it is, in my opinion, a total misconception of psychology to believe that it is primarily, or perhaps even exclusively, a science based on

1pp methods. Such a view absurdly narrows both the domain of psychology and its explanatory power as a discipline.

Many of the key psychic processes studied by psychology are in fact inaccessible to this kind of introspective or subjective methodology. Thus pure introspection gives us no access to what might be called the undercurrents or underpinnings of consciousness. Much empirical evidence has been gathered to show, for example, that we ourselves have not the slightest idea as to how we in fact process information, and that our subjective reports of the way in which we function mentally and emotionally will frequently turn out to be wrong. Often we will turn out to be in a quite different state, seen from an objective psychological perspective, from the one we suppose ourselves to be in

However, although there are numerous medium- and low-level processes which we cannot introspect – to which, in other words, we have no 1pp access – these low-level and medium-level processes, are not only constitutive of the high-level psyche, but are organized by it (see Chapter 4, Figure 4.5). Thus the two questions as to what constitutes consciousness, on the one hand, and how it is organized, on the other, require separate discussion. Narrow and superficial as my introspective view of them may be, the fact remains that these parallel or sequential processes may have been organized by me. Indeed, they may even have been organized by the content-simplifying (and perhaps, from a 3pp perspective, misleading) models I have made of my own consciousness. The fact that I myself cannot know, or form a detailed phenomenological model of, what I am doing in the entire continuum of my psyche, from the higher levels of my consciousness to the most elementary constitutive levels, does not mean that, from perspective of high-level psychology, this activity ceases to be something which I do (becoming, instead, something done to me). No – it is I who do it. Even though I may have no real idea of what it is that I am doing (see Chapter 5, Figure 5.2).

Consciousness: The easy problem, the hard problem, and the seemingly very hard problem

Chalmers (1996a and 1996b), commenting on the epistemological questions raised by consciousness, has suggested that we need to distinguish between what he calls the 'hard' and the 'easy' problems involved. The easy problem concerns the development of theories and explanations at the functional levels of consciousness (see also Chapter 4 on different types of explanation). These basic levels of consciousness can be understood and explained as functional mechanisms. Provided that we can identify the specific mechanisms that perform the functions of consciousness in question, such explanations will be sufficient. By way of example, Chalmers mentions, in this regard, our ability to discriminate between, categorize, and respond to stimuli in our surroundings (in other words, the way in which our cognitive system integrates information); or the features characterizing a state of sleep and a state of wakefulness; or the mechanisms brought into play when we focus attention, and so on. We have come a fair way already in explaining these functional aspects of consciousness, and it is only a question of time before we can provide complete explanations of the mechanisms involved. So, at least in principle, this kind of phenomenon presents no problem.

The hard problem relates to our actual experience as conscious beings: to the fact that, in Nagel's words, there is a way of being conscious. Chalmers presents the problem thus: how is it that all these ingenious functional mechanisms of the brain do not simply remain physical and chemical processes? What is it, among all these processes, that gives rise to consciousness? No matter how well-developed our explanations for our various functional capacities may be, we will not have explained the nature of consciousness itself or in what sense all these functional mechanisms are our consciousness. Even if we were able to provide a complete functional account of the brain, this further question would still remain.

To use Levine's term (1983), it would seem that there is an explanatory gap between functionality and experience, a gap which we are not yet able to bridge, and which corresponds to the gap between the first-person perspective of consciousness and the third-person perspective.

In addition to what Chalmers calls the 'hard problem', however, it would seem that there is also a 'very hard' problem in which Chalmers himself is trapped, namely that of understanding that consciousness cannot be explained merely as something 'within' us. In his formulation of the problem of consciousness, Chalmers constantly returns to the basic picture of a brain that functions in such a way as to allow the phenomenon of consciousness to emerge from within.

Further on in the present chapter, however, we will see that the concept of consciousness can be formulated in terms of the taxonomy we have presented so far. This means, in the first instance, that it can be viewed from both the 'top-down' perspective of high-level psychology and from the 'bottom-up' perspective of low-level psychology. But consciousness emerges not only through this vertical connection between the low-level processes of the brain and the higher organizing processes of the psyche. It emerges, in addition, through the horizontal connectedness between an organism and its surroundings. Consciousness is not just something within us, but a phenomenon that arises from the way in which we are connected, and relate, to the world that surrounds us. As an aspect of the psychic connection between an organism and its surrounding environment, therefore, consciousness must also be understood from this horizontal perspective: both 'inside-out' and 'outside-in'.

On qualia and reason

In addition, we may ask whether qualia, as a central feature of our consciousness, are susceptible to scientific analysis and explanation. According to one view, the phenomenological content of consciousness is not describable or explicable in scientific terms, and is bound to remain mysterious. Alternatively, one may argue – as I will below – that qualia must necessarily be related to our basic way of connecting with the world and directing our activities at/by the objects in our surroundings, and as such they must also be susceptible to explanation.

In identifying what it is like to be conscious in the way we are, we by definition refer to the phenomenological qualities of consciousness. From a philosophical perspective, we may also refer to reflexivity and rationality as the particular hallmarks of human consciousness: these features, in particular, help to explain what it is like to be a human being. Nevertheless, the qualia dimension is central to our daily lives, as, for example, when we seek to exchange experiences in our communication with others: how the food tastes, whether the new sofa is comfortable, what it was like to dance together, what impressions we got from the soundtrack and visuals of a film, how we would describe the feeling of the woods in the autumn, and so on. Generally speaking, if I seek to become aware of my being in the world, at this very minute, I will not, in the first instance, have recourse to philosophy or psychological rationalization. I see my surroundings, feel my physical being, sense the temperature of the surrounding air, feel the pressure of the wind, smell the wet leaves, hear the rustling of the treetops. To describe these sensations is to say – at least partially – what it is like to be me, right now: in the presentative state of consciousness in which the key elements are qualia.

Of course, in describing what it is like to be me, I might also refer to such things as speculations about mortgages, interpersonal troubles in marriage, pedagogical disputes with my children's teachers, moral dilemmas, annoyance at my work place, psychodynamic troubles with myself, my self-confidence and self-esteem, and so on. But none of these forms of reflection has, in itself, a phenomenological quality, though they may give rise to emotions, such as anxiety, that can be experienced at a phenomenological level. As mental processes they belong to the domain of our rationality, exemplifying the various troubles that arise from our very existence as social beings capable of self-conscious reflection. These may well be the kinds of troubles that many other social beings (biological, artificially created or, for that matter, extraterrestrial) pester themselves and each other with, but even if we knew this to be the case, it would not give us any greater insight into what it is like to be any one of these creatures. Intelligent, social bats from Alpha Centauri might well be preoccupied with the same kinds of moral dilemmas as we are, because the very fact of being social and reflective gives rise to such dilemmas. In this respect, there might indeed be no difference between their way of being and ours. The difference, however, would immediately become evident if we turned to the feelings and sensations attached to the state of moral dilemma that we, or the clever bats, respectively found ourselves in. Similarly, the next generation of computers, as intelligent, socially-directed machines, may well get into the same kinds of moral dilemmas that we experience in our human interaction. But they may well feel nothing at all in response to these dilemmas – or their reactions may be of a kind that does not correspond in any respect to our human understanding of emotion. We might even be able to explain such reactions, but we could hardly understand them.

The basic characteristics of consciousness: resonance and first-person perspective

Resonance

As a first step to dealing with the problems involved in formulating a scientific psychological model of consciousness, let us look first at the question of where, and how, consciousness arises. Here I will introduce the concept of a *proto-consciousness* to refer to the most simple organization of the basic constituents of consciousness. In its embryonic and most elementary form, this proto-consciousness must include the key elements that are identifiably present in the organized form of consciousness.

As we have seen, the two basic characteristics of consciousness are: (1) that it has a phenomenological quality in the form of qualia, and (2) that it is directed at/by something, or, to put it another way, that it has an intentio or first-person aspect. In other words, there is a someone who is conscious.

Let us first take a closer look at the phenomenological element. To identify any object, even in the simplest terms, is to describe the ways in which it connects to the surrounding world. Its particular qualities – what might be called its qualitative identity – derive(s) from its particular forms of connectedness. The characteristics of any object, in other words, are defined by its connections with the characteristics of other objects and, ultimately, those of the entire universe (see Østerberg 1966). Any quality of that object is also, therefore, an expression of, or carries a resonance of, something else.

A snowflake, for example, will, by its very existence, offer information about temperature conditions outside (the fact that the snowflake has not melted is evidence that it is cold). Similarly, the myriad ways in which ice crystals combine to form snowflakes contain information about, or carry a resonance of, how each snowflake was formed in the cloud it originates from. The same is true even for objects that seem virtually impervious to their surroundings, such as diamonds. The crystalline structure of the diamond carries a resonance of the general physical conditions of the universe. Everything has resonance, from the most fundamental atomic structures to the functioning of a thermostat, which switches heat on and off in response to alterations in the surrounding temperature. Likewise, the morphology and behavioural patterns of biological organisms carry resonances of the conditions that surround them. The shape of the penguin bears witness to the gruelling conditions of life in the Antarctic, while its behavioural breeding strategy tells us something about the availability of food under these conditions at different times of year.

At the most fundamental levels of reality we find the resonances of non-organic matter (the characteristics of snowflakes are examples of these deep resonances). Among the higher species of animal life we discover resonances in the form of the morphology, metabolism and behaviour of the organisms, but gradually also in the form of qualia in still more developed organisms, which can be seen as phenomenological resonances of the organism's psychic connections with the surrounding world. Qualia – understood as the particular way in which a given individual experiences, for example, the redness of a tomato – can be defined quite simply as a highly organized, that is to say psychic, form of resonance. Qualia are experiential phenomena that arise as resonances from the psychic connections between higher biological organisms and their environment.

I have chosen the term 'resonance' because it suggests that something reverberates as a result of something else, as the string of a violin starts to vibrate and produces a sound in response to another, similar sound in the room. Thus the term indicates that from the qualities of a given object we learn something not only about the object itself, but about the way in which it connects with the surrounding world. An object 'resonates' with the surrounding world because it is connected with it.

The contention here is that the phenomenon of resonance is a constant in the natural world which can be found throughout the existential spectrum, from inanimate diamonds and thermostats, through the elementary forms of organic life, to high-level, conscious organisms such as human beings.

We are now able to provide a first definition of proto-consciousness. First of all, it must be a specific form of resonance that reflects the particular connectedness between a given organism and its surroundings. Bats have a specific resonance, as do dogs, and human beings, by virtue of their particular forms of constitution and their ways of biological and behavioural connecting with the surrounding world.

The idea that consciousness arises, in a non-mystical sense, from the basic laws of nature is often termed pan-psychism. Pan-psychism has a long history that can probably be traced to Democritus (460–370 BC), and perhaps even further back. Subsequent versions of it were expounded by, among others, Spinoza (1632–1677) and Diderot (1713–1784). During the nineteenth century and the beginning of the twentieth century, a materialist version of the concept was forged, relating it to the idea of reflection. Thus the specific characteristics of an object were seen as a reflection of the surrounding world; similarly, the psyche was considered to reflect the world outside. In the twentieth century, pan-psychism has been championed by Whitehead (1861–1947) and, most recently by Chalmers (1996).

Biological organisms do not only resonate with the surrounding world, they actively direct themselves at/by their surroundings, and this quality of intentionality, as we have seen, is precisely what differentiates them, not only from inorganic nature, but from artificially created mechanisms, such as thermostats, or, for that matter, from the elementary, physiological processes of which the biological organism is constituted. Any intentional being, as we have argued, involves a someone who is resonant.

These two elements: (1) resonance (which, in its more developed form, includes qualia), and (2) directedness (including an intentio first-person perspective) are thus the constitutive elements of the proto-consciousness and the consciousness. An entity that is only resonant cannot be proto-conscious. Only entities that are both resonant and directed – that have, in other words, a first-person perspective – can be said to have a proto-consciousness.

Strangeness, perspective distance, and resonance

With the concept of resonance now in our armoury, we may return to addressing the difficulties which we encounter, as human beings, if we seek to understand what it is like to be a bat or another conscious being. An important feature of resonance is that it belongs, so to speak, to the individual: one cannot 'be in' (share) the resonance of another without being this other. In order truly to understand what it is like to be a bat, one must connect and 'resonate with' the surrounding world in the way that a bat does: one must, in other words, be a bat oneself or just like a bat. To the extent that we do not share the same kind of connectedness or resonance, we will remain more or less removed from the other's experience and, to a greater or lesser degree, will find it difficult to assume their first-person perspective. Depending on the degree of difference – the degree of our 'estrangement' – this 'perspective distance' will be greater or smaller.

As suggested earlier, cultural differences are one cause of perspective distance between human beings. We are indeed ethnocentric creatures: although we may be willing, in principle, to acquire the customs and ways of other peoples and cultures, we find it difficult to do so. The process of 'learning' another culture, is, for most of us, a long-winded business, and while it is still in progress the 'others' whose culture we are trying to acquire are bound to remain strangers to us. The more unfamiliar and strange the others' culture seems, the harder it will be for us to put ourselves in their place and assume their perspective – and the greater the perspective distance between us will appear.

Yet how significant, in fact, is the distance created by differences in culture? After all, we are all human beings with the same basic constitution. We share the same cognitive capacities for experiencing the world, the same basic emotions, the same desire for attachment, and, fundamentally, the same socially centred connectedness. As members of the same species we are in resonance in the same way. Although, as a Western European, one may have difficulty in fully understanding how an Australian Aboriginal thinks about life and the world, one will surely know, when it comes down to basics, when the Aboriginal is sad, happy, angry, afraid or filled with loathing. Nor will one doubt that he, like ourselves, is socially directed to form allegiances and attachments and that he, in turn, will be able to recognize in us fellow human beings to whom care and consideration are due. Seen from this perspective, the distance between human beings from different cultures may be no more than superficial 'wrinkles' on the deep ocean of experiences we hold in common.

A different kind of perspective distance is created by the constitutional differences between species. In many of our basic endeavours, and many of our ways of apprehending and 'resonating with' the world, we are, to be sure, not so very different from bonobos; indeed, in these respects, we do not differ greatly from most other mammals. However, the further away we move in the animal kingdom, the fewer constitutive elements do we appear to have in common. Snakes are much more distant from us, perspective-wise, than cats, and ants are more distant still.

Even here, however, we may ask how significant the differences really are between the ways in which the various species resonate and connect with the world. Perhaps the distinctly human characteristics are not, after all, so distinct from those of chimpanzees – despite the apparent distance between our perspectives? Perhaps we and the bonobos, for example, resonate with the world in the same fundamental way? Perhaps, indeed, any biological organism, at the most general level, resonates with the surrounding world in the same basic way, so that the differences between us and other mammals, for example, are negligible? Further, it may be that the decisive factor that makes us, as human beings, resonate the way we do consists of our being, at the most fundamental level of all, constructed on the basis of carbon chemistry. Perhaps it is this that makes the crucial difference between us and machines or artificial organisms based on silicon. At the level of quantum physics, different elements will give rise to different ways of functioning, which in turn will have consequences for the nature of consciousness. The implications of this are currently being investigated by neurophysiologists and neuropsychologists – see, for example, Hameroff 1997 and Conrad and Conrad 1997. It may be that fundamentally different types of organisms (the 'carbon-based' and the 'silicon-based') will eventually develop sufficiently similar forms of psyche to be able to exchange scientific insights, engage in a common moral and social discourse, and establish shared values and a practical ethics, yet remain utterly different in terms of their phenomenological experience and 'resonance': their way, in short, of being someone. Thus the perspective distance between these two forms of organism will prove to be far greater, and more crucial, than that between, for example, a bat and a human being, both of whom share the same fundamental chemistry (who could be said, both literally and metaphorically, to have a much greater 'chemistry' between them).

Are thermostats conscious?

How far down the line of living creatures and inorganic objects can we go before consciousness fades to nothingness?

There is no doubt that we are conscious ourselves. Mice are probably conscious as well – it is perfectly plausible that there is 'a way of being a mouse'. Further down the animal scale we can believe this to be true for lizards, fish and snails as well. There is no reason to believe that consciousness fades out at any point of the scale so far.

Chalmers (1996: 293ff) proceeds: what if we descend even further, moving from these 'lower' creatures to neural networks and even thermostats? Do we have any reason to believe that the consciousness will fade out at some point and eventually disappear? Why should there not be a way of being a thermostat?

The answer is straightforward: as we have seen, proto-consciousness requires not only resonance but intentionality. Thermostats are functional systems, and like everything else in the universe – they have resonance. By the way in which they function, they carry information about their surroundings and are activated by that information alternately to cool or heat the surrounding air. But they do not possess intentionality. They do not actively direct themselves at a goal in the way that mice, snails and the smallest self-propelling single-celled creatures do (see Chapter 4, the section 'Transition from functionality to intentionality'). Since thermostats, though functional and resonant, are not intentional, it follows that they cannot be conscious. Not even proto-conscious. Because they have no intentio, there is no 'way of being a thermostat' or 'resonating in a thermostat way'. Resonance in itself, though necessary for consciousness, is not sufficient. Only with the addition of intentionality can consciousness emerge.

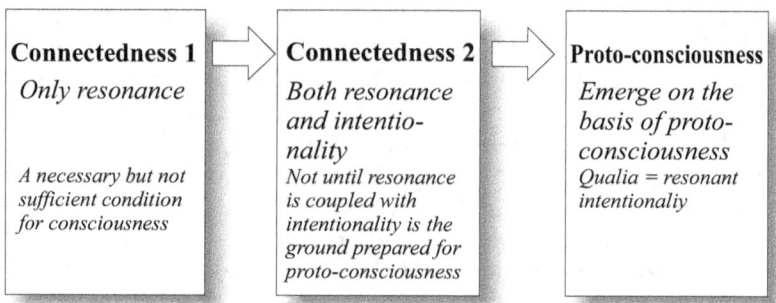

Figure 6.2 *illustrates the development from the simple resonance that arises through the connections between any objects or organisms in the world, and the proto-conscious resonance that arises from intentional connectednesses.*

Summary: The constitutive elements and earliest phylogenesis of consciousness

These considerations concerning proto-consciousness and, in particular, the constitution and nature of human resonance and human directedness, lead us to the following developmental model: the particular quality of a given organism's, or object's, connectedness with the surrounding world can be expressed in terms of its resonance. It is only when this connectedness has an intentional quality, or a quality of directedness, that it can be said to be proto-conscious. Intentionality *is* the structure of this protoconsciousness, while resonance is its content (see Figure 6.2).

What then is consciousness?

On the basis of these definitions of proto-consciousness, we may now move to a consideration of consciousness itself. To be conscious means to be directed at/by something in a resonant way, or, conversely, to resonate with the world on the basis of one's first-person perspective.

In order properly to understand what consciousness is, one must thus understand what it means to be in resonance – that is, to be in connectedness to something, which makes an impression on one: in the strong sense that one is this resonant impression. To be conscious, as we have seen, is to be conscious of something – for example, a tree, and that, in turn, means the impression it makes and our being in resonance with it. Set out in words, this may seem rather intricate, and it may at first be difficult to apprehend what it means: to be in resonance. But the state we are referring to is not in any sense mystical or miraculous: on the contrary, it defines our everyday way of connecting with the world around us.

It should be borne in mind that what we are defining here is consciousness, rather than the narrower domain of self-consciousness, meaning the highly organized consciousness of adult human beings. Thus babies, bonobos, dogs, bats, snails or amoebas can all be admitted to the company of conscious organisms – whereas passive plants and thermostats are decisively excluded.

Consciousness as phenomenological model formation

Since we are conscious of things in this directed- and qualia-based way, the world is presented and represented to us as a phenomenologically coherent unit. We do not apprehend the world, through consciousness, as a formless bundle of disparate and unconnected phenomena – on the contrary, we are conscious of the world as a coherent entity in which we involve ourselves through our thoughts and feelings, and our active, willed endeavour to establish connection with it. As we walk along the beach, for example, we are aware of that involvement in the very act of walking, of being in that particular place, of sensing the beach. Whether our consciousness extends to the entire beach, or is focussed on the lapping of the waves against our feet, we will continue to experience the world itself as a unity. The work of processing the impressions we receive is distributed among numerous different functions of the brain: thus our awareness, for example, that a blue ball is bouncing across the table is based on one brain process that registers movement (in this case 'bouncing'), another that 'specialises' in colours only (in this case 'blue'), yet another that deals with shapes ('round'), and so on. It is a scientific problem in itself (one referred to as 'the binding problem') to understand how all these processes join together to produce a single, coherent experience of a bouncing, blue ball. But it is a matter of psychological fact that we do experience all these different aspects of reality as a whole rather than separately.

The fact that the world is experienced, through our consciousness, as a unitary and unified whole could be understood through the concept of phenomenological model formation. Models, as we saw in Chapter 1, work by presenting, in a tangible or transparent form, selected salient features of a given object. In other words, they neither can nor should present every aspect of the object or situation in question, but only a judicious choice of those features that are relevant for the purpose. In addition to this process of selection and abstraction, an attempt is made to reveal the interrelatedness of the different elements within the model and the coherence of the whole.

A similar process takes place in our consciousness when we have a phenomenological experience of something. Obviously, we cannot consciously experience all that there is to experience in a given social situation, or even when a wave washes over our feet. Each such situation includes an infinite number of features and characteristics which we perceive unconsciously (in so far as they are perceptible at all), but only very few directly form a part of our phenomenological consciousness of the object or situation in question

A further characteristic of models is that they are operational (see again the first part of Chapter 1, for example Figures 1.5. and 1.6). They present objects or situations in terms that enable us to systematically identify and conceptualize them on the basis of what we need from them and do with them. In its formation of phenomenological models, consciousness operates in a similar way. What we experience is an abstract 'model' of the situation we are in or the object we are confronted with, including only those features of it which are of use or interest to us: a model based, in other words, on our particular involvement in, commitment to, the situation or object, and the way that we are directed at/by it.

A further feature of consciousness formed by the phenomenological models is that it is transparent. Our models appear not merely as a simulacrum of a reality that remains, in itself, inscrutable. We have the absolute sense of looking at reality itself. When we walk along the beach, and consciously take in our surroundings, we do not have the sense that we are looking at a film on a screen. We experience the beach and the entire situation directly. Although to be conscious of a situation means, by definition, to form a phenomenological model of it, we are not conscious of or attentive to the model as such; rather, we are conscious because of this model. Such is the transparency of our phenomenological experience, that we have a sense of complete realism: when we experience something, we experience it directly; we are conscious of this reality, this slice of life.

The concept of consciousness as a means, or source, of engagement with the world through a process of phenomenological modelling is also in accordance with our evolutionary view of psychology. It seems clear, or at least credible, that this way of engaging with the relevant parts of one's world (those that are essential and meaningful to the organism) is of functional value to animals, presenting them with a direct impression of what, for them, are the key features of their surroundings, and with a ready-made scenario that tells them directly – without any need for further, time-consuming cognitive processing – what they should concern themselves with in the here-and-now, and what behaviour they should initiate. This capacity, surely, has a survival value. A given animal will be able to control and optimise its behaviour much more successfully, we must assume, if its 'life-world' (meaning those features of the world that are particularly relevant to a given organism) is directly presented in the form of 'instructions': 'enemy too close! run! now!' or 'good food! Over there! go there! eat!' – in other words, in the form of a model, or scenario, for involvement and action. Such a system, surely, works much more efficiently than one that would require the animal, on each new occasion, to process numerous disparate details and to figure out, on that basis, what a given situation was all about and what its optimal behaviour would be. As it is, these considerations take place instantly, through the formation of phenomenological models that directly make the situation clear and suggest the best course of action (see the earlier discussion of will and action, Figure 5.5 in particular).

Two degenerate versions of the concept of consciousness as model formation

The concept of consciousness, like that of free will, can best be defined in relation to two degenerate or extreme versions.

At one end of the scale, we find the (social) constructionist concept of consciousness, and at the other, a concept championed by, among others, Churchland (for example in Churchland 1979, 1995).

According to the (social) constructionists, our experience of, for example, a beautiful red sunset is no more than a construction based on socially acquired concepts of the world. We have no knowledge of what the world in itself is like, so the argument goes, and our models, therefore, cannot be said either to present or to represent the reality of that world. Our models only reproduce certain agreed narratives about that reality. In the Middle Ages, people actually saw the sun sink below the horizon and, for that matter, so do we on summer nights when we experience the spectacle from the sand dunes. But, unlike the people of Medieval times, we can tell a different story, namely, that the earth turns on its axis, and as it does so the horizon comes up and hides the sun from view. And indeed, if one focuses on that story, one can actually also see how the horizon rises (try it sometime), just as, formerly, we saw how the sun sank down. The social constructionists argue that this story is no truer than the previous one – though it may be, in one way or another, a more efficient and useful narrative to some members of a particular culture (for example, the technology-centred cultures of the Western world: it is much easier to calculate the track of a rocket on the basis of the new astronomic world picture than on the basis of the old one).

As we saw in Chapter 1, this type of theory necessarily involves an anti-realist ontology: consciousness and its contents, structures and insights have nothing to do with the world, but a great deal to do with culture, language and the rules of narrative. Accordingly, the quality of the pain experienced by a person who burns his fingers in a flame is generated by his culture's way of speaking of pain. Is it possible to articulate the pain in such a way that it will disappear? It is quite true that, for instance, a person can considerably modify his/her own pain threshold and degree of bodily tension in connection with the pain, simply by being more relaxed and less hysterical. Cancer patients, for example, report that deep and chronic pains can be modified and will become more tolerable if, for example, they are experienced in a different frame: 're-framed', for instance, as 'the music of the body'. And yet: nobody can make the pain go away by 'explaining it' away. Nor can anyone walk through a rock wall merely by telling tall tales and saying 'open sesame'. The world is. This is the fact we must relate to, and one way or another this is what the models formed by our consciousness are all about.

It is true that the way we think about sex, for example, has quite a lot to do with how our culture 'articulates' sex. It is well known, for instance, that what is deemed attractive, in men's and women's appearance, changes from one culture to the next as well as over time. Nevertheless, the core of one person's sexual attraction to another cannot be explained purely in terms of the prevailing cultural fashion. The way in which two people are attracted to one another, the way they 'turn each other on', has a great deal to do with the way in which they 'resonate' as biological organisms. Moreover, it seems that certain features of human appearance tend to evoke the same resonances throughout the human species, regardless of fashion or culture: thus, for example, symmetry between the various duplicated parts of the body, such as eyes and limbs, is universally regarded as attractive, and is more fundamental to our appreciation of beauty, or otherwise, than more superficial characteristics (such as the degree of plumpness) whose value does indeed vary from culture to culture. It is true, too, that each culture 'tunes the instrument of the body' in different ways through different narratives concerning the body, sex and sexuality. In some cases, indeed, a specific culture may deliberately 'mis-tune' the body so that it will resonate in ways that trigger off frightened avoidance, repression or outrage. But the more fundamental features of the body will remain at the core of the resonance and sense of connectedness between two persons who are mutually attracted, irrespective of the particular narratives they may invent to describe one another or themselves. To be 'turned on', after all, is not the same as to 'talk about'.

Churchland, among others, goes to the opposite extreme. In one sense, he agrees with the social constructionists that our conscious models of the world are cultural artefacts. The way we experience a red sunset, and the model we form of it in our consciousness, are thus culturally acquired. But, rightly speaking, as Churchland would say, what is actually happening when we experience a sunset is that a bundle of electro magnetic waves is hitting a system of nervous cells (the eye) that passes on impulses to other systems of nervous cells (the brain). Churchland believes that we need to unlearn the naive models which dictate our experience of red sunsets, and replace them with natural scientific models that present matters the way they really are. Thus we would cease to model the event in a pre-scientific way as a beautiful sunset gradually turning the sky crimson as the sun sets beyond the ocean. Instead, in accordance with reality, we would experience the relative movements of the celestial bodies towards one another and the various refractions of the electro-magnetic waves resulting from an increased number of gas molecules as the angle of the sun rays in relation to the atmosphere gradually flattens out. Indeed, as our scientific insight into the neural basis of consciousness gradually develops, we will be able to experience directly how these refracted electro-magnetic waves activate different brain functions. We might, for example, be able to say something like 'these electro-magnetic effects will trigger off functional processes in, among others, the colour-processing and movement-processing areas of the brain, which in turn will trigger off activities in other brain areas. In the old days these activities would, somewhat naively, have been called emotions.'

One of the things that Churchland obviously does not take into consideration is that consciousness is not just a *re*presentation of reality from which we select intellectual models for illustrating certain events and connectednesses with the surrounding world. Churchland confuses the models formed in our consciousness with the kind of rational, abstract models formulated in the scientific articles academics write for one another. However, our phenomenological, conscious models of the world are neither pre-scientific nor scientific articulations of reality. Nor are they either pre-academic poetry or academic reports. They are forms of resonance in a biologically and culturally formed organism. The phenomenological models of our consciousness are resonant impressions of the world.

It is true that, as we develop our cultural understanding of the surrounding world, we also develop and expand the way in which the world makes an impression on us: we develop and re-tune our entire resonant system. For instance, we can gradually learn to taste wine: suddenly, it's no longer just a question of being 'quite nice': we can detect a tiny hint of an autumn forest here and a tiny bit of sulphur there. Similarly, we can learn to listen to music: the piece of music which used just to sound like 'something baroque' is opened up to us, revealing infinite depths, tensions and flirtatious interactions between the instruments. We also know that Inuit are much better able than city-dwellers to distinguish the slight differences between various qualities of snow. By and large, city-dwellers can only discriminate between the fresh white newly fallen snow in the parks and the brownish slush on the salted streets.

Although by acquiring more cultural meanings, we will experience, experiment with and develop still further personal senses (see Chapter 4, the section on 'The levels of psychology'), so that more and more of the world's variegated aspects are revealed to us, the objection to social constructionism remains: our phenomenological models will always emerge through our connectedness and resonance with the real world – irrespective of the narratives we may construct about that world. Two problems, in particular, arise from Churchland's reductive constructionism.

First of all, he clearly misses the point that the modelling that takes place in consciousness will always be a phenomenon arising from our connectedness with the world. Phenomenological models emerge through that connectedness; indeed, they are themselves a form of connection with the world. Thus Churchland's objection to our ways of modelling a red sunset as naïve, erroneous and insufficiently overly models, is absurd, because this is simply the impression that one part of the world (the astrophysical) as a matter of fact makes on another (the human organism). Nothing is more real than these real impressions in the shape of our phenomenological models: the astrophysical and electromagnetic events are also a red sun setting on the horizon, and this model of reality is not less true than that presented in the differential equations of physicists. Enriched by science, the models formed in our consciousness may perhaps be more comprehensive and 'truer' in the sense discussed in Chapter 1, that is, more useful for a given purpose. However, one cannot conclude from this that such models are truer to reality. That would simply be a fallacy.

Second, it would seem that Churchland is interested only in the abstract third-person viewpoint – the universal perspective from which a given phenomenon, such as a sunset, may be recognized by any conscious creature, be it a human being or an intelligent bat from another solar system. In this sense, Churchland's 3pp-reductionistic constructionism shares a common problem with social constructionism: neither grasps that our consciousness is a form of phenomenological modelling that is also determined, in a way that is unique to us as human beings, by our resonance as carbon-based organisms, and our ways of connecting, as such organisms, with the world around us. No matter how much we may enrich our ways of resonating and connecting with the world, the resonance we enrich will still be specific to us as the organisms we are, and will still be based on our fundamental constitution.

In other words, the phenomenological models entailed by consciousness are not just a construct of a particular culture, but a form of resonant connectedness with reality, and in this sense they are a part of that reality themselves. Moreover, one kind of modelling (in the form of differential equations, for example) is not necessarily truer than another (such as that based on a more poetic or impressionistic perception of the world).

We are bound, as I have argued, to reject the anti-realist ontology of constructionism. Yet the considerations raised by social constructionism contain an important element of truth. We will now take a closer look at these considerations.

Proto-consciousness and social constructions

To be proto-conscious, as we have seen, means both to be resonant and to be directed at/by something in an intentional way. Thus defined, proto-consciousness is a prelinguistic reality – unless, of course, one takes the concept of language to an extreme, allowing it to comprise any form of active relationship to one's surroundings.

This definition of the structure of proto-consciousness as a pre-linguistic, and, for that matter, a pre-social reality, is in sharp contrast to at least the most radical versions of social constructionism, which claim that consciousness is fundamentally socially created. The content of consciousness, it is argued, is a socially constructed phenomenon that will change as society itself changes, from one epoch to the next and from one culture to the next. Indeed, the very phenomenon of consciousness is a social construct, and even the nature of individual consciousness in a given society is defined by the linguistic constructions of the society in question.

The argument of the present book is, on the contrary, that human consciousness is not merely a social or linguistic construct, nor does its nature and existence depend on the form of the society and the kind of thinking prevalent in the particular culture in which it is conceived. For consciousness is rooted in proto-consciousness, something that we have in common with every other living creature, even those that have no language at all in the proper sense of the word that do not live in societies, and that are not brought up in a cultural-historical context (amoebas, foxes and so on).

Having said this, however, it must be admitted that, to a large extent, the consciousness of human beings is socially formed. In order to make clear how this statement is to be understood, we need to differentiate between discourse and structure.

A discourse is a method for constructing arguments. It provides the framework for what can be recognized as substantial, useful and acceptable arguments concerning how to act and why one acts the way one does. On the basis of Mead's understanding of consciousness, one might say that discourse provides the framework for, and the content of, our communications about one another, and therefore also the framework for, and content of, our communications about ourselves, which in turn determine our self-understanding and our rationales for acting the way we do and leading the lives we live. Discourses are indeed created by society and as such are culturally and historically variable. Each epoch, each geographic location, each culture on Earth, each philosophical tradition, indeed each short-lived trend, has a discourse of its own and will thus provide its own linguistic frameworks for discussing others and oneself. It is through such discourses that the individual (albeit tacitly) identifies his/her own reasons for being the person he/she is or wants to be, and his/her judgements as to what constitutes the good life. From the point of view of discourse, it is true that consciousness is first and foremost a social construction.

However, the structure of consciousness, by which the proto-consciousness is defined, provides the fundamental frame, the basic ontological conditions, that make possible the existence of that kind of consciousness in general, and social discourses on consciousness in particular. Any such discourse is an intentional, resonant phenomenon and – obviously – must be structured as such. If the structure were different it would not be consciousness.

However, it is too easy to dismiss a theory, in this case, social constructionism, by addressing only its most extreme representatives. Let us take a look instead at the picture presented by Burns and Engedahl (1998), who offer a more moderate social-constructionist concept of consciousness based on Mead's symbolic interactionism, and to some extent also on Berger and Luckmann's elaboration of this theory. Burns' and Engedahl's prime concern is to counteract the tendency to treat consciousness exclusively as a phenomenon of the brain. They note the striking failure, on the part of the extreme materialists, to include any sociological categories in their theory of consciousness, and set out to redress this trend.

A key aspect of their model is that they differentiate between consciousness and awareness. Consciousness, for them, consists of socially constructed cognitive representations and self-consciousness in linguistic representations; whereas awareness, in their theory, refers to sense perception and phenomenological processes that are not immediately accessible, as such, to consciousness: they are not something that have the quality of being reflected upon. Finally, they identify a further level, underlying both consciousness and awareness that consists in purely physical or material processes: that is to say, the biological, neuro-physiological, perceptual and cognitive functions of the organism. By and large, these processes operate independently of both awareness and self-conscious reflection.

In broad terms, Burns' and Engedahl's argument can be outlined as follows: on the one hand, the cultural framework that is generated and sustained by members of society, provides a common stock of cognitive concepts, definitions and practical directions for action, orientating us in how to understand a given situation, relate to it and act accordingly. The social activity of human beings (including reflection) is organized and regulated by socially-produced rules and regulatory systems. Above all, social institutions – understood as the system of expectations and sanctions by which a society controls the behaviour of individuals – serve to structure, and provide the content of, individuals' ways of thinking about and relating to a given social situation. By giving meaningful answers to a number of fundamental questions: what is going on? what kind of activity are we talking about? what kind of activity is required of me? what will happen if I do this or that? and so on, institutions, understood in this general sense, are indeed what make it possible for us to form a conception of a given situation, and relate to it, at all.

Likewise, Burns and Engedahl argue that our understanding of persons is constructed within this institutional framework. Through their relations with other persons, individuals acquire linguistically based, collective representations of themselves. First, a socially created, linguistic framework provides the possibility for others to conceive of, and relate to, the being and activity of the individual. Second, the self-conception of the individual (which for Burns and Engedahl is equivalent to reflective consciousness) arises from his/her acquisition of other people's ways of referring to him/her. Hence, the individual is involved in an ongoing conversation about, and discussion of, him/herself, and this external conversation in turn forms the basis for the individual's internal conversation about him/herself. Thus the basic material or framework for the individual to develop a self-conception is provided by external social institutions. Or, to put it another way, in Burns' and Engedahl's sociological conception (which is in turn based on Mead's), the self is ultimately constructed from linguistically based, institutional material. Their main hypothesis is that individual reflectivity – as a defining form of consciousness – is derived from collective processes.

From their primarily sociological perspective, Burns and Engedahl assume that the phenomena of consciousness are hierarchically structured, and the structure they put forward may be compared to the kind of hierarchical structure I have outlined above. The scheme illustrated in Figure 6.3 shows how the various stages in their hierarchy relate to the concepts of the low-, medium- and high-level psyche (see Figure 4.5).

As will be evident from the above, Burns and Engedahl are concerned with the discourse of consciousness and self-consciousness: the social content that provides the raw material for our self-consciousness and the framework for developing an acceptable way of understanding ourselves: acceptable, that is, to our culture and hence to ourselves as socially-adapted human beings (or to those parts of ourselves that are socially-adapted). This social content provides us with the reasons for doing what we do, and for intending or desiring to do certain things. One culture may differ from another in terms of this discourse and the framework it sets up for what constitutes an acceptable self-understanding and/or acceptable life project.

But we can see, too, that Burns and Engedahl have no concept of proto-consciousness as a universal, non-linguistic, non-sociological, non-institutional phenomenon. They deal exclusively with the sociological dimensions of a purely human consciousness, first and foremost at the level of high-level psychology and the upper reaches of the medium-level psyche, which we hardly share with even the highest of the other animal species.

High-level psyche	***Linguististically-based reflective consciousness***
	Nature: Linguistically-based, collective concepts and models of our physical and biological life conditions, our natural resources or lack of resources and our economic conditions. **Culture 1:** Linguistically-based, collective concepts and models of good and evil, truth, morality, etc. **Culture 2:** Linguistically-based, collective concepts and models of collective representations, knowledge, institutions. *Burns & Engedahl argue that self-reference, and hence consciousness (in their meaning of the term) develops on the basis of Culture 2 concerning the sociological dimensions of life.*
Medium level-psyche	***Non-linguistically-based awareness***
	Nature: At this level, we experience and conceptualise our physical and biological life conditions in a non-reflective way. From a socio-biological view, this occurs through group experience: factors such as resources or lack of resources help to determine the way in which we tacitly orientate ourselves, but there is no collective representation of this process. **Culture 1:** Impressionistic feelings for and evaluations of group life based on group and individual experiences, but no collective articulation or conceptualisation of these. **Culture 2:** Group and individual experience of and feelings about life as such, but no articulated understanding of or explanations of the complex patterns of life.
Low-level psyche	Here we are below the threshold of consciousness; there is no immediate access to the material: the biological functions, the hormonal system, the cognitive and emotional capacities of the nervous system, etc.

Figure 6.3 *Adapted from Burns and Engedahl 1998: 79.*

They have nothing to say about the rest of the consciousness continuum, where the concept of discourse does not apply.

Second, while it is true that Burns and Engedahl have chosen a sociological rather than a neurophysiological perspective, their reflections on the role of sociological discourse in shaping consciousness nevertheless give primacy to the third-person perspective. In other words, they have replaced the purely neurophysiological third person perspective with one based on sociological/socio-psychological considerations, but they have come no closer to addressing the first person perspective.

In sum, this kind of social constructionist approach to consciousness deals only with the high-level phenomena of consciousness and is not concerned with the first-person perspective. Burns and Engedahl's account of the way in which individual human self-understanding is created on the basis of a culturally defined discourse still offers no description or explanation as to what it is like to be an individual who becomes conscious within this discourse. Only the discursive forming of intentionality is touched upon, not its distinctly human resonance.

The ontogenesis of consciousness

The development of consciousness during the first years of life

We can now take a closer look at the ontogenesis of human consciousness, that is, at the way in which consciousness develops within the individual human being, primarily during the first years of life (see Bertelsen 1999, where the developmental model is presented in more detail and with extensive reference to empirical research in child development).

From the very beginning, to however small a degree, an infant's behaviour is directed at objects in its surroundings which it may relate to and start to use (though its ability to use them is initially very limited). A dummy, for instance, can be seen, touched, felt, tasted, and so on, and as such becomes special to the child. From the inside-out perspective (intentio $\Rightarrow$ intentum) we can say that the object is made meaningful when it is made use of; its meaning becomes apparent from its use. Making use of an object creates, in this sense, an important resonance within the child, who comes to understand that this particular object can be used in this particular way, or these ways, and not others. From the outside-in perspective, on the other hand (intentio $\Leftarrow$ intentum), one may say that the objects already have a meaning before the child makes use of them, a meaning which the object has acquired through its use in the human world at large. The meanings of objects in this sense can be demonstrated to the child; parents, for instance, may show or make clear to the child how to use a baby walker: 'look, this is how you can use it – you stand here, hold there and push.' (See Wittgenstein 1971; also Chapter 3 of this book, the section on the centred life, and Chapter 4, the section on the levels of psychology).

To begin with, the infant will direct its behaviour primarily at the immediate meaning of the objects, but from the age of about 12 to 18 months, children will gradually develop, through play, their skills in handling and investigating objects and making use of them in a great variety of experiential ways. Gradually, a new form of play will appear in which the child makes use of the object, not only literally (sucking the dummy because that is what it is made for), but metaphorically. In his/her play, the child metaphorically pretends that the object is something else (the stones represent Daddy, Mummy and the children; the twig represents the food which Daddy gives to the child, and so on). The child approaches the objects in his/her own way and finds his/her own methods for establishing their possible meanings. At the same time, the child, in experimenting with these objects, invests them with his/her own sense. (See Chapter 4 on the distinction between meaning and sense). The child's directedness at the object in terms of its sense is still based on his/her directedness at it in terms of its meaning – he/she does not lose sight of the real meaning of the stone even as he/she pretends that it is a person. If a child were totally to lose his/her grip of the factual meaning of an object, he/she would be hallucinating.

The way in which the child connects to the world through meaning cannot arbitrarily be chosen by the child him/herself, but is determined by meanings established in advance: both those that derive from the physical characteristics of objects (a dummy has a weight, shape, colour, and so on) and those that are culturally-historically created (the dummy has been produced for sucking). But as the child experiments with a given object in pretend play, he/she will gradually become more independent from these established meanings, and acquire a greater degree of freedom in finding his/her own ways of making use of objects and investing them with his/her personal sense. For example, the dummy can also be dropped on the floor so that Daddy will constantly have to pick it up and make funny faces. Thus, while the way in which the child directs his/her behaviour at an object in terms of its meaning is not up to him/her to decide, to an increasing degree he/she has the freedom to direct his/her behaviour on the basis of the personal sense that he/she has invested in the object.

On this basis we can make a first rough outline of the ontogenetic development of consciousness.

From 0 to 18 months: an emerging sense-directed intentionality. During this period, the child will remain primarily in a dyadic, socially centred form of connectedness, based on the one-to-one relationship between infant and adult. We see how child and adult continually attune themselves to each other – one will make a sound, the other will make a sound; one will smile, the other will smile; one will lift an arm, the other will do likewise. From the very beginning, the child and the adult are profoundly resonant to one another in a socially centred way, so that each of them will also be particularly directed at/by the directedness of the other, both in relation to him/herself and in relation to the surrounding world.

This directedness at/by directedness will gradually become more and more complex and profound, ranging from simple imitations of facial expressions or limb movements to long behavioural sequences, initiated by the child him/herself, which involve going through a complex choreography of movements, body positions, eye contact, and so on, while waiting intensely for the reaction of the other.

Towards the end of this period, this kind of behaviour will have become a game in its own right – a common third party between the child and the adult. Through gesticulation and the beginnings of language, the child will create other common third parties, drawing the adult's attention to something beyond the two of them: a toy, for instance, or an event outside the window, so that they may share the experience. The dyad has become a triad. Being together is no longer 'just' a given fact to the child, but has turned into an event in which the child actively participates; being together has turned into doing things together. The self-active directedness at/by directedness (of the other) becomes, with increasing degrees of freedom, meaningful.

From 1½ to 3 or 4 years of age: completed meaning-directed and emerging sense-directed intentionality. Once a triadic relationship is established, objects will no longer simply have meaning, they will also make sense – and not just sense to the child him/herself, as is the case in experimental pretend play. Moreover, the child will now discover that the same object, with the same common meaning, may nevertheless have an entirely different *sense* to another person. For instance, the child may be curiously engaged in something, only to discover that Mummy is signalling warnings of danger. Or perhaps Mummy shows no interest whatsoever in the object, or is amused by it while the child is still somewhat frightened. This is how the dimension of sense emerges gradually, in the child's directedness, from the dimension of meaning.

From 3 or 4 years of age and onwards: completed, sense-directed intentionality. During this period, meaning-directed intentionality is consolidated. To an increasing degree, the child will be directed at/by the fact that the other, or others, direct their behaviour in another way. At the same time, the child's realisation that the directedness of others is different from his/her own will be the catalyst for discovering that his/her own ways of directing his/her behaviour at and by others is unique to him/her. In realising, moreover, that other individuals direct their behaviour in relation to their own directedness, so the child will discover and develop his/her ability to direct his/her behaviour according to his/her own directedness.

Through this process, the child will be given the opportunity to become absorbed, or engaged, in him/herself and in his/her own directedness. In other words, the child's consciousness will become individuated (see also Figure 3.8).

During the first period, from the age of approximately 12 to 18 months, in which the child's connectedness with the surrounding world is social in character and based primarily on the profound, dyadic togetherness with another (adult) being, the child and his/her form of consciousness are predominantly centred (see Chapter 3). During the next period, from the age of 1½ to 3 or 4 years, there will be an explosion in the child's behavioural capacities and, now that he/she has the physical capacity to go exploring, while being able constantly to return to the safety of the 'home base' with Mother and Father, he/she will seek, of his/her own accord, to move away from the dyad. The child's way of relating to the world, and its form of consciousness, will become increasingly decentred. Not until the age of 3 to 4 years or more, will the forms of connectedness have become sufficiently organized and self-consciously directed to allow us to speak of a properly individuated form of consciousness: one that will gradually become more sophisticated in the years to come and indeed throughout the child's adult life.

At the beginning of its life, as its directedness in relation to meaning begins to emerge, the infant's consciousness will consist of factual, phenomenological models. To the infant who reaches for its dummy, a dummy is a dummy and nothing else. The meaning of the dummy will become clear to the child to the extent that it (the dummy) becomes resonant through use. Similarly, the child's consciousness of a cup will, to begin with, consist in a factual phenomenological model – a cup is a cup is a cup. But when the child begins to engage in pretend play, other objects may gradually come to be used as metaphorical cups. For instance, the child may pretend that a fir cone is a cup. A fir cone has a great deal in common with a cup: it can be grasped in the same way and lifted to the mouth so that one can pretend to drink from it, and it can be placed on the table along with other cups to serve as a pretend coffee set. Likewise, Daddy and Mummy may be represented by stones, and so on. In order to pretend that the fir cone is a cup, it will suffice to add just a few, or perhaps just a single pretend characteristic to the fir cone, for example that it is supposed to contain a drink. In other words, in playing with the fir cone, and directing his/her behaviour at it in accordance with a particular sense of what the fir cone is, the child has formed a model: that is what his/her consciousness of the fir cone consists in. It is true that it is not quite a factual phenomenological model, but, give or take a few degrees of abstraction, it is close to being one. This formation of phenomenological models in an emerging sense-directed consciousness can thus be termed realistic phenomenological model formation, albeit based on a rather concrete original object (the fir cone).

The adult's imaginative models, in contrast to the infant's, can depart much more radically from the material or existing world. When an adult imagines something, or reflects on people, things and events that are not immediately present, or daydreams about some hypothetical occurrence, he/she is directed at/by something in a way that, in contrast to the child's, does not immediately model reality. We may call this way of forming phenomenological models an ideal, or abstract, model formation.

Because they are highly abstract, it is precisely these 'ideal' models that will enable the child to direct him/herself in relation to the directedness evident in another's action or behaviour. This directedness is not a mysterious or impalpable element in the other's act – it is quite simply and clearly implied by the act itself and its evident goal-directedness (see again our earlier considerations on will and action, for example in Figure 5.5). Nevertheless, it takes a highly developed capacity to abstract the directedness of the act and turn it into something one can relate to as such. (Similarly, whereas only relatively simple mathematics is required to describe the speed of a movement, more advanced mathematics is necessary to describe its acceleration – even though this change in speed is just as directly implied by the movement as is the speed). Only when we have such ideal model formations can directedness – both that of others and one's own – be modelled as a psychological quality in its own right. In other words, it is only when the child is able to perform this advanced form of abstract modelling, that he/she can identify and relate to directedness itself as the quality which, from a psychological perspective, characterizes both one's own mind and the mind and intentions of the other (for further details, see Bertelsen 1999, and Chapter 3 of the present book, especially the section 'Development of protosociality, protomorality and directedness at/by the directedness of others', as well as Figure 3.9).

Summary of the development of consciousness

Thus far we have outlined the ontogenesis of consciousness in terms of the following developmental stages:

- The emerging, factual, meaning-directed intentionality of 12- to 18-month-olds: the child's directedness is organized by an emerging, factual, phenomenological model-forming consciousness ('a fir cone is a fir cone is a fir cone').
- During this period, the infant is directed at/by concrete things in the form of objects and the behaviour of others, including the directedness evident in the behaviour of others.
- The completion of meaning-directed intentionality and the emergence of sense-directed intentionality in 1½ to 3- or 4-year-old children. The

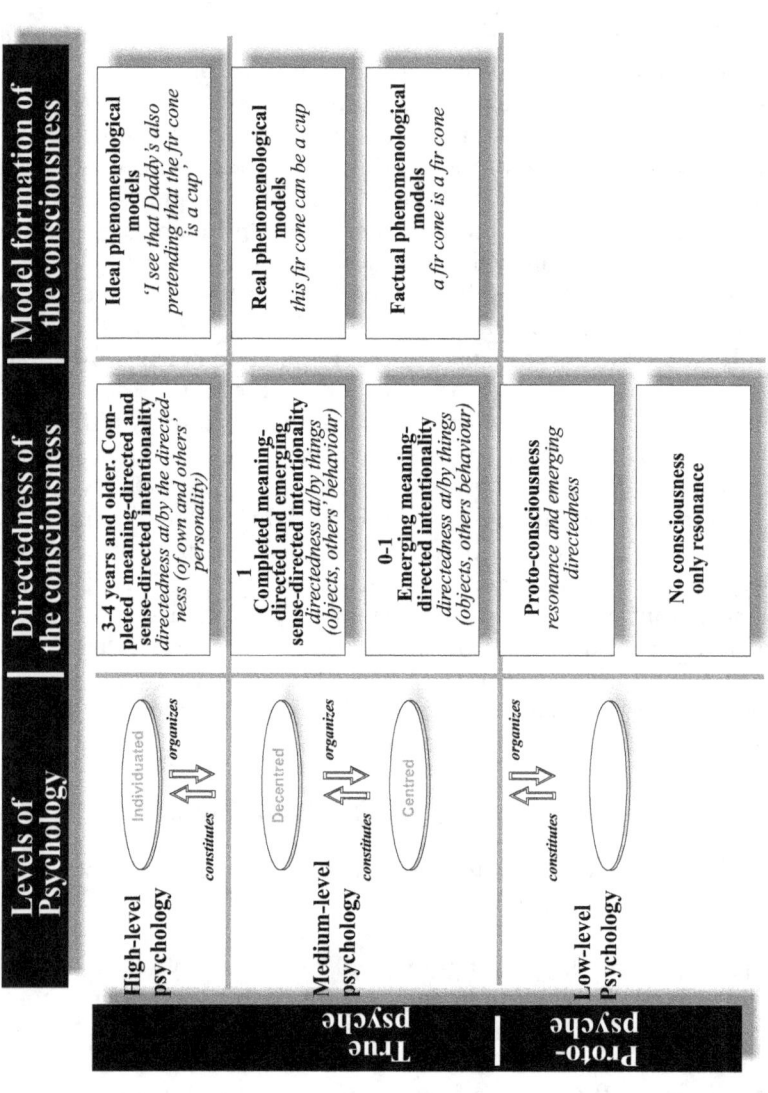

Figure 6.4 shows how proto-consciousness is a feature of low-level psychology while real consciousness is found at the level of the true psyche. At this level various further gradations of consciousness can be identified, corresponding to the centred and decentred medium-level psyche and the individuated high-level psyche.

child's directedness is organized by a now complete, factual model-forming consciousness and an emergent, realistic model-forming consciousness ('this fir cone is supposed to be a mug'). Again, albeit at a more advanced level, the child is directed at/by concrete things in the form of objects and the behaviour of others, including the directedness evident in others' behaviour.
- The completed, sense-directed intentionality of four-year-olds and older children. The directedness is the expression of an organized, ideal model-forming consciousness based on factual and realistic model formation ('I see that Daddy is pretending that the fir cone is a cup; he's imagining that it's a mug').

This kind of directedness develops into a directedness at/by the directedness that is observed in, and abstracted from, both the child's own acts and those of others, and at/by the relatively stable personality expressed by these acts over time and across various situations.

These considerations, which are illustrated in Figure 6.4, can now be incorporated into our taxonomic model. It should be noted, with regard to the figure, that the various stages in the ontogenetic development of consciousness are set alongside the various levels of psychology and the psyche that are used to characterize the various stages of phylogenetic development; however, this does not mean that animals, or for that matter our earliest ancestors, whose psyche could be characterized as 'medium-level' and who live, or lived, a centred mode of life, only had the maturity of a 0–1-year-old present-day child, or that those early human beings who led a decentred mode of life had the level of maturity of modern 1- to 4-year-old children. Had that been the case, neither animals nor our ancestors would have survived. Thus, no reference is made in this scheme to the general level of maturity, ability or intelligence of human beings or animals at these various levels, but solely to the nature of the directedness and the form of consciousness. The figure shows, for example, that our ancestors at the decentred stage who, despite possessing more mature and developed cognitive skills, had the level of intentionality of modern 3- or 4-year-old children, lived on the threshold of a modern, reflexive form of consciousness, in which their behaviour and actions were directed at/by the directedness evident in others and themselves: in other words, they were on the threshold of being able to form ideal phenomenological models and thus of becoming conscious of consciousness.

Consciousness, organization, and resonant belonging to the world

A Cartesian theatre? A Darwin machine?

Generally, we tend to assume that consciousness is a single object, or an experience of the here-and-now, or a particular place within us. Dennet (1984) has called this idea 'the Cartesian Theatre' because it can be compared to a staged event, where the essential thing is not what goes on behind the scenes, or after the curtain has fallen, but what happens on stage. There may be many roles and many individual scenes, but all of them are strictly controlled by a director, and the course of the drama is determined beforehand by the playwright. Thus the meaning of any staged event has been decided in advance by a central authority.

Dennet's alternative conception is closely bound up with the concept of the so-called Darwin machine (see Flanagan 1992). According to this concept, no central authority exists to give meaning to what happens in our consciousness and to decide what is going to happen. There is no main stream of consciousness. On the contrary, consciousness consists of a system of numerous channels, numerous impulses, each having an activity of its own, and each offering, so to speak, its own draft of what is going to happen on stage/in the consciousness. The vast majorities of these drafts are short-lived and will never even get close to being 'staged': that is, becoming conscious. Only the most hard-to-kill drafts will fight for a place in our conscious awareness. Just as the Darwinian concept of evolution does not involve a superior authority that chooses which species should survive (see also the section on explanations in Chapter 4), so there is no superior authority (the soul, the self, the 'I' or whatever) to choose which drafts will actually pop up as the content of consciousness. In each case the question of which draft will proceed further is decided by the relative strength and mutual dynamics of the contenders.

Dennett's concept offers a bottom-up perspective on consciousness and, in this sense, makes an important contribution, helping to get rid of the mystical understanding of consciousness as something sui generis and distinct from everything else that exists in the world. It also helps puts paid to the Victorian, rationalist concept of the will, which maintains that we are in full control of everything that happens within us. Thus it helps dispose of the notion that we, as selves, have absolute creative power to decide what enters our consciousness. Though in essence it is not new, Dennett's point is important as it presents, in a more modern form, the points made by the romantic philosophers and further developed, in psychology, by Freud.

As we shall see, however, things go astray if this preoccupation with the bottom-up perspective leads us to over-emphasise it at the expense of the top-down perspective.

If we keep to the double perspective of consciousness (incorporating both the bottom-up and top-down views), the acknowledgement of the 'view from the top' need not involve us in some form of Cartesian Theatre or speculative rationalism, in which consciousness is represented as an omnipotent authority which, quite independently of the world, defines its own content and the direction in which it will flow. It is true that the reflective consciousness is liberated from its basis in so far as it is not solely determined from the bottom up, but it is not detached from its basis. Reflection is indeed reflection on something, that is to say, on what one is, on what one wishes to become, on the situation one is in, and so on. We will return to this in Chapter 7.

Resonance versus *'existential loneliness'*

Once we understand that the core of personality consists of resonance in the vertical continuum, the entire concept of 'existential loneliness' as a basic human condition becomes absurd, or at least speculative and without real anchoring. Indeed, the notion of sublime loneliness is conceited, in several senses of the word. Loneliness of this kind – the loneliness that stems from never quite being reached by others and never quite being able to reach others – could only be claimed on the basis of the most extreme form of individuation and authenticity seeking, through a discourse that confined one to an almost claustrophobic relation to oneself and where one is cut one off from (proper) contact with one's own resonant vertical continuum. In reality, as we have seen, the resonance by virtue of which we become someone in the first place can only emerge from our absolute connectedness with the surrounding world. Since this resonance and connectedness with the surrounding world lie at the very core of our being, it is simply impossible for us to be existentially lonely. For better or worse, we live in the midst of our world, our culture, our commitments as individuals, and we are resonant with all these forms of connection. We belong inescapably to the world, to our culture, to life. At any one time we are also faced with a huge variety of possibilities. But we experience loneliness only if we develop discourses of the self that lead us to dissociate ourselves from, and desensitise ourselves to, our own resonance, making ourselves elaborately rationalistic and cutting off our insight into the very core of our nature.

The cure for this ailment lies in a self-organizing and life-organizing discourse that will serve to remind us of our resonant, directed connectedness with the world. General psychology, as a discipline concerned with the entire psyche and its connectedness, on all levels, with the surrounding world, is well placed to advance our self-understanding by opening up a realistic discourse on what it is to be human – a discourse which takes in both the horizontal continuum of our interrelation with the surrounding world, and the vertical continuum of the different levels within our consciousness.

Consciousness and free will

Our taxonomy of consciousness, as represented in Figure 6.4, can now be incorporated into our taxonomy of the will, as presented in the previous chapter (see also Figure 5.10).

As we recall, the free will has the following three characteristics: (1) it is directed with a certain strength and intensity – what we call willpower, (2) it is directed at something in particular, in an organized way. The greater the degree of downward organization, the greater the freedom of the will, and (3) it consists of a process. A person willing something may either be somewhere in the intentionalization phase, concentrating on clarification and decision, or somewhere in the realization phase, where a decision is taken and an action initiated to achieve a certain goal.

Likewise, consciousness has the structure of intentionality: it is about something, it concentrates and focuses on something.

If we combine these concepts of will and consciousness, we can say that it is in the intentionalization phase of the will that the consciousness is engaged in model formation. The will has a specific focus, it is concentrated on a specific object; thus, in the process of willing, we are consciously directed at/by something, and thereby form our phenomenological models. The relationship between will and consciousness can be described as follows:

- Consciousness about a certain object is characterized by a higher or lower degree of willpower in its directedness at/by that object. For instance, one may be more or less continuously preoccupied with one and the same thing, so that the phenomenological models present in one's consciousness will likewise remain more or less the same (as opposed to the constantly changing, experience-based models successively presented in associative streams of consciousness).
- Consciousness plays an organizing role: either in the intentionality phase of the will, where it offers a more or less concentrated and more or less well-focused phenomenological model of a given object – or as consciousness about something to which one actively relates.
- Consciousness is found both in the centred or decentred medium-level psyche, or in the individuated, reflective high-level psyche. At the level of

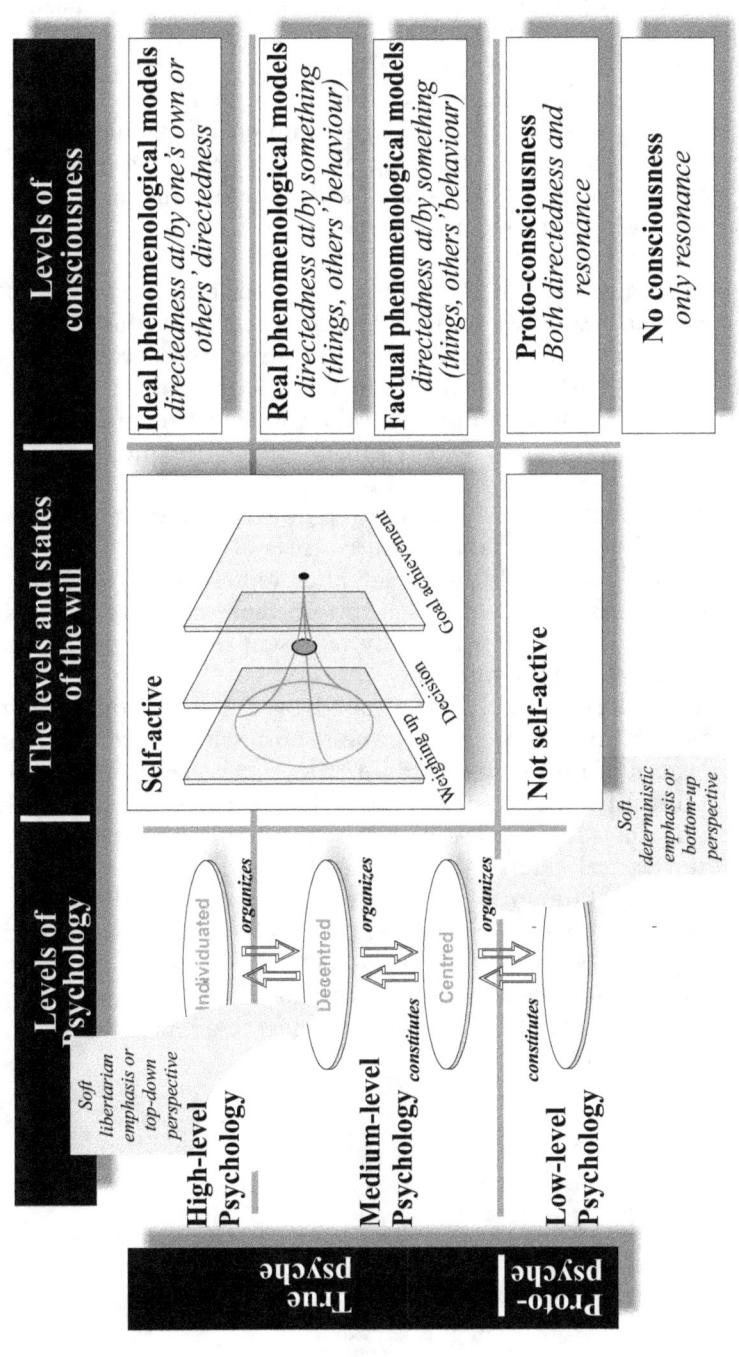

Figure 6.5 shows the relation between the different levels of consciousness and the free will, meaning both the free will as in its top-down organizing role, and the will in the phases both of intentionalization and realization.

the medium-level psyche the phenomenological models are factual or real, as for example when an adult human being is merely preoccupied with and absorbed in something without actually reflecting in any self-conscious way on the matter; or when an animal is directed at/by something in a willed and conscious manner, displaying increased intentionality or actual goal-realizing behaviour involving more or less persistent willpower. At the high-level psyche, on the other hand, human beings make ideal or abstract models.

In Figure 6.5., an attempt is made to illustrate the relationship between free will and consciousness. If we look at consciousness from the bottom-up perspective – from the point of view of what constitutes it – consciousness consists of myriad different functions. In other words, much more takes place in the psyche – at several levels – than we can become reflectively (reflexively?) conscious of by means of our abstract phenomenological models.

If we look at consciousness from the top-down perspective – from the point of view of how it is organized – it consists of free-willed, organized phenomenological models. Ideal models thus represent arrangements of the constitutive realistic models, which in turn represent arrangements of constitutive factual models, which, finally, represent arrangements of proto-conscious resonance and intentionality.

In this sense the free will is facilitated by the directedness of the phenomenological models of consciousness, both with regard to strength and to its degrees of organizing freedom. The highest level of free will is facilitated at the individuated level of the high-level psyche, which involves the formation of abstract models of directedness at/by directedness. This points to the classical (Kantian) idea that the highest peak or the most developed form of humanity is to be found in the social and moral consciousness of free-willed, self-conscious, individuated, authenticity-seeking beings. Indeed, it is the very fact of our social and moral connectedness that both demands and makes possible the organization of the self-conscious free will. This leads us to the next chapter in which we take a closer look at the self.

Chapter 7

The Self and the Life Project

One way or the other we engage in life, each other, and ourselves. We are concerned with how life will be for ourselves and for each other, and we involve ourselves in how we and other people are as human beings. Most of us do not reflect on these things all the time. Sometimes we do, and during those periods of our lives in which everything is revised, we do so a great deal – but, most of the time, this engagement manifests itself more in the form of the tacit, social, and psychological directedness of our actions, our behaviour, our way of thinking and our emotions. Our engagement manifests itself in the way we do things, and in the way we sustain and frame our daily lives, right down to the simple and dull routines. Whether we are reflectively conscious of it or not, we want something from our lives, each other and ourselves. Another way of expressing this would be: at any given moment we will be engaged in the project of experiencing life: engaged in a *life project*. The life project is not just an anonymous, universal process – there is a someone who has this project, a person such as you or me. This way of being a someone and of being in an intentio or first-person perspective is captured by the concept of *'the self'*.

The phenomenological structure of the self

The intentionality-structure of the self

Such an understanding of the self is based on the conception that the self will always be in an intentioned connectedness. Intentionality is a coherent, indivisible unity that can be viewed from two perspectives: the inside-out perspective which has the character of intentio, and the outside-in perspective which has the character of intentum. (See also Chapter 4).

When intentional connectedness is viewed as intentio (inside-out), it will be characterized by our directedness at something. Our connectedness is seen from this perspective as an active driving force: we seize life, fulfil ourselves, and express ourselves. By actively expressing ourselves, we make an impression on the world – we model, produce, and create it. By expressing ourselves we also, to a greater or lesser degree, for better or worse, consciously or unconsciously, make an impression on other human beings. On the basis of the impressions we make on them, others will relate to us in one way or another. Hence we can see ourselves in the impressions we make on the world and other people. We are mirrored in the world, and this reflection is essential to us, not just as confirmation of our worth or existence, but, more fundamentally, as that which enables us to feel ourselves, to know ourselves, to become conscious of ourselves – indeed, to become a self at all. The essence of being a self is to be a someone. A someone who, with regard to consciousness, can be characterized as having a first-person perspective on the world, on others, and on him/herself. A someone is someone who, with regard to dynamics, can be characterized as having a driving force, as being active, searching, engaged in trying to seize the world, and as a self-reflective being who models and organizes his/her own life on the basis of the impressions he/she makes on the world and other people.

When intentional connectedness is viewed from the other perspective, inside-out, as intentum, it is characterized by our directedness by something. The key feature of our connectedness, seen from this perspective, is that we are not simply propelled, by our driving force and our need for self-expression, to direct ourselves wildly, blindly and haphazardly at things. We are directed by what is important to us. We are also directed by what has meaning to us in terms of our biological, cultural and life history. The fundamental, physical and biological elements of our life-world are meaningful to us, as biological creatures who are, at the most basic level, organically connected with these elements. We are also, as members of the human species – and not just as members of some particular tribe or culture – connected, just as fundamentally, to the culturally produced elements of our life-world. Likewise, we are directed by those things, people, and events that have acquired a special meaning for us in our personal life history, the things which – within their biologically and cultural-historically established frames of meaning – we have given a personal sense. These various meanings and senses that make up our life-world are also what attract our directedness – it is precisely these meanings and senses that we are directed by.

This means that our life-world consists, not only of the impressions made on the world by our expressions of ourselves (in the widest sense, ranging from the ways in which we relate to and manipulate the world as producers and creators of things, to the impressions other people get of us), it also consists of its own expressions (the world as it is, irrespective of what we do with it; other people as they are in themselves, and so on).

Hence, to a greater or lesser degree, for better or for worse, consciously or unconsciously, we are directed by those things that have meaning for us and in that sense represent an ideal, something which we strive towards. We are and want to be a part of this ideal, it is of value to us, and in this sense it directs us or gives us direction in life. We idealize it as particularly meaningful and 'sense-ful' to us: thus when we are children we idealise our parents, and as adults we may have colleagues and friends who represent an ideal to us. Certain artefacts of our culture – art, science and social institutions, including institutions on a small scale, such as a barbecue night with the neighbours – may also play this role.

This means that we will always be in a state of connectedness with the world in which we are directed at/by something. We are dynamically connected with the world via the mirroring self-expression of the intentio aspect, whereby we see ourselves in the impression we make on others. We are also dynamically connected via the idealizing intentum aspect that gives us a sense of affiliation, fullness and direction. Without mirroring, we are not a someone, and without idealization life is not a 'something', but is empty, meaningless, and senseless as well as directionless.

The fact that what is involved here are not merely 'dead', mechanical, or functional connections, but a someone who is connected in this way, is captured by the statement that this connectedness has a first-person perspective (see Chapter 6). The basic form of the self can be defined as the

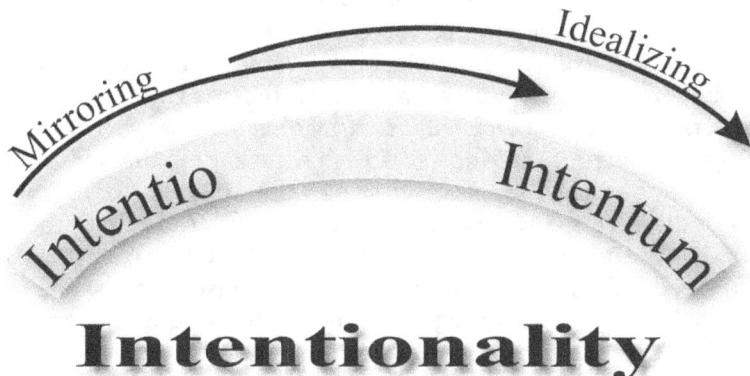

Figure 7.1 *illustrates the intentionality, its mirroring intentio, and its idealization of the intentum. This way of modelling the self is inspired by Kohut's self-psychology but is transformed into the frame of phenomenology (this transformation of self-psychology is worked out in detail in Bertelsen 1996).*

intentio or first-person perspective of an individual – a person or any organism – in its immediate directedness at/by something.

Further, we may now distinguish between what I call the first-order self and the second-order self. The *first-order self* is represented by the immediate, non-self-mirroring, intentioned connectedness in which one is immediately directed at/by someone or something. Or, to put it another way, an intentioned connectedness between an organism and its surroundings has by definition an intentio aspect. Hence an organism that is connected in this intentioned way is by definition also a someone and by definition therefore has a self – no matter how rudimentary this self may be. On the basis of this definition alone, it makes sense, from a logical point of view, to apply a concept of the self even at this immediate, first-order level.

The question, however, is whether it is not, after all, counter-intuitive to use the term 'self' at this immediate level, where there is no self-reflection, only an immediate abandonment to the sense of being present in the world together with other things. Intuitively, one tends to identify the self with self-consciousness. However, it may nonetheless make sense to refer to the self at the level of non-reflective consciousness. Even at this level there is, after all, a conscious someone who has a first-person perspective. This intentio or first-person-perspective aspect must necessarily be present, even where there is little or no capacity for self-reflection or self-centredness. (See also our considerations concerning proto-consciousness in Chapter 6).

Self-consciousness and self-reflection are to be found only in the *second-order self*, which is defined by its capacity for directedness at/by directedness as such, as, for example, when a person reflects on the way in which he/she is directed in a particular situation or in life in general.

So the definition of self in this context is that the self of the first order is the someone who exists as immediate and devoted directness's first person perspective, and the self of the second order is the one who exists as the first person perspective in the directedness at/by directedness.

From such a definition follows, as we have seen: (1) the self of the first order does not emerge because it becomes the object for or intentum in the directedness of the second order self. The self of the first order exists independently and before the self of the second order occurs. (2) The self is determined independently of the concept of consciousness. The self is a way of being directed, including a way in which the consciousness can be directed. The self of the first order is under no circumstances self-conscious, nor does it become so because the self of the second order is directed at/by it. Self-consciousness emerges as the second order self's directedness. Consequently, the first person perspective (or intentio in the directedness) that is, that there is a way in which one are someone, does not equal self-consciousness. Self-consciousness emerges because of the second order self's directedness, consequently, not even the first person perspective in the second order self is self-conscious.

The levels of the self: horizontal connectedness

The above model of the self is, as explained, based on two dimensions in an organism's – and thus the human self's – connectedness to the surroundings: a horizontal and a vertical dimension. Together these types of connectedness substantiate realism rather than constructivism, both when it comes to the scientific design of our empirical studies and theoretical, explanatory models with regards to the self as a psychological object, as well as in relation to our own personal understanding of the ways of being a self.

As mentioned, intentional beings are basically connected to their surroundings – where the actual intentionality constitutes an unbreakable non-dualistic entity. The self – that one is someone with a first person perspective – is a resonant expression of how the world is a significant and meaningful something. And not just that. The world is something in itself, which we are directed at, but the world is also something because we are directed at the world in ways whereby we change it, produce, transform and leave our marks on it.

In exactly this fact lies realism's design obligation to both empiricism and theory in relation to psychological phenomena generally, and self in particular. We cannot examine the self nor explain it, unless our study designs are created to examine the self as connectedness, and examine its various aspects as shaped by the ways in which it is at once created as expression and resonant impressions of the world.

In the same fact also lies realism's obligation in relation to one's own understanding: that we are not who we are, because we separately (i.e., horizontally unconnected) construct ourselves like that, but because we are connected the way we are. The way we are a self is basically constituted by how we are, horizontally speaking, in connectedness with the inevitable ontological double intentio/intentum character, which they happen to have.

The levels of the self: vertical connectedness

As seen, there is also a vertical dimension to the self's connectedness. The second order self relates to its horizontal types of connectedness by seeking insight in its ways of being immediately and horizontally directed at, and by developing and changing these ways. Together insight and change thereby constitute the way in which the second order self organizes its own constitutive foundation.

Here it is important to keep in mind that the second order self occurs as an intentional connectedness. So an unbreakable entity where being directed at something cannot exist without at the same time being directed by something. This means that the second order self cannot be a random (dualistic) construction, which quite unintegratedly just directs itself at the horizontal connectedness. The second order self is also directed by (or rather, realistically obligated and framed by) these horizontal types of connectedness. This means that the second order self exists as constituted in the horizontal connectedness, at which it is directed.

It is crucial to keep these double dynamics in mind in order to understand, examine and explain the second order self. On the one hand (vertically bottom-up), the second order self is constituted by horizontal intentional types of connectedness and the intentio aspects of these in the shape of first order selves. On the other hand (vertically top-down), the second order self is the very way in which this constitutive foundation is organized – a way and an organization which noticeably does not occur until the second order level. Without constitution no organization – and without organization there would not have been this type of constitution either.

This ontology invites a clearly, realistic and anti-constructivist design, both in our empirical studies and in our theoretical explanations and personal self-understanding. We simply have no (proper) idea about what a self is, if we in a constructivist way believe that the second order self is a separate (that is, horizontally and vertically unconnected) construction.

This consideration of the self's vertical, hierarchical structure leads to the following model:

- **The development of the first order self.** The self of the first order is the first person perspective in active connection with the surroundings, characterized by the directedness at/by the daily myriads of small and major tasks. We set ourselves small and major goals, we become involved in them with certain types of directedness, they present themselves to us in a particularly meaningful way and as something we can act in relation to in certain ways. As we saw in Chapter 6 we have certain models of action in which and whereby we see our surroundings; models of action whereby we also shape our concrete actions in relation to these tasks. The development of the first order self's level is based on the development of these connections to the surroundings, which take place via feedback loops between the models of action and the tasks. On the one hand, these models of action shape the efforts to carry out the tasks. On the other hand, these models of action can continuously be adjusted from successful and unsuccessful experiences of carrying out the tasks. The development of models of action/the first order self does not automatically involve the development of the superior organizing life project/ second order self. That is, changes and developments of models of action/first order self can easily take place and continue to be generally

directed and organized by one and the same (maybe inappropriate, wrong and unbeneficial) superior life project.
- **The development of the second order self.** The self of the second order is the first person perspective in active connection with the surroundings, characterized by the directedness at/by directedness. Here the development takes the shape of a development of the very superior (conscious and unconscious) life project, that is, the superior organization of all the first order level's myriads of tasks, that give life a personal directedness and meaning. The development of the second order self's level is based on the development that takes place via feedback loops between the life project (or projects) and the immediate models of action, both unconsciously (or as a barely consciously reflected change in the person's general intentions, projects, values, etc.), and as a more consciously reflected change of one's own life contents.
- **The development of the third order self.** The third order self is the first person perspective in the more general organization, in which we are consciously, reflectively, directed at/by 'what is important'. That is, reflections of an ethical, legal, social, political, psychological, etc. sort. Deliberations about what is important in life and how to reflect deeper and more competently on this. The development of reflections of the type 'what is important' and of the third order self means that the development of the life project and the second order self does not happen blindly and as pure trial and error.

Perspectives of the self

Having determined the self by its intentional structure and the levels of this, we will now look at how the self is created, exists, and has different perspectives; in other words, the different ways in which the self is connected to its surroundings, the different ways in which we 'experience the world', 'see it', 'regard it' and 'are shaped by our surroundings'. We can distinguish between the self's existence and creation in, respectively, third person perspectives, second person perspectives, first person perspectives, and zero person perspectives.

- **In Connectedness with a second person perspective (1pp–2pp).** What it means to be connected with our first person perspective to a second person perspective should be quite clear. It is when we are connected to someone else, another person with his/her own first person perspective. When this other person relates to us with his/her first person perspective, that person's perspective is a second person perspective to us. This can be written as 1pp–2pp. An important part of our personal development and continuous shaping of our personality happens precisely in the interaction with other people and their perspectives on and directedness

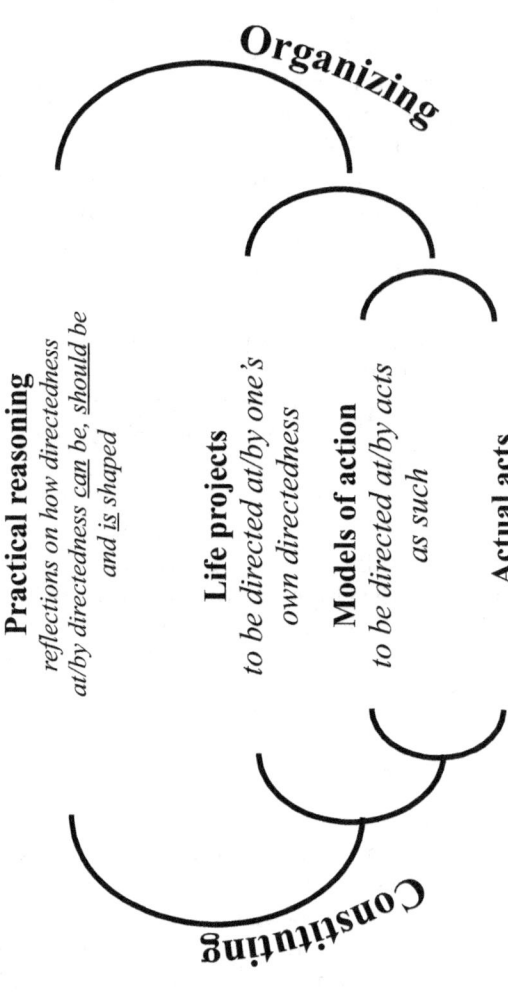

Figure 7.2 shows three subordinate levels of the high-level psyche. The first loop (indicated with the lowest placed double arrows) is between the model of action and actual acts. The next loop is between all these models of action of the world and the more generally organized life project (indicated as the next set of double arrows that comes from and leads to the lower system of arrows). The top loop is between the organizing life projects and, overall, organizing practical reasoning – that is, reasoning about which life projects one ought to strive towards.

at/by the world – and their perspectives on and directedness at/by us and our own directedness. When the other has his/her first person perspective (which is a second person perspective to us) directed at/by us and thereby his/herself, then his/her first person perspective is part of the shaping of our own self, it could be said that that person plans a 'project human being' with us (whether the person wants to or not, and whether the person is conscious of it or not). A central part of developing as a human being, to become a self, takes place in this interaction, in which we meet each other as selves with a first person perspective directed at/by each other.

- **In Connectedness with a zero person perspective (1pp–0pp).** We are not just directed at/by other people, other selves. We are also directed at nature, and generally the world which has no perspective, no self, which is nobody. Our self is also created and thrives in our silent non-psychical surroundings. Our home with its interior decorating, the great quietness in Norwegian forests, colour explosions in a coral reef in the Red Sea, or the lawn or the street with its cars. None of this has in itself a perspective or any project human being planned for us either. Nonetheless, we are also shaped through such connections with 0pp, which can be written as 1pp–0pp.

- **In Connectedness with a third person perspective (1pp–3pp).** Parts of our cultural and social surroundings 'speak' to us. Art, science, ideology, religion, all the myriads of social norms, rules, laws and institutions all contain vital and shaping meaning and sense, which we are also shaped by and shape ourselves in relation to. The experience of great literature, for example, opens our eyes to new aspects of life, shows us a new meaning in life, and makes things senseful in a deeper way. These aspects of our life world put our existence into perspective, put our first person perspective into perspective and direct it. They shape our selves in way s other than the very silent natural things in the zero person perspective surrounding us. Although, our social and cultural products (in the widest sense) like natural things in themselves are not intentional, are not someone and consequently can not plan a shaping project human being for us. They are, as mentioned, meaningful and full of sense in a particular human way. They express what we together, through cultural history, develop, maintain, experience, realize, understand, want, strive for, love, despise, fear, abhor, or are curious about. As such they have nobody's perspective particularly, or rather they have everybody's perspective. So the difference is that none of us can have a zero person perspective (there is no way in which to be a stone); each of us is an individual person with each our unique self and therefore with each our unique second person perspective in relation to each other; each of us can, however, assume the same scientific perspective or political perspective of something. In principle, we can all understand/explain a natural phenomenon like thunder in the way a theoretical theory does (although we each in our own perspective may experience it very differently). In principle, we can all assume a number of political perspectives and views, for example racism problems, from different angles. To assume such a perspective is to be a general someone, to assume a general, or if you like an 'impersonal', third person perspective – but still a perspective as opposed to the perspective-less zero person perspective. Thus, the third person perspectives that we are connected to express in great and small ways what is important in life, they carry to a higher or lower degree the different discursive versions of 'project human being'.

- **In Connectedness with a first person perspective (1pp–1pp).** Naturally, in our reflective deliberations we can strive towards shaping ourselves, hold back sides of ourselves, emphasize others, be part of specific self-developing relationships, which we assume will make us thrive and develop. All of it is regulated by our directedness at/by our own directedness, which can be expressed as the self's connectedness to itself in a first person to first person relationship. To some, but not everybody (not all the time and not always equally consciously focused), one important aspect of life can be the 'project human being' one has with oneself.

Hereby the general features of the model of the self are in place.

The natural and cultural history of the self

Cultural history of the self

The above considerations concerning the formation and discourse of the consciousness can now be combined with our general model of the evolution of the human psyche, as presented in Chapter 3. Figure 7.3 outlines how the development of the distinctly human consciousness-based forms of connectedness (the connectedness between the first-person perspective and the zero-, second- and third-person perspective, respectively) follow the fundamental, intentioned forms of connectedness common to all animate creatures. These range from the centred, to the decentred, to the individuated forms of intentionality. The central human characteristics of the self are formed in the course of this phylogenetic development.

In the centred mode of life, we find the self in the format of nature. This self is based on the mode of life of the earliest hominids and human species. In this context, consciousness-based connectedness exists mainly as a connection between the first-person perspective and the anonymous zero-order perspective of nature, 1pp–0pp. This means that the ability to put oneself in the place of others in a conscious, mirroring way, does not play a

Form of connectedness	Format of life and self	Emerging distinct features of the self
1pp-0pp Until 150,000 BC	**Centered mode of life:** *The self in the format of nature* Activity is centred around the behaviour and practical life of the group and regulated by the group only in direct spatio-temporal contact.	(a) Proto-self. (b) 1pp of first order. (c) No actual actual discourse, no real 'human project' - more the project of a certain way of life.
1pp-3pp *Began from around 150,000 BC, completed around 60,000-40,000 BC.*	**Emerging decentered mode of life:** *The self in the format of myths* Division of labour, emerging culture. The individual bears the meanings of the culture with him/her and hence cooperative behaviour can be regulated by the group even at a spatio-temporal distance	(a) Completed first-order self (b) 1pp of first order (c) Cultural discourse implying an embedded anonymous 'human project' (no 'someone' who can engage in the discourse as a mutual project); this kind of life is based on the law of nature/god.
1pp-2pp *Began to emerge perhaps around 60,000 - 40,000 BC, crystallized as philosophical discourse around 400 BC*	**Completed, decentred mode of life. Emerging proto-individuated mode of life:** *The self in the format of dialogues* Cultural discourse not only as a form of behaviour regulation, but also in the form of a personal, reflective discourse concerning the right kind of life.	(a) Completed first-order self and proto second-order self (b) 1pp of first order, emerging 1pp of second order (c) Cultural discourse including both an emerging genuine personified 'human project'.
1pp-1pp *Began to emerge from around 400 BC, crystallized in completed form around 400 AC*	**Completed individuated mode of life:** *The self in existential format* Only here do we find genuine directedness at/by one's own (and others) directedness as a free-willed and reflectively organizing agent; understanding oneself in a life-historical discourse based on choices of lifestyle and endeavours to achieve authenticity.	(a) Completed first- and second-order self (b) 1pp of first as well as second order (c) Cultural discourse implying individual authenticity and a genuine 'project human' created in dialogue with other people and in existential dialogue.

Figure 7.3 *Overview of the evolution of the human with special reference to the relation between mode of life, form of connectedness, and form of the self.*

decisive role in life, although there is every reason to believe that this capacity exists in embryonic form in, for example, chimpanzees. Chimpanzees know what a mirror image is, and on a small scale they may occasionally also deliberately deceive each other, that is, set out to give the other a false impression of something. This implies that, to some extent, the deceiving individual is able to imagine how the other individual *would* be inclined to understand a situation, and how this understanding can be tricked. It also means that we are dealing here primarily with a first-person, non-mirroring perspective which belongs to the first order. Likewise, the further we descend down the line of animal species, the more we find only an emerging self or proto-self. The decentred mode of life has no real, formulated discourse and no real 'human project' as an explicit guide to what constitutes the good life.

In time, this self will develop into the self in the format of myths, based on the decentred lifestyle. Elementary versions of this decentred lifestyle date back to approximately 150,000 years ago, and lasted until possibly 60,000/40,000 years ago. Here we will find, in emerging form, the beginning of real discourse and of a genuine, though still not explicitly formulated, 'human project'. This exists primarily in the anonymous form of the meanings embedded in cultural artefacts: tools, funeral rites, the infrastructure of the home base, and so on. We also find an embryonic form of 'narrative': that is to say, works of art and other artefacts which serve no immediate technological purpose and which therefore presumably mirror the emergence of other kinds of 'independent' meanings and institutions in the form of rites and myths. In this way, certain general, common (and 'immanent') meanings or third-person perspectives on nature, life and other people are generated. Here, the self's consciousness-based connectedness with these meanings can be seen in terms of a first-person/third-person perspective, 1pp–3pp. At this level, then, we have a completed first-order self. However, there is still no someone to whom the formulation of a self-organizing discourse of life and the self can be attributed, and no someone that is engaged in a 'human project' involving both the self and other people.

During the following 60,000/40,000 years, both the decentred mode of life and the decentred self were consolidated and completed. During the same period, we see the gradual emergence of a genuinely individuated mode of life. Towards the end of this period, around 1,000 years BC, a period which saw the appearance of explicit religious and philosophical discourses, we find the self in the format of dialogues. Discourses concerning the good life were now formulated in writing, and became the explicit subject of religious and philosophical rhetoric, discussions and dialogues, in which different explanations and interpretations were offered and disputed. The form of consciousness-based connectedness that now emerges is that between the individual's own first-person perspective and that of another individual, which is seen as a second-person perspective: 1pp–2pp. Through this explicit insight into the individual and personal perspective of the other, the individual gains insight into the fact that other, different perspectives exist in general, and that one may have one's own perspective. In other words, he/she gains genuine reflexive insight: thus we see the birth of a real, second-order, first-person perspective and hence of a second-order self.

From an evolutionary point of view, this was probably in the making for a long time and originated in other species of mammal (see above). However, the proto-form of this second-order self did not crystallize into the fully-fledged version until around 400 BC, the period of the Greek city-state philosophers (the most outstanding of whom was Plato). At that period, the discourse concerning the self and life took on the form of an interpersonal dialogue, and it is here that we see the emergence, in outline, of a specific 'human project'; not just the more or less anonymous lore embodied in religion, myth and the great stories of a particular culture, but a discourse formulated in terms of individual projects for the betterment of humankind. Thus Plato's dialogues, for instance, are presented entirely in terms of Socrates' personal project to deal with and enlighten his (unreasonable) listeners and sparring partners.

The self-organizing discourse of the completed second-order self, the self in the existential format, is dynamically modelled by what it actually chooses – in an explicit, self-conscious and free-willing way – to do with itself and its own life. As we saw in Chapter 5, this completed, second-order self was crystallized, about 800 years after the Greek philosophers, in the Augustinian discourse of around 400 AD. It is only at this stage that we find a cultural discourse implying an individuated endeavour to achieve authenticity, and the emergence of a real 'human project' explicitly aimed at guiding the individual's own directedness and first-person perspective as well as those of others. Here, we are no longer dealing with a Socratic dialogue between 'experts', in which the reasonable person lays bare the unreasonableness of the other, and then proceeds therapeutically and educationally to introduce some of the basic rules governing reason. Rather, we are led respectfully to examine our own first-person perspective and that of others in an endeavour to complete our quest for reason.

The very significant transition from the self in the format of dialogues, to the self in the existential format – that is, the development 1pp–2pp ⇒ 1pp–1pp – was probably facilitated by the belief in a personified god (for further details, see Bertelsen 2002). The origins of the Christian concept of God lay in the personified God of the Jews – a god that has his own will and is engaged in projects involving the world and human beings that are beyond our human understanding. The frames of this discourse thus came to form the basis for St Augustine's thinking. In the event, Augustine's entire self-organizing discourse – his deeply sincere dialogues with his God, and his wrestling with the very concept of a divine plan for his life – led him to the radical concept that what mattered was what the individual (with the grace of God) *chose himself* to *will* with his life. Thus it could be argued that the discursive concept of a personified god formed a transitional object in the developmental process towards the completed, individuated human being.

The self's organization, dynamics and discourse

The concept of self is crucial to psychology because through this concept we can achieve insight of a vital aspect to the human psycho-dynamics' self-organization. With the concept of *discourse* we can then further try in terms of contents to characterize the way in which we in an organizing manner direct ourselves at/by the directedness – both our own and others'. Social psychologically speaking, one can say that the discourse provides the frameworks, and in terms of contents, the understanding and concepts of how we relate to each other and talk about each other. Thereby, the discourse also provides the frameworks and contents for how we relate and talk about ourselves. Basically, therefore, the discourse also provides the frameworks and contents for how we give reasons for our acts and ways of being and relating, in other words, the discourse provides the frameworks and contents to how we are directed.

However, it must not be understood – like it is in constructivism – to mean that the personal way of being and relating is merely created by society, originating from the ways we have agreed to talk about and to each other. It cannot be deducted either that the self (including the self-organizing dynamics' discursive frameworks and contents) is thereby just a social construction.

Furthermore, that discourse is not, as is often seen in constructivist ways of thinking, mistaken for a self. The concept of discourse and the models of our social and culture-specific discourses are merely about contents. We still need the concept of the self to emphasize the very central point that we can be someone with a first-person perspective in the first place, and that on the basis of this reality, and not as a consequence of this or that constructed discourse, we are beings that are directed at/by the world and at/by our own and each others' directedness. Therefore, it is not a consequence of this or that discourse that we in a self-organizing and co-organizing way can intend 'project human being' for ourselves and each other. Rather it is because we, ontologically speaking, are a piece of reality that can be directed at/by something in general, and directed at/by directedness specifically.

Having said this, can we then in return, also on the basis of realism (as opposed to constructivism), admit the concept of discourse to a quite central role in the understanding of humans and self, both with regards to individual psychological and cultural psychological variations?

Discourse and cultural variations – a western and an eastern self?

The discourse determines how the self is structured and more precisely, how it organizes itself top-down, and as it is directed at/by its own directedness, the following is a possibility:

Discourses may be culture specific. How the self looks inside a culture varies from one sub-cultural discourse to another. How we understand ourselves, each other, life and people from other cultures varies according to whether we stand in Nazi environments, liberalistic high school environments or the extreme left wing. We find similar major variations in the shaping of the self and thereby in ways of being and relating to ourselves, each other, life, and the world from one major culture to the other, e.g., between East and West.

Precisely because of cultural variations in the discourses there is the danger of ethnocentricity. That is, there is the danger of elevating one culture's, (e.g., the Western), or even a sub-culture's type of self, (e.g., middle-aged, white, conservative, highly educated men) to the universal type of self. In other words, completely ignoring the possibilities of how people in other cultures, and with other discourses, live other lives and have other ways of being directed at/by the world and each other. The very problem of such ethnocentricity is one of the points in which constructivism sees clearly (a clear vision shared by realism).

How deep are these cultural differences, are they compatible with the concept of a universal self, or must we do as constructivism and assume that there is a number of selves, even that the individual can change selves when the person moves from one sub-cultural environment to another? How meaningful is one of time's constructivist claims that it is all about developing super-flexible multiple selves so one can quickly and efficiently adjust and keep up with the changeable pulse of reality? Let us see if it even makes sense to talk about different selves.

Much psychological, sociological, and social anthropological research has presented convincing evidence that there are significant differences between the Asian self and the Western self. It seems that the Western self is very much influenced by the emphasis on autonomy and a free will self, to be conscious of and in control of one's own individual life, actively influence, manipulate and re-create one's surroundings (as well as people, society, and world resources) according to one's own needs and pleasure (not least according to the principle of maximum profit). Alternatively, it seems that the Eastern or Asian self is influenced by an endeavour to adjust in a harmonious and self-denying connectedness with one's own surroundings (family, culture, nature).

The difference is also sometimes expressed as the difference between a (Western) I-culture and an (Eastern) we-culture. The self in the I-cultural discourse is first and foremost directed at/by its own directedness. The aim is to achieve insight to one's own needs and how to fulfill them; the aim is to find oneself, fulfill or actualize oneself; it is about showing independence, autonomy and individual characteristics; about focusing on one's *own* life project, one's own life style and to be in control of one's surroundings and life conditions.

The self in the we-culture is first and foremost directed at/by others' directedness in particular, and at/by the family, culture, and nature generally. It is about the ability to read and adjust to others' and the community's needs, about being aware of what oneself can do to fulfill these needs; it is not a question of being unique or leaving marks in the world, but a question of adjusting, adapting, and belonging to a community. The focus of the life project is here on what the surroundings call for, and how to be in harmony with one's surroundings.

It may, however, seem that we thereby have two distinctly different selves. One self whose directedness at/by the directedness is characterized by (1) being or striving to become oneself by being enough in oneself, and (2) a self whose directedness at/by the directedness is characterized by being/becoming oneself through devotion and self-denial. However, looking at the matter in light of the model of self presented above with its horizontal and vertical dimensions, it seems more probable that we are dealing with the one and same self with the same intentional basic structure. It is just that this universal structure of self is organized differently in different cultures and discursive contexts

The point of departure for this understanding of cultural variations is precisely the self's intentional structure and thereby the universal intentio/intentum structure: that the self is, on the one hand, directed *at* the world in an effort to leave a mark and in an effort to reflect itself in the results and reactions to this, and on the other hand, that the self is directed *by* the world. So the cultural differences do not appear from different selves with different basic structures, on the contrary, it depends on how the intentio and intentum aspects are discursively emphasized in relation to each other.

Thus, the Western self with its I-discourse can be theoretically explained as a self where the intentio aspect is discursively in the foreground, with its driving force of reflective directedness at/by the directedness, this means that the self is put into perspective and discursively views itself from inside-out. However, that does not change the fact that the other side, the harmonizing and affinity-seeking intentum aspect, must always and necessarily be in the background. It also means that for the driving force of the I-orientated and reflective person, it is not just a question of leaving one's own autonomous marks on the world, but also about sensing the meaning that basically comes with belonging to a normative and ethical human community.

Alternatively, the Eastern self with its we-discourse can theoretically be explained as a self where the intentum aspects are discursively in the forefront. This is a self that is put into perspective and discursively views itself from outside-in, first and foremost in the light of an idealized directedness at/by the directedness. However, here it also applies that even though the idealizing intentum aspect is in the foreground, such a self will also, in its very affinity-seeking, harmonizing and culture fulfilling efforts, necessarily always be a driving force, leave marks, understand itself and reflect itself in others' reactions.

This type of cultural difference, which is often characterized as an East/West difference is thus, not of a fundamentally, categorical kind. Basically, the human self is one and the same self; but it may vary culturally and discursively with regards to which of the two aspects of intentionality that is in the foreground and which is in the background.

In this connection it is probably right to point out that this difference between the 'Eastern' and 'Western' selves may also be to a high extent a difference in sub-cultural styles, e.g., also within the Western culture. Strictly speaking, the I/we-discourse is a question of differences in personality style. Indeed, it may even be differences in personality style in the same individual, according to which situation the person finds him/herself in. A person, who in one situation must have his workplace's and organization's interests and continued survival at heart, may well be influenced by the we-cultural discourse; while in another situation where the person's own career is at stake, he/she may be just as influenced by an I-culture's discourse. The point is that such differences do not require such concepts as multiple selves or relativist, constructivist explanatory frameworks. Differences and the rich human variation can, as shown, be explained from a concept of a universal self and the explanatory frameworks of realism.

In practice this distinction, which is theoretically approached, can be the basis of examining and theoretically explaining the diversified cultural image that has occurred in Denmark (and naturally the rest of the world). For example, one could distinguish between 'respect cultures' and 'underplay cultures'. In the respect culture the individual's efforts are to a very high extent about achieving others' respect, as the intentionality predominantly has the intentio perspective (the reflective inside-out perspective) in the foreground. The underplay culture is, on the contrary, about putting aside, or at least underplaying oneself and one's own individual significance for the benefit of the community, the family, or clan because the intentum perspective (the idealizing outside-in perspective) is predominantly in the foreground.

In the meeting of these cultures it is crucial to understand one's own role as 'the other' in such a self-other relationship. In the first culture it is important to meet in a mutually, reflective respect. If you cannot or will not be such a respectful other, then you do not simply provoke a cultural discursive construction (discourses can be overcome, as mentioned). The problem lies deeper because it is quite simply the very intentionality that is at stake, the very way in which we are completely capable of understanding and relating to the world. A breach of the reflecting respect requirement does not merely shake the individual's concepts (read: constructions), but his/her foundation.

Naturally, such a 'respect culture' can degenerate and the efforts to achieve others' respect and have them in a confirming way reflect us, can naturally develop into madness. Thereby not saying that this state cannot be changed (through psychological intervention); but it does mean that what we are looking at here does not originate from what the individual culture or subculture might construct of discourses regarding the individual, but, on the contrary, from deep ontological structures in the way that we can even be a self. What is at stake is the very intentional relationship's intentio/intentum emphasis (regarding foreground/background) and 'project human being' that is connected to it.

A similar deliberation concerns the meeting with a person from an 'underplay culture' where our task as the 'other' is to enter a relationship in which the first person underplays his/her own significance and simultaneously assigns us the task of 'central person' about whom the whole situation revolves. This can also develop into total self-underplay and to the complete elevation of the other as an idealized guru, who offers directions for life, and without whom the idealizing individual would sink into emptiness and meaninglessness. Again it is extremely important to understand what we are dealing with dynamically. This is not merely a question of agreement, to try to talk about the mutual situation in another way, or installing a new narrative that communicates the relationship in a different way. Again it is about the deepest dynamics regarding the ontological structures in the very intentionality.

What basically goes wrong when such cultural meetings fail, is project human being. Project human being – and the very sense of the other's self – fails if we (1) as 'the other', for our own dynamic reasons, cannot assume the right starting position as reflecting or potential ideal (e.g., if we are so preoccupied with obtaining respect that we are incapable of showing respect, or if due to our own self-effacing position we are incapable of directing the other), or (2) because of constructivist delusions, we believe that it is all just a question of persuading the other. Things go wrong when, with such strategies of persuasion, we make ourselves completely blind to 'project human being' and the deeper structures of self that we are dealing with.

A self that is put in perspective by first, second, and third person

Another central difference in how the self can be constructed, and which is not captured with persuasive constructivist concepts, is the difference in the perspective in which the self is shaped. As seen above, the following perspectives emerge:

- *First person–zero person connectedness.* It is a connectedness characterized by an individual with an intentional self which is directed at/by things, which on their side are not directed at/by the individual's directedness. For example, a self in quiet devotion to a sunset.
- *First person–third person connectedness.* We find ourselves in such types of connectedness when we connect to cultural artifacts: articles for everyday use, art, discourses, science, etc.
- *First person–second person connectedness.* A self-developing connectedness in which the individual's directedness is partly shaped by the other's directedness at/by the first individual's directedness.
- *First person–first person connectedness.* We are directed at/by our own directedness.

This aspect of the model of self invites various cultural variations. There is a decisive difference between the cultural self-discourses, according to which type of connectedness it is based on.

A self which primarily bases its self-creation on third person types of connectedness understands itself in light of scientific and/or artistic and/or crafted products' discourses. It will be a self whose whole discourse and striving to become itself, to gain an insight of itself and achieve possibilities of self-development, most of all are directed at and shaped by relating to culture's 'project human being'. So to become oneself and understand the humanity about oneself through scientific studies, art experiences, practical activities, which are not characterized by actual interaction, etc. Such a 'third person self' will have another character than a self which is primarily based on actual conversations and closeness to other people. A self, which is in a genuine interactional culture and discourse – a 'second person self' – will strive towards finding itself, achieving insight of itself and developing through dialogues with other people, conversations with dear and close friends and colleagues, discussions with colleagues, and also dialogues with professional councilors, spiritual advisors, psycho-therapists, etc. Finally, there is the 'first person self' whose striving towards his/her own self is first and foremost a contemplative activity, that is, an introspective search to find ways to sense, formulate and shape him/herself as a self.

Which of these perspectives/aspects of the self's connectedness are in the foreground and have the greatest significance, and which ones are silently and anonymously in the background, varies for the individual at different times in life, in different life contexts and in different cultural contexts. In one sense we are dealing with cultural and sub-cultural variations. However, the point is that these are variations based on the self's deep universal structures and the universal, general perspectives in which any self with one or the other foreground or background emphasis is created. Consequently, it is not separated (i.e., horizontally and vertically unconnected) social constructions, which the individual or the individual culture invent and agree on.

Content variations

All that remains is to look at the purely content-wise variations in the self's discourse. It is naturally enormous and leads to infinite variation in the types of human self. There is an enormous difference between the content-wise discourse in American legal environments that have specialized in buying and emptying values from companies and an Afghan society of fundamentalists to whom just being on the internet, indeed even watching TV, are deeply indecent excesses. However, in the light of the above even these impressive and thought-provoking differences are mere 'ripples' on the surface, that render no reason to assume the existence of fundamentally different human selves. Regardless of these content-wise differences, there are some deep structures in the self that originate from the ontological fact that the self is intentionally with horizontal intentio/intentum reality connectedness and vertical constitutive/organizing connectedness. While the superficial content-wise ripples may lead to, and settle for, a purely constructivist description of the self and its abundance of variations, the deep structures show us the actual and essential variations.

These structures have, as seen above, a horizontal and vertical dimension. Thus, we can also follow the development of the self's discourse – discourse-carried way of being someone – in these two dimensions.

Vertically speaking, the self is developed in a vertical continuum, that is, simultaneously towards the increasingly elevated (the increasingly more sublime discursive and organized understanding of human existence in the world), and towards the increasingly grounded (the increasingly better contact and acceptance of one's own constitutional foundation all the way down through the very deepest and most fundamental types of universal connectedness).

Horizontally speaking, the development can take place as a development of the horizontal connectedness' involvement in life, and again in two directions: towards an increasing devotion to an increasingly more complex and widespread life world, and towards an increasing authenticity-creating, self-profiling, or stepping-into-existence as precisely this someone who is thus connected, involved, and devoted.

The self and the vertical continuum

The self and the irreplaceable

A seagull can recognize its young among ten thousand other young seagulls in the colony; yet it would make no difference to the seagull if its young were replaced by sufficiently identical clones. It would make no difference to the seagull because it would simply not comprehend what it would mean that these were not in fact its young. A human being might also be deceived by a sufficiently refined clone of his/her child if the nuances were finer than the human senses are able to distinguish. But, unlike the seagull, we would also feel utterly deceived (not to mention all the other feelings we would go through) if we were told that our child was just a clone. In contrast to the seagull, we would immediately understand the subtlety that this was not the same child, despite the fact that to all intents and purposes it was identical, and our emotions would stem from the fact that we are attached to the original child as irreplaceable (see also Mammen 1983, 1986). Indeed, the distinctly human characteristics are closely bound up with the concept of irreplaceability.

In Chapter 4 (see also Figure 4.1), we distinguished between two different ways of being connected with the world. We can identify an object or another human being by sensory criteria alone (sense-categorically, in Mammen's words). The other's appearances, the sound of his/her voice, and so on, comply with our criteria for identity, resembling those of the person in question to such a degree that it must be him/her. Where the connection with another is of this kind, it suffices that the resemblance is strong enough, if there is no difference between this child and our own child, or if the differences are so nuanced and minute that we would never be able to identify them, it would not matter at all if the child were in fact some other than our own – indeed, where this kind of connectedness is concerned, the child before us will indeed be our child.

At the same time, however, we have another important way of connecting with others, in which we do not identify the other by this kind of algorithmic pattern recognition, and in which the complete fulfilment of the sensory criteria does not matter.

Take my pocket knife, for instance. I have carried it for fifteen years now and used it for many purposes: to open bottles in Tokyo, to slit open fish after scuba diving in the Red Sea, to open Christmas gifts in Norway, to cut off my dog's matted hair in Denmark, and so on. I am connected with this knife, it is mine, and indeed it is so because of the particular history we share. I might be deceived if someone decided to make an exactly identical copy of my knife, made of the same kind of dark-hued wood, with the same marks of wear and tear, and so on. But if I found out that I had been deceived, it would matter to me – the knife that I would now have in my pocket would not be the same knife. The point being that all those things that made it my knife, all the uses of it which made up our common history, are unique and cannot be repeated. If I lose the knife I can buy a new one, but it will never be the same – in that sense my pocket knife is irreplaceable. When I take it out of my pocket to look at it, I identify it immediately (sense-categorically). For instance, I immediately recognize the quality of the steel when I open it, but I also identify it in another way because of all the historically made choices I now connect it with. In this sense, I categorize it in terms of those choices.

If these considerations apply to a simple object such as my pocket knife, an object which you cannot even interact with, they are all the more true, of course, in relation to the people with whom we share a life-history – our near and dear. It might be possible to copy them by means of cloning and all sorts of smart biochemical and genetic techniques, but precisely this person, with whom we have shared a whole series of unique and unrepeatable experiences, great or small, will nonetheless be forever irreplaceable. By the same token, it is precisely the irreplaceable and unrepeatable nature of our life-history that makes us the people we are. Of course, a human being will sustain and continue his life on the basis of countless replaceable objects in his/her surroundings (a steak is a steak is a steak, and one steak may be as good as another), but real human depth is provided only by the historically created, irreplaceable forms of connectedness which emerge through jointly creating a slice of life history.

The irreplaceable things and people in our lives provide the self with a sense of fullness in the double dynamic of mirroring and idealization. *Reflection*, in this context, refers to the irreplaceable impressions the individual makes on another (or to his/her cultivation of things), by means of which the self comes to know itself and becomes a someone. The idealization of an irreplaceable person stems from the fact that the self relates to, is a part of, and is directed by precisely this irreplaceable other, the most valuable, directing and meaning-creating other. This is how others become 'someone(s)', and how the surrounding world and life become 'something(s)'.

To recognise another person as irreplaceable means to respect, submit and defer to (1) what the other is in him/herself, as well as to (2) the fact that the other is at the core of our very constitution as selves. We owe our own existence to this other as a someone/something, and we owe our life to him/her/it as a someone/something that has fullness and direction. The trees, the rivers, the birds, other people, the artefacts of our culture and ideas should all be understood as the irreplaceable elements they really are. They demand the natural deference which is due to them solely by virtue of their existence and because we are able to become a someone, and to make our life a 'something', only through this mirroring and idealizing relation.

Irreplaceable objects, and persons, can be found in all forms of connectedness. They are present in our 1pp–0pp relations, that is, in our relationship with nature. More precisely, they are present with those inanimate parts of nature that do not have a perspective of their own, which cannot in themselves be a someone, and which are not in themselves directed at/by us, and consequently cannot be engaged with us in any 'human project'.

Irreplaceable elements can be found, too, in 1pp–3pp relations, that is, in our relation to the artefacts of human culture and not least in relation to the ideas (in the widest cultural and scientific sense) put forward by human beings. I refer here, of course, not to the Platonic concept of ideas as entities that have no existence in our world, but belong to another realm altogether. On the contrary, the ideas that express and guide us have thoroughly material origins: they have arisen because generations of human beings have actively struggled to grasp, manipulate, and explain the surrounding world. However, no mutual human project is implied in 1pp–3pp relations. Certain ideas may have a very central meaning and sense to us, but they are not directed at/by our directedness.

Only in 1pp–2pp relations – that is, in our relations with other people – do we find genuine mutual 'human projects'. It is here that we find the self existing, and coming into being, in connectedness with a someone that has an intentio or first-person perspective that can be directed at/by our own directedness. Another person, that is, who can be engaged in projects with ourselves; who is directed at/by our own first-person perspective, whether constructively and respectfully, or – as is sometimes regrettably the case – destructively and manipulatively. Another person who can/ /should/wants or dares to enter with us into the human project: that is, into the project mutually to humanize one another, on a greater or lesser scale, for better or worse, consciously or unconsciously. Thus in 1pp–2pp relations we are concerned precisely with irreplaceable persons, with those individuals who provide us with an irreplaceable sense of fullness, and without whom we could not acquire the form and character of the someone we are, or are in the process of becoming.

Indeed, we can see the meaning of irreplaceability even in 1pp–1pp relations: in other words, in the directedness at/by our own directedness. This does not imply some negative egocentism – on the contrary. It is precisely a person's history with him/herself – the fullness that comes from self-knowledge and from being able to feel oneself in the concrete experience of life itself – that makes an individual into a someone, a self. The sense of what it is to be the person one is embedded in the narratives told about the particular, unique events of our lives – narratives that can easily be distorted or replaced through the misinterpretations or ideological idiosyncrasies of well-intentioned interlocutors. If these constructed narratives neglect or distort the irreplaceable elements of our life history, those people or things that have helped us to become the someone we are, we experience it as a form of psychic violation.

To become oneself, to be oneself, means retrospectively to accept oneself, to show care and tolerance towards one's own being, to feel the fullness of one's irreplaceable life history as the being one is, for better or for worse, without letting this prevent one from also looking forward to the further free-willed, self-conscious, and creative endeavours that lie ahead. It is only by grasping and acknowledging these irreplaceable elements of one's lifeand self (both retrospectively and prospectively)– and by thus becoming able to direct onself at/by one's own essential directedness that one can truly come to experience oneself as, and indeed be, a someone in relation to oneself and in relation to another someone.

The self and the human project

Let us take a closer look at the 1pp–2pp relation in which the other is him/herself a someone who can be directed at/by ourselves and therefore can engage with us in a human project.

From the *intentio* perspective ('inside-out'), the relation to the other may be either flexible or rigid. If the relationship is flexible, the individual self will be susceptible to, and mindful of, the other. He/she will try to attune him/herself to the way the other is, both as a consequence of his/her particular relation to our own self, and as a consequence of those relations of the other, which it is not up to us to co-create. The self is able to mirror in and idealize the other in a way that allows the other to direct him/herself on the basis of his/her own personal and unique character. Engaged in this relationship, the self becomes part of a mutual human project with the other in which both selves thrive and develop. Through symmetrical dialogue and mutual attunement, both may direct themselves at, and be directed by, the directedness of the other in ways that provide space for the well-being and development of both. Both are in a state of surplus, and both can be, and become, a someone in such a relationship, just as both can grant that possibility to the other.

When the relationship is rigid, by contrast, the self is in deficit and experiences a state of need in relation to the other. In order to thrive and develop into a more flexible character, the self needs to be mirrored in the other. In order to grow in the relationship, the self needs to find itself, to know itself, to consolidate itself as a someone, by seeing itself expressed in the approval of the other (through a pat on the shoulder, a confirmation), and this need may be constant. Here, the self will need to grow to a level at which it can enter into a more flexible mutuality. In this state of deficit, it will primarily enter into one-sided human projects, the course of which will primarily be from the other to the self.

Similarly, when the rigid self is in a state of deficit, it will be in extreme need of attachment to the other as ideal, director, and guide. Moreover, it will also have a great need to experience itself as attached to another, as part of another, in order to avoid a sense of emptiness and loneliness. This other must be able to contain (Winnicott's term) our idealizing self and to allow him/herself (continually, and over a long period of time) to be idealized; and it must be able to make the effort to hold (Winnicott's term) us, so that, through this kind of nourishing relationship, our own self becomes capable of a more flexible and reciprocal relationship. Here too, the human project takes a primarily one-sided course, with the direction coming from the other.

Rigid relationships such as these imply a demand. When we encounter another self in this state of dynamic deficit, a demand is made on us to be able to contain and hold the other in a patient and persevering one-sided human project. This may involve continuously, and over a long period, reflecting or mirroring the self of the other, and allowing oneself to be idealized, until the self of the other reaches a state of surplus, and there is a possibility for the human project to become mutual. When this level of mutuality is reached, both selves can see themselves expressed by the impressions made on the self of the other. At this level of mutuality, the dialogue concerning one's values and trajectory in life, can be full of personal sense to both parties, and give guidance to both.

The self relates not only to real others, but to imaginary ones, which are the product of the self's intentionality and its mirroring and idealising of the other. These relationships are just as complex, just as laden with sense and meaning, and just as crucial to the self's being and becoming as are its relationships with real persons. One may flinch or gloat, be pleased or grieved in imaginary inner dialogues with imaginary persons. One may wake up from a dream feeling upset or, on the contrary, strengthened in a way that will have an effect on one's future directedness. One may be just as curious, fearful, and hopeful about the outcome of fictitious events in a novel as are the heroes of the novel themselves, to whom one may ascribe details of appearance, life, and personality beyond those supplied by the author him/herself. Great literature may forever help to direct or re-direct one's own directedness. To imagine the other is to form a conscious, ideal model of that other.

The question is, then: will one's model of the other serve in a profitable way to open up the self and make it more flexible? Or will it, on the contrary, serve to close up the self and make it more rigid? Or indeed, will it cause an already closed and rigid self to remain in a self-perpetuating deficit?

We may express this in terms of the dynamics of intentio mirroring: is one's model of the other of a kind that will place the other in a superior position, so that the other will be able to say to us: 'Do not think you are something (or someone) special'? If so, the self is forming a state of 1pp–2pp directedness, in which its self-expression is inhibited, is not allowed to unfold and will remain in a state of deficit – of not knowing itself properly as a someone. In this perpetual state of deficit, the self will go on endeavouring to become a someone: endeavouring, that is, to get itself mirrored as a someone by real others in all its various activities in life. This kind of model of the other will do the self no good, from a psychological point of view. The self will continue to be directed by its deficit, its need for mirroring. First, it will prevent a real, fully personified and willing other from breaking through to form a genuine, mutual relationship, and from co-opting the self in a real, surplus-increasing human project. At the same time, this kind of model of the self will prevent the individual from directing him/herself in an open manner at/by the other.

It is true for all of us, however, that directedness at, insight into, and an understanding of what is irreplaceable in our lives may contribute to the self's ability to enter into a self-other relationship in which it can thrive, grow, and escape from its vicious circles. In some cases an opening model of the other may yield the desired result: the self will succeed in escaping from its self-perpetuating state of uncertainty and self-doubt into a state in which its being a someone, its worthiness of self-esteem, becomes evident and will no longer have to be mirrored so intensely, so continuously, and so one-sidedly.

Alternatively, one may look at the question in terms of the dynamics of idealization (intentum): is one's model of the other of a kind that will likewise keep the self in deficit through idealization? If so, the self will be locked in a position where it cannot direct itself in a way that will provide it with a sense of fullness or repletion (the opposite of emptiness and depression) and with a sense of direction in its general social interaction with other human beings. Instead, it will persist in exaggerating the status of others, in guru worship, in the idolization of ideal others or over-idealized aspects of nature or culture. The self, here, is rigidly locked into a 1pp–2pp directedness which will not allow the other to break through with a genuine, surplus-increasing human project, nor allow the self to break through to true mutuality.

Moreover, flexible openness and mutuality require a second-order self that is capable of directing itself at/by its own directedness, through developing new insight and changing its self-organization accordingly. In other words, a self that is capable of engaging in a human project in relation to the individual's own life: a project that is performed, both by the self alone and by the self together with the other in the 1pp–2pp relationship. Here, too, one's model of the other may intervene negatively, if it does not allow room to imagine this kind of free-willed and creative self-organization by a second-order self.

Perhaps it would be appropriate to add that, although the good 1pp–2pp self, from a psychological point of view, is a self in a symmetrical relation, and although a second-order self has the freedom to organize its own relation to itself, this does not mean that the self will therefore grow sky-high or endeavour to become all-powerful. It is our very sense of the irreplaceable as irreplaceable that constitutes us as a someone, and this sets a natural limit to our self-assertive search for mirroring, while the dynamic of idealization assures us a natural and genuine sense of fullness and direction which protects us against senselessness, lack of direction, and emptiness.

We might further add that of course the self represents 'the other' to another human being – to enter any relationship in which one willingly joins with another in a human project, is to be required to direct oneself at, and be directed by, the directedness of the other. This entails putting oneself in the other's place and using one's empathy as a substitute for the introspection, self-insight, and self-organization that the other is not yet capable of, or has not yet reached in directing him/herself by his/her own directedness (see Kohut 1977, 1984). The human project in which the self is directed at the other, must therefore be such as to open the other up, enrich the other and arouse something in him/her (Fromm 1979).

Self-psychology, life psychology, personality psychology, and social psychology

The *psychology of the self* deals with the distinctly human ways of being a self/oneself: the capacity self-consciously to experience oneself, to think of oneself as a someone, to feel something in that regard, and to exercise a certain degree of freedom, and hence a certain degree of free will, in the endeavour to be or become a someone. Thus the psychology of the self deals with the distinctly human feature of creating, sustaining and continuously developing oneself/one's self.

A *life psychology*, then, could be said to deal with how, in being oneself, the individual endeavours to live a certain kind of life and to create, sustain, and continuously develop it; that is, to engage in a life project in a way that gives both sense and meaning, making life into a 'something' with a fullness of its own. In this sense there is a close connection between being oneself and being engaged in a life project.

This is why discourse is central in this connection: discourse meaning the way one thinks of, feels for, and wants something from oneself and one's life, and the extent to which one can, should, or dares to direct oneself at/by oneself and one's life. There is the discourse of the self that enables us in an organizing way to think of ourselves as ourselves, and the discourse of the life project that enables us to reflect on ourselves, and hence consciously to exercise our will in organizing ourselves. The question as to what elements go into this organization, and how they are arranged or composed, is decisive to our understanding of the self. In dynamic terms, we may ask which components have been crystallized and how, on the basis of these components, we are able to think, feel, and will something through a certain discourse concerning ourselves and our lives. In terms of psycho-history, we may ask when the different components crystallized as phenomenologically operative and self-dynamically organizing (see Bertelsen 2002).

It is in these respects that the psychology of the self differs as a discipline from personality psychology, although the two disciplines are interrelated in significant ways. The psychology of the self deals with the intentional quality, in itself, of being a someone at different levels (see the first- and second-order self). Personality psychology deals with the personal element of being a self. Personality is the organization of the most general and constant components of the personality, which (1) descriptively characterize a person as a human being, and at the same time distinguish that person from other persons, (2) help to explain both the general and the individual features of that person's nature and behaviour, and (3) form the basis for a normative judgement of this particular individual's way of being and acting. Thus personality psychology deals with the concrete, material conditions under which the self emerges as a human being and an individual, and without which there would be no such thing as the self at all.

Similarly, life psychology must be distinguished as a discipline from social psychology, though the two disciplines intersect in essential ways. Life psychology deals with the sense and meanings which emerge in the dynamic field in which the self operates as a someone relating to the world, and to life, in all their fullness as 'things' in their own right, and relating likewise to others as subjects, each of whom is a someone in his/her own right. By contrast, social psychology deals with the material reality of the interactions (with others, with social institutions, with society) which the personality enters into, and in which he/she emerges as, and becomes, him/herself; interactions in which, finally, the personality is engaged in a pro-social (or, for that matter, anti-social) way, operating him/herself as an agent that creates and changes the society in which he/she lives.

The self, authenticity, and what the human project is about

We will now attempt to combine the above considerations concerning the self with the taxonomy we have developed up till now. The result is illustrated in Figure 7.4.

To be oneself is to be in the unbroken vertical continuum that ranges from the second-order self at the highest level of the psyche, via the first-order self at the medium level, to the emergent self at the lowest level of the psyche, in the border area between the true psyche and the proto-psyche.

Viewed bottom-up in the unbroken continuum of self-consciousness. To look at the self from the bottom-up perspective is to see that the authentic self-consciousness of the high-level psyche requires the capacity and the daring to attend to, and to recognize, all the layers of resonance that go to make up

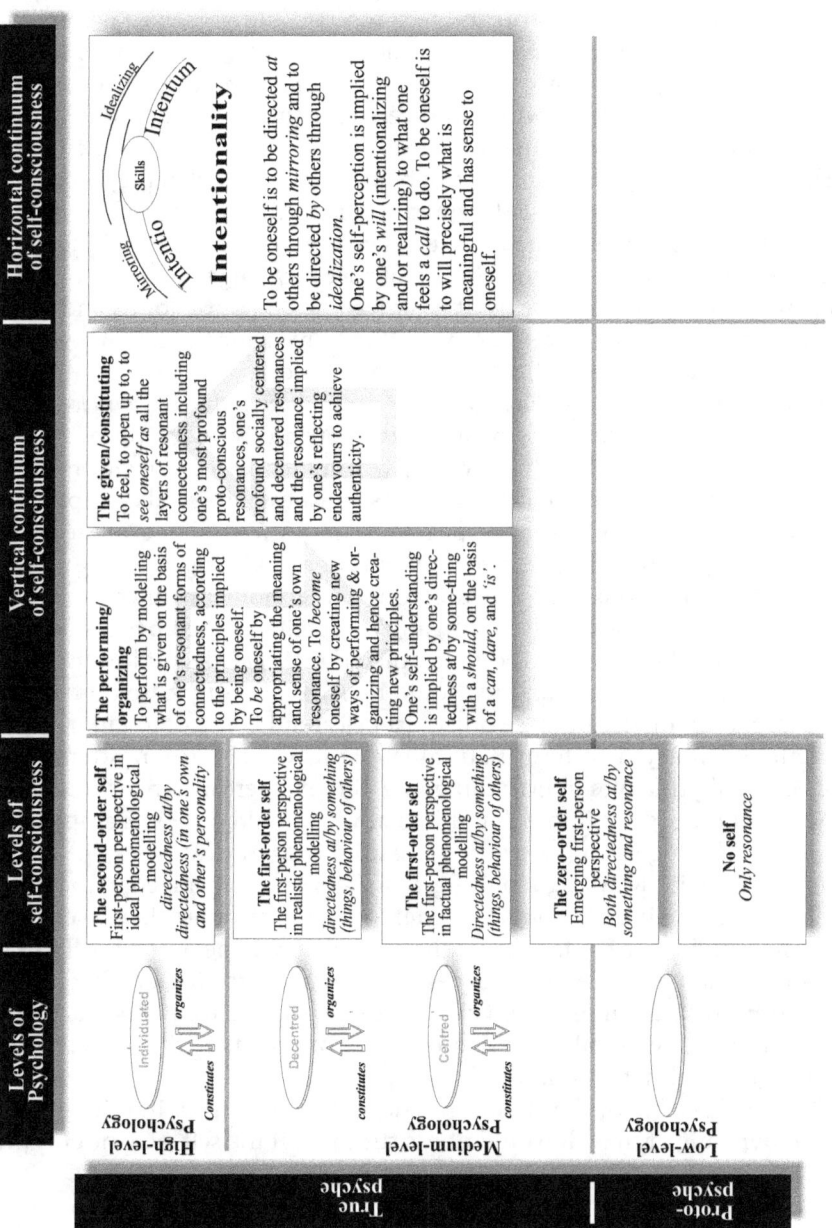

Figure 7.4 shows the taxonomic connection between the levels and forms of directedness of the self and of the psyche.

our real self – that are oneself. To be oneself is to recognize oneself in terms of these resonances, including those from the most profound, proto-conscious level, no matter how these elements are composed and organized within our personal constitution in terms of the degrees of joy, fear, sensuality, or inquisitive intelligence with which we approach the world. To be oneself is also to recognize the ways in which the deep resonances formed through one's various interconnections with the world, at the centred, decentred, and situational level, constitute one's way of being oneself, and that they represent the way in which, as free-willed beings, we have mirrored ourselves in our surroundings, and allowed ourselves, through the dynamic of idealisation, to be directed at/by the things and people that have meaning to us. To be oneself, in other words, is to recognize what has meaning and sense for us and to be directed accordingly. Finally, to be oneself is to recognize one's own way of endeavouring to become authentically individuated.

Viewed top-down in the unbroken vertical continuum of the self-consciousness. This perspective enables us to organize the constitutive parts of the self as revealed to one self. This downward psychodynamic organization takes place through the performance of self-consciousness. From this perspective, to be oneself in the unbroken vertical continuum means to exercise one's free will in organizing the given constituents of one's being, drawing on the various layers of resonance formed by one's intentioned connections with the world. To be oneself is also to organize oneself, through performing as, the person one should be. This can be called the *'should'* dynamic of the self.

In this vertical continuum, the should dynamic is partly based on an *'is'*. 'Is' in quotation marks, because one must be careful here not to fall into the naturalistic fallacy. The term naturalistic fallacy refers to an attempt to ascribe moral principles to how things are. But the mere fact that something *is* the way it is does not imply that this is how it should be. For example, the fact that, as biological creatures we are naturall*y* aggressive, does not mean that aggression is always a good thing, if aggression is organized in the form of violence. Sometimes it would be better to hold back rather than to express aggression in this form. Or, the fact that our society *is* the way it is offers no guarantee that it is the best of societies. The moral principles for what is best – and for how something should be, cannot be derived from how it actually is, and at times the moral 'should' must act to oppose the 'is', intervening to organize it in a different manner.

On the other hand, the moral questions and principles implied in the should dynamic of the self would not occur to us, if the self were not deeply socially centred and resonant to the common humanity of others in the world: in this sense the 'should' indeed arises from a fact of our existence as human beings. To use Mary Midgley's (Midgley 1994) term we are sympathetically minded; moreover, she argues, this sympathy is conatively presented in terms of our endeavour, or our will, to get to know the existential and social aspects of other living creatures. Our basic directedness and capacity for sympathy (in other words, our resonance) enables us to feel/know, or provides us with the opportunity to feel/know, what it is like to be other people. Emotionally, this sympathy reveals itself in a preoccupation with how others feel, and how they feel for one. Cognitively, it shows itself in our preoccupation with, and ability to absorb, other people's cognitive perspectives on, and thoughts concerning, the world and ourselves.

Here we may introduce a distinction between what might be called respectively a medium-level and a high-level morality. Medium-level morality is to be found in the medium-level forms of psychic connectedness. Here, in the way we have indicated above the 'should' consists precisely in the *is* of our deepest impulses to social centredness. This medium-level morality is the most profound intentio mirroring of the self: fundamentally, we see ourselves, and the way we are, through the expression of ourselves in our social surroundings. Our medium-level morality is implied, moreover, by our deepest intentum ideals: the meaningfulness of life which makes it a something for us at/by which we can direct ourselves. From the very beginning of mankind, this morality and common social sympathy has been closely bound up with the survival of the group (see Chapter 3 on the evolutionary development of connectedness). This is what one might term a morality of survival. High-level morality, by contrast, is not simply a morality of survival, but a 'surplus' morality which is at once constituted by the elements of medium-level morality, and serves to organize these constitutive elements into a more highly developed form.

The should dynamic of the self is also based on a 'can', indeed, the former presupposes the latter. We should not expect ourselves or others to perform something which cannot be performed, either because it is beyond our abilities (or those of the other individal concerned) or because we (or the person concerned) are in a critical situation which does not provide the necessary freedom for action.

Finally, the should dynamic also presupposes a dare. Paraphrasing Fink (1995), one might say that a self that approaches the world in general, and his/her own directedness and that of others in particular, with a should, but does so without the necessary courage, will be paralysed. In Fink's words, between should and do there will always be a dare. The dare without the should will lack direction and be little more than recklessness, while should without dare has no power. To dare is a precondition for being able to perform, that is, for exercising the will to organize oneself in certain forms of connectedness, both in the phase of intentionalization and in that of realization (see Chapter 5).

To endeavour to be an authentic self, using one's free will to direct oneself with a should that is based on an 'is', a 'can', and a 'dare', is the central psychodynamic of human life.

Free will, consciousness, and the self

The self and the forms of free will

Self-organization is not an anonymous, mechanical device, nor is it a dynamic that operates tacitly within us. It is something we do, something we perform ourselves, in so far as we reflect self-consciously on our lives and form phenomenological models of the way they are, the way they could or should be, and the way we dare to let them develop. This is how free will, the consciousness and the self form a synthesis in conscious self-organization.

We can distinguish between three aspects of conscious self-organization or free will:

(1) free will as *insight into necessity*
(2) free will as *creation*
(3) free will as *disentangling*

The self and free will as insight into necessity. The conception of free will as insight into necessity goes back to the time of the Greek stoics. Stoicism teaches us that the scope of our freedom will not be increased by scratching our nails till they bleed on something that it is not up to us to change. We become free only when we can give up on this impossible struggle. Kierkegaard was also drawn to this version of the free will: to choose oneself, or to become oneself, is to organize, on the basis of the high-level, second-order self, the various decentred and separate constituents of one's being, in the form of our low- and medium-level forms of connectedness. By engaging in this weak form of downward organization (see Chapter 4), the self does not create anything new: it merely organizes its consituent parts. This view of the way in which human beings function accords entirely with Kierkegaard's; indeed, for Kirekegaard it would have been blasphemous to attribute to humans the ability to create anything entirely new (only God can create in this sense).

However, it is unnecessarily reductionist to confine free will to this form of downward organization alone. This reductionism arises from an inadequate understanding of the dynamic of medium, downward organization (again, see Chapter 4 and Bertelsen (2002) for details concerning the Christian dilemmas arising from this). At the same time, it is precisely our insight into necessity that constitutes the best answer to libertarianism or Sartrean existentialism (see Chapter 5). Real insight into necessity, as represented by the fundamental forms of connectedness and resonance that constitute us as human beings, serves to strengthen insight into one's constitutional, conditional possibilities, and this self-insight, in turn, feeds the individuating discourse through which the self-organizing dynamic emerges as self-consciousness.

The self, the life project and free will as creation and development. However, to define free will only in terms of insight into necessity, or to regard this as the only form of free will that is worthy of notice, could result in a kind of fatalism. It would be an ontological simplification, and would reduce our understanding of life, to neglect or deny the human power to create. Indeed, the freedom of the second-order self to develop a genuine life project consists precisely in the fact that the particular way in which our elementary, constitutive forms of connectedness are organized by the high-level self is not determined in advance. It is this organizational freedom that allows us the possibility to develop genuinely new forms of the self and life projects that are not determined, and could not have been predicted, beforehand. As organizers of our selves, in other words, we are also creators. This is not to say that their free will, in this sense, gives human beings absolute power to create themselves and the world in whatever way they want. By no means. A central, existential task for the self is precisely to balance the creative freedom of the self, and of the life project, with the freedom, or acceptance, born of insight into necessity.

The self, the life project and free will as disentangling. There are two main ways in which the self, and the life project, can become entangled. First, one may be unclear and confused about one's identity and aims in life, or have found oneself in a moral or political dilemma. These classic dilemmas will in most cases have been experienced by others who have found their own ways to disentangle and perhaps resolve them. In such cases, one may be able to gain insight into one's own confusion by engaging in existential conversations with others, or by reading books that offer various types of disentangling strategy. In some cases, however, there may be no such disentangling strategies to hand, or those that exist are not accessible to the person in question. It will then be left to him/her to seek insight within him/herself and to create new, strategic forms of self-organization. In such cases the entangling or dilemma may prove to have been productive in so far as it created the dynamic state of tension which led the person to move forward existentially, both demanding and making possible new, dynamic, self-forming and life-forming discourses.

This kind of confusion or entanglement at the level of the second-order self may, however, be accompanied by a dynamic resistance to any kind of disentangling. This is the case with – indeed it is almost a defining characteristic of – neurotic confusion of a self-deceiving kind. Gullestad (1992, Chapter 9) describes, for instance, the case of Even, a man in his midthirties, who decided to consult a therapist because of problems with assertiveness and his inability to back out of a situation that he finds undesirable. Even is extremely preoccupied with and dependent on other people's opinion of him. In the therapeutic situation, he is, to use Gullestad's words, extremely 'up to' the therapist. He expresses his gratitude that the therapist has spared him time to discuss his problems and he hopes that his being there is not too much trouble to the therapist. At the same time, the therapeutic interview shows that there is, so to speak, 'another Even'; someone whom he does not like to present openly. For instance, though he is apparently willing to listen to what the therapist has to say, he does not seem to take it in entirely. A saboteur appears to hide behind the cooperative Even. This side of Even is actually very anxious to be assertive, to stand out in entirely his own way, to be contrary, and to assert his right not to share the views of other people. All the evidence suggests that the rather self-apologetic, cooperative Even conceals another Even who insists on his own views and rights. This other Even is willing to present himself, but only covertly. In other words, the 'real' Even is not prepared to come out into the open and introduce himself. In Gullestad's expression, he is not a mid-field player, but only wants to play from the touchline. His intentions are thus primarily expressed through an indirect and hidden attitude of protest.

The key point here is that Even appears, even to himself, to be the socially minded, cooperative, friendly, confirming and good Even. The model he has formed of his engagement with the world and other people simply leaves no room for another kind of engagement, in which he would have the freedom to will something and to initiate projects, including projects with other people. And it is certainly not part of his self-conscious, formulated engagement in the world that 'his own self' should instead burst out from time to time in the form of contrary, stubborn, sabotaging, and non-social behaviour. In this sense, the model of himself, and his engagement with the world that he clings to and consciously dares to present, is based on self-deceit.

In the light of the present model, self-deceit and resistance to getting out of a situation can be understood as follows: each self has a multitude of conflicting engagements, forms of directedness or wills to act. The prototype of a neurosis is that the basic $will_A$ (the will to be pro-social, cooperative, and so on) is of a kind that (1) conflicts with something else that one wants from one's life: a basic $will_B$ (to be assertive, have driving force, and so on), and (2), in addition, is of a kind that prevents $will_B$ from being a part of the conscious, self-reflective modelling of the second-order self. Theories based on similar principles can be found in the works of writers as different as, for example, Sartre (1969), Fingarette (1969), Shapiro (1989), and Boss (1990). This other will, the basic $will_B$ (to hold one's own, to express oneself, to impress others) is still acted out, despite the resistance of the second-order self against acknowledging its existence, and it will still be a co-organizer of the way in which the person acts and directs his life during certain periods of his life. Thus the person does the willing, even where this is covert and unacknowledged; he/she is not simply at the mercy of some anonymous force.

Such conflicts are rooted in discourses of the self which variously support or deny these wills for engagement in the world – discourses which themselves are rooted in both cultural and individual life history. In the above example, it may be that the basic will$_A$, the one for which the person dares answer and believes to be acceptable, is embedded in a discourse which can be formulated somewhat as follows: 'to be pro-social implies that one cannot be assertive as well'. This discourse distorts the expression of assertiveness, making it purely contrary, sabotaging, and stubborn, while at the same time the person lacks the capacity to formulate that this is actually what happens.

This does not necessarily mean that Even, in order to live a more rounded life, must emerge as a rhetorical, assertive, and flamboyant entertainer in all sorts of social situations. If his constitution *is not* that of being a mid-field player, a should of that kind would only do violence to him. If he were to demand this kind of action from himself, it would be a form of self-betrayal; nor would it be proper for another person to demand that kind of action from him. If he is not constituted to be a mid-field player, he can and should do something else, namely work with an existential disentangling of the discourse underlying his self-deceiving model of his own personality: a model that does not and cannot contain the necessary driving force, the intentio, the capacity for mirroring which could eventually lead him to a sense of fullness as a someone. This kind of disentangling will provide him with freedom in the form of insight into his own constitution – his own necessity – and will also give him the freedom to create another discourse on the meaning of pro-sociality. Through this innovative discourse, his second-order self will be able, to a far greater extent, to organize his overall intentionality, his personality, and the social interactivity in which it exists. Insight will give him the freedom to form his personal position, neither outside the field nor mid-field, but his position from which he can develop and interact in an authentic way.

The dynamic tension resulting from the tug of different wills in different directions may be negative in so far as it locks a person into an unsatisfying and neurotic life. It may also, however, be a productive tension in so far as the person succeeds, perhaps through disentangling conversations with others, in fighting his/her own resistance to realizing that a basic will$_B$ is also at work.

Let us imagine that a person has performed an act or has been engaged with the world in a way that did not live up to his/her own standards and self-expectations, or which may even have been contrary to these standards and expectations. The person will then experience an aspect of his/herself (namely, that implied by the undesirable action or engagement) that is, in one way or another, contrary to the part of him/herself implied by the moral standards and psychological expectations that he/she has formulated or articulated.

The person may then do one of two things: he/she can deny the action or engagement in question by denying his/her involvement or denying that it expressed any part of his/her true self. Or the person may recognize that he/she did indeed act or engage in this way, and that this expressed a perhaps hitherto hidden aspect of his/her self.

If the person denies, or does not realize, that this aspect of his/her self was actually expressed by this particular action, it means that this aspect of his/her personality is denied from being part of the person's conscious and free-willing organization. Unrecognised, and therefore not susceptible to consciously willed elaboration, this aspect of the self will continue, nevertheless, to contribute to the way that the person feels about himself and his life, and will continue to determine the person's action and engagement. Because the existence of this aspect of the self is denied, however, the person will tend to distort the action or engagement in question to make it look as if it is the expression of another, more acceptable aspect of the self. In other cases, reasons and justifications are found for the action: either it is construed, retrospectively, as the expression, after all, of an acceptable aspect of the self, or perhaps an attempt is made to make it look as if it was forced by outer circumstances beyond the person's control. Irrespective of how the denial is expressed, it is a way of blocking the person's authenticity.

By contrast, the person's acknowledgement that this aspect really *is* an aspect of his/her self will bring it within reach of his/her consciously willed self-organization. However, this insight may be characterised by either a self-indulgent or a self-destructive attitude. To have a self-destructive attitude means to despise oneself for having this aspect of personality, and is a way of making life uncomfortable and of squeezing freedom out of one's life project.

A self-indulgent attitude may develop in two different ways. First, the previously hidden aspect can be reorganized, thus eliminating the cause of a particular kind of action or engagement that does not accord with the person's standards. This kind of self-indulgent recognition will result in a change of behaviour, so that this aspect of the self is brought into line with the person's moral standards and psychological expectations.

Alternatively, it may be that this aspect of the self cannot be immediately reorganized, and will remain a part of the self, but one that is clearly identifiable to oneself and of which one is clearly conscious. Thus it is not removed, but in some way kept under control. One knows that this aspect of the self exists, and that one will, so to speak, have to make a willed effort to reduce its influence on how one feels, what one does and how one engages in life. In this way, it may come to be seen as the 'contrast' within oneself in relation to which one may strengthen those aspects, those actions and those forms of engagement one really wills, on the basis of one's standards and expectations.

In sum, to deny the 'dark' sides of one's self is to let them live on as reasons for how one feels, acts and engages with the world – they live on as reasons, or causes, over which one exerts no control, and as such will choke the self, depriving it of freedom and authenticity. By contrast, to realize and stand by one's 'dark' aspects means, at least in principle, to bring them within reach of one's free-willing and conscious self-organizing capacities. Whether this self-organization consists in neutralizing these dark aspects, or in using them as a contrast to the sides of oneself that one wishes to develop, and in 'making an effort' to keep their influence under control, it is a precondition for enabling the person, through the conscious and free-willing second-order self, to take responsibility for his/her life, his/her sense of identity, and his/her actions and engagement with the world.

In addition to the kinds of entanglement described above, a person may experience feelings of entanglement or inadequacy in his/her self or life projects that result from underlying, constitutive problems. In such cases we are no longer at the high-level domain addressed by clinical psychology, but at the medium- or even low-level domain, where it is a matter of either working with the basic, constitutional relations of the psyche and/or developing compensatory, constitutive structures which may after all make life tolerable. But that is quite another story which we will not concern ourselves with here.

Free will, consciousness, and the self

Together, free will and the modelling consciousness thus form a synthesis, constituting a someone, a self, that apprehends and connects with life as a something containing both meaning and sense.

The existence of and continued development of free will as (1) insight into necessity, (2) creation and (3) existential explanation, is manifested by the fact that we care for ourselves and for the other people in our lives, and in this sense are directed at/by not only our own directedness, but also the directedness of others. This kind of caring self-organization gains energy from the dynamic tension between the constitutive, upward dynamic of the self, based on who we can be, biologically and culturally, and the organizing, downward dynamic, based on who we should and dare to be – through the free-willing, self-organizing dynamic of self-consciousness.

Free will as an experience of the self and free will as an ontological fact concerning the self

Chapter 5 dealt primarily with free will as an ontological fact. The question raised was how the world can be constituted and organized in such a way as to allow the existence of free will – irrespective of whether we experience ourselves as free or not. In other words, the question concerning the ontological fact of free will was separated from the question concerning the individual's experience of his/her will as free. Although we can, as a matter of fact, have free will, some people are unable to recognize it and/or do not experience their will as free; still others, for religious or philosophical reasons, may deny the existence of free will, arguing, for example, that only God can truly have free will

A typical immediate objection, based on experience, against the existence of the free will goes as follows: 'If I actually have free will, how can it be that I cannot will what I want to do? How can it be that I continue to mess about with my life and that I am not feeling well? Why is that I can't just will to feel well?' Audible in such a question are the words of St. Paul: 'The good which I will to do, I do not do, and the evil which I will not do, I do'.

Another reason why we may be inclined not to feel that we have free will is that it is probably pragmatically useful that our conscious models of the world are constituted in such a way that we experience, on the one hand, that the world behaves as it necessarily has to behave, and in accordance with our expectations, as if it had been firmly placed on a deterministic track (that is to say, we have a deterministic world view). On the other hand, we experience that we can act and choose ourselves what we will to do (that is, we have a libertarianistic self-view). It appears that this combination provides us with an optimal basis on which to manoeuvre in relation to the daily routines of life, equipping us with both a sense of ontological security, in the belief that daily life and the world run on predictable rails, and, at the same time, giving us a feeling of freedom in being able to choose, within this secure framework, the optimal course of action for ourselves, and the goals we want to achieve – in each case with a sense that our choice will have predictable consequences. Thus our ancestors may have thought somewhat as follows: a herd of horses will do as a herd usually does, when startled, they will run away in a body. Should we then choose to chase them into the narrow cleft over there or onto the hillside over there?

This pragmatically useful, yet self-contradictory, experience presents no problem in pre-scientific thinking – nor, indeed, is it problematic within a social-constructionist view that demands no coherence from our systems of belief, or within a dualistic philosophy in which freedom is said to belong to another, spiritual, realm. However, to the scientific mind, which adheres to realism and monism and demands of a theory that it be coherent and free of contradiction, it is, of course, problematic to claim at once that the *entire* world is deterministically constituted; and that one part of this entire world (the human being) is an exception to the rule.

To a person with a scientific cast of mind who (1) is trained in the deterministic line of thought; (2) wants to build his/her scientific explanations only on the basis of a simple concept of causality (see Chapter 4, the section: 'Downward causality and the dynamics of organization'; (3) nevertheless believes that it makes sense to operate with a concept of free will in the human being, and, finally, (4) would like to bring his/her own personal experience and scientific thinking into line, soft determinism (see Chapter 5) probably seems the least contradictory model: 'I can do what I will, and this is in no way affected by the fact that whatever I will, will always have a cause; all that matters is that the various causes underlying my will have converged at that point in the world which is me'.

However, a simple concept of causality that can, at best, uphold the soft determinist concept of quasi-freedom, is not the only available concept to build our explanations upon. As we have seen, the concept of dynamic downward causality and organizational freedom offers us a model of free will that also accords with the personal experience of our self as a single vertical continuum. In this way of thinking, a scientific explanation that allows room for the existence of genuine free will, is combined with our personal awareness of ourselves as possessing free will, both in terms of our insight into necessity, and in the form of innovation.

The core of personality and the resonant, vertical continuum of the self – from a first-person perspective

In the light of the above considerations, it will also become clearer what we mean by the statement that human resonance lies at the core of personality. We are that resonance. We consist of, feel, and relate to our resonance, which is the way in which our connectedness with the surrounding world makes an impression upon us. To become oneself is to realize and feel oneself as a resonant system in the entire vertical continuum, and to experience the resonances at all the levels of the self: individuated, decentred, and centred.

Through introspection, and through feeling one's own resonances with the surrounding world, we can discover three dimensions or directions by which we can feel and recognize ourselves as the persons we are in relation to the world. There is, first, the dimension of natural history in which our resonance consists of the phenomenological categories we form of the body/nature. Here, we are concerned with the very basic, biological/human way in which the world in the form of resonance makes an impression on us. Next, there is the dimension of cultural history in which our resonance is couched in the discursive forms of our culture, and experienced in these terms. Finally, there is the dimension of life history in which our resonance takes the form of our own life-historical engagements with the world and our life project.

Within each of these dimensions one can look downwards (or, if you like, upwards) through the layers of the vertical continuum. In Figures 7.5 and 7.6, an attempt is made to illustrate this connection. Figure 7.5 shows the connection schematically, and Figure 7.6, as an illustrative model of the three dimensions of resonance down through the three layers, outlines the connection in a more 'analogous' way.

	Life history	Cultural history	Natural history
Individuated	One's own engagement	One's own cultural discourse	One's own categories of the body/nature
Decentred	The many possible engagements	The many possible subcultural discourses	The many forms of connectedness with nature
Centred	To belong by virtue of human engagement	To belong in the discourse of one's culture	To belong with the body in nature

Figure 7.5 *The core of personality. The figure shows the resonance of the vertical continuum in the form of a table. There are three dimensions in this resonance (the dimensions of life history, cultural history, and natural history). Furthermore, resonance exists at three different levels: centred, decentred, and individuated.*

At the deep, centred level, the phenomenology of resonance – the way one feels oneself and the world – consists of a sense of belonging: belonging to the world (from the perspective of natural history), belonging to one's culture (from the perspective of cultural history) and belonging to life (from the perspective of life history). At the decentred level, the phenomenology of resonance consists of feeling that one exists amidst a multitude of possibilities and amidst the complex variety of the world, culture, and life (here complexity refers precisely to those things that cannot be viewed from one perspective only, but need to be approached from many different angles). At the individuated level, the phenomenology of resonance, the way one feels oneself and the world, consists of experiencing the various categories of the body/nature in the specific form in which one has appropriated and organized them as one's own; and, just as one feels oneself as a someone in the forms of nature and the body, so the phenomenology of resonance at this level consists, too, in the way that one appropriates a cultural discourse as one's own discourse; experiences one's engagement with the world, in the course of one's life, as specifically one's own, and senses oneself as a someone through the medium of one's life project.

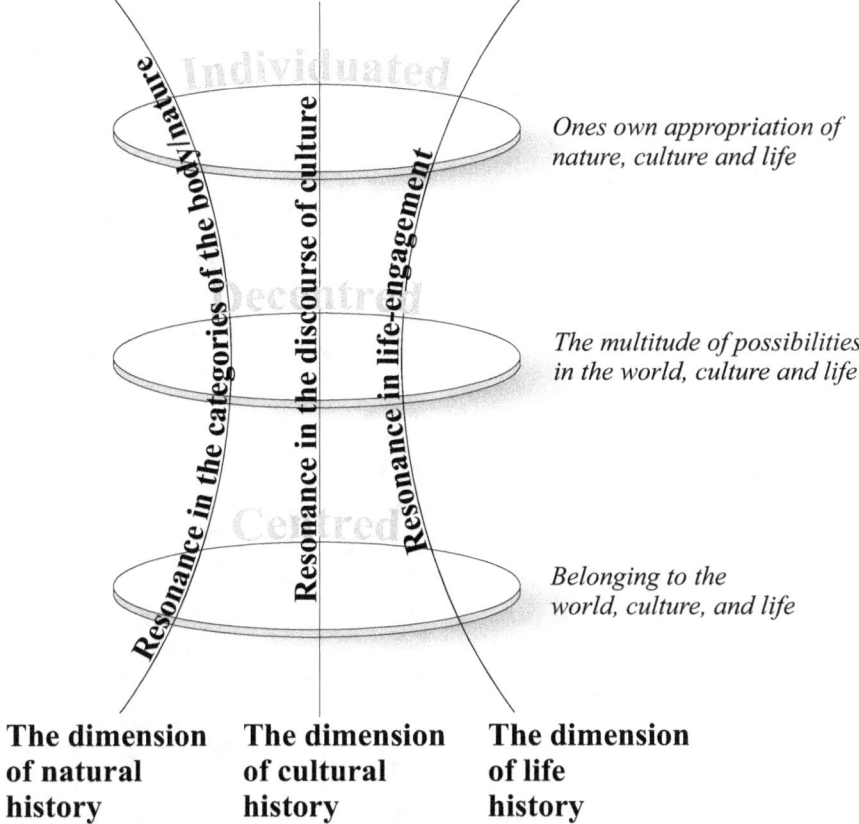

Figure 7.6 *Similar to Figure 7.5, but here an attempt is made to illustrate the resonance of the vertical continuum in the form of a more analogously designed figure.*

Chapter 8

An Anthropological-psychological Taxonomy

What does it mean to be human – and how can psychology contribute to our understanding of humanity?

The central questions in this book have been: How are we as humans able to participate in a moral and societal life built on co-existence? What should a theoretical model look like that is able to identify and explain the core aspects of human competencies and qualities by which we are able to participate in a moral and societal life? And how, that is, by which methodologies, on what kind of scientific foundation, and with the aid of which explanatory styles, can such theoretical models of the human condition be constructed?

This book attempts to answer the above questions by presenting a basic anthropological model of human psychological connectedness to surroundings, especially with regards to the directedness at/by the directedness in certain phenomena: free will, consciousness and self.

The book's project has been to present this basic anthropological model and thereby show that it is a good proposition for a 'critical tolerance on the basis of co-existence', that it is a good proposition for a 'critical realistic universalism', and as mentioned, a proposition of psychology's contribution to a general anthropology.

As shown, the psychological contribution and the basic anthropological model is not like a specific catalogue of contents of central phenomena, motives, values, etc., which would almost certainly be limited to a more or less pseudo-universalistic and in actual fact, an ethnocentric (Western) catalogue. The basic anthropological model is, on the contrary, presented as a taxonomy and a research strategy that is established on very few basic assumptions, which are then claimed to be genuinely universalistic and genuine starting points for a realistic and critical anthropological psychology (and its contribution to a genuinely critical general anthropology). The main idea is:

- that a human being is a being that exists in connectedness with its surroundings generally, and a life of co-existence in particular,
- and that this human connectedness is realized in the form of relations of action, which are always intentional, i.e., always directed at/by something in general and directed at/by the directedness (one's own and others') in particular.

In the first chapter, general psychology was defined by, among other things, the central question to which it must try to find an answer: is psychology a coherent science? We showed that, from a methodological point of view, we can answer this question positively in so far as we succeed in demonstrating the potential compatibility of different areas of psychological knowledge. In order to do this, we need to build an overall model to show the interrelation between the different insights achieved by the various branches of psychology and the applied disciplines, and to provide an overall framework within which to formulate new concepts, models, and theories. In the second chapter, we took a closer look at the requirement that this framework for our concepts, models and theories should be of an anthropological-psychological nature to ensure that these theories address the distinctly human aspect of the psyche.

For this purpose, we applied the MAT method, which consists in creating general Models Of Taxonomic Attributes. The method was described in the Introduction: it involves (1) choosing a number of phenomena which for empirically and theoretically well-founded reasons can be assumed to be related to the distinctly human qualities of the psyche; (2) analysing these models with regard to their overall characteristics, and (3) putting forward, on this basis, a general model of at least certain distinguishing aspects of human nature from a psychological point of view.

In the following chapters we proceeded to formulate and crystallise an overall anthropological-psychological framework or taxonomy. There are three coherent aspects of this taxonomy, and for the sake of clarity, each of these aspects will be summarized separately.

Three overall aspects of an anthropological-psychological taxonomy

First aspect: inner side, outer side, top side, underside

We have seen that, from the perspective of anthropological psychology, the phenomenon of connectedness is one of the most fundamental and all-pervasive distinguishing elements of the human psyche. Connectedness is thus one of the central elements to be considered in tracing the biological and cultural evolution of the distinctive human characteristics, and is included in our considerations concerning the self-understanding of modern human beings and their endeavour to achieve authenticity.

In *the horizontal dimension of connectedness*, we distinguish between, on the one hand: (1) the mirroring, inside-out direction of the intentio, and (2) the outside-in direction of the intentum, in which the self is directed, in its search for goals, values, meaning and sense by idealised objects or other people. From an ontological point of view, this horizontal double directedness is an indivisible unity.

Despite the recognition, in both scientific and popular psychology, and indeed in our own personal self-understanding, that this horizontal double directedness represents an indivisible, ontological unity, we are apt to adopt a one-sided perspective. Methodological reduction, though often necessary,

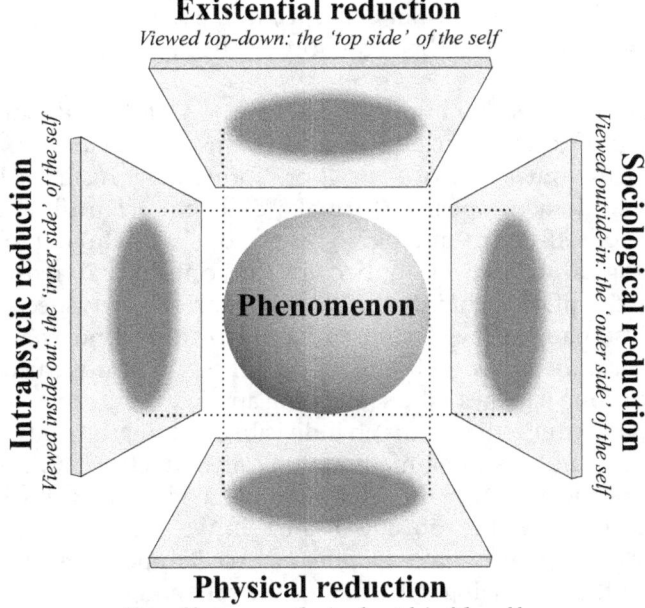

Figure 8.1 *shows the self (or another psychic phenomenon) in its horizontal and vertical forms of connectednesss. The self is viewed from four different, methodologically reduced perspectives, each of which provides a model of the self. The figure should be read as follows: the sphere casts a shadow or projection on four of the surfaces – each shadow indicates a certain abstracting or reductive approach to the unity.*

may lead us to concentrate on the 'inside-out' perspective, and to make models and concepts of the self and other psychological phenomena from this reducing perspective alone. This may be termed intra-psychic reduction, in so far as it refers, so to speak, to the inner side of the self alone. There is no harm in applying this kind of methodological reduction, nor in formulating psychological theories from this intra-psychic perspective, nor indeed in using this inner-side reduction as a personal discourse for developing one's own self and self-understanding. Things start going wrong, however, when we confuse recognition with ontology and are led to believe that this reductive scientific model or discourse for self-understanding offers a sufficient account of the self's ontological presence in the world. This leads to a gross ontological reduction and hence to a disregard for all the other sides of the self and its dynamics that can be understood only from other perspectives than the intra-psychic.

In looking at the concepts, models, and theories advanced by the specific theoretical and applied disciplines, it is important to establish the particular methodological reduction and perspective that they are based on – whether, in other words, these particular concepts, models, and theories concerning human characteristics have been put forward from an intra-psychic or some other perspective.

Similarly, it is possible to make what I call a sociological reduction that focuses on the outside-in perspective. From this perspective, concepts concerning the outer side of the self are formulated. Again, it is possible from this limited perspective to make excellent scientific models and discourses for self-understanding, so long as one is careful not to allow this methodological reduction to become an ontological reduction that precludes scientific insight into the other dimensions and aspects of the self, and thus also narrows the discourse for one's own self-understanding.

The vertical dimension of connectedness. If we look now at the vertical dynamic of connectedness, the same thing applies. Here, too, one can speak of a dual directedness that forms an indivisible, ontological unity, and which can also be approached in a methodologically reductive way. If we look at the existence and actions of the self from the top down, we will see primarily what might be called the top side of the self. We might refer to this as the *spiritual reduction*, which may well offer an excellent perspective from which to focus on the organizing dynamics of the self, and, similarly, provide an excellent discourse for self-understanding, in so far as one wishes to focus on the self-conscious self. But again, if this approach results in an ontological reduction, it will narrow the scope both of one's scientific explanations and one's personal insight into the self. From a scientific point of view, it will result in a mystic and/or dualistic and/or idealistic model of the self-consciousness, as something entirely different in kind from, and separated from, rather than constituted by, the world in general and our own corporality in particular. Likewise, this kind of ontological reduction will result in a narrow discourse of self-understanding that entirely eliminates the constitutive basis and conditions of the self.

Conversely, if we take a bottom-up perspective it will be the underside of the self, so to speak, that we focus on. We might call this the physical reduction, which, again, may provide us with an excellent scientific approach to the basic, constitutive conditions of the self, just as it gives us a discourse for focusing on the physical constitution of the psyche and on the most fundamental elements underpinning the vertical continuum of the self. Once again, however, we must ensure that this methodological reduction does not lead to an ontological reduction that precludes awareness of the other dimensions of the self, and indeed results in a denial of the self, presenting it as an illusion with no foundation in reality.

Second aspect: my side, your side, nobody's side, everybody's side

As we have seen, especially in Chapters 6 and 7, the self is constructed on the basis of four key forms of relationship between the self and the world.

First-person – zero-person (1pp–0pp): In this relationship the other to whom one relates does not have a perspective of its own which can be directed at/by one's own first-person perspective. In other words, there is no someone who is directed at/by one's self. This relationship might also be called an I-that relationship.

- First-person – first-person (1pp–1pp): Here, one is directed at/by one's own directedness. In this case there is a real, specific someone who is directed at/by one's self. This relationship might also be called an I-me relationship.
- First-person – second-person (1pp–2pp): In this relationship one is directed at/by another who has his/her/its own first-person perspective, which in turn is directed at/by one's own perspective. This might also be called an I-you relationship.
- First-person – third-person (1pp–3pp): Here, finally, one is directed at/by the common meanings of one's group or society in the widest scientific and cultural sense; these relationships contain human perspectives, but do not include a someone who is directed at/by one's self. This might also be called an I-'we' relationship ('we' in quotation marks because there is no real, specific someone in this relationship).

As we have seen, we cannot ourselves assume the zero-person perspective: in other words, there is no way of recognizing, experiencing, or understanding how the world 'looks' from this perspective. It is, however, possible to assume the other perspectives – and indeed, they represent the various methodological vantage points from which one can gain both greater personal self-awareness and a scientific understanding of the nature of the self (and of other psychic phenomena).

To assume a first-person perspective is to understand and recognize introspectively what it is like to be a human self. It is an excellent, methodological reduction to use introspection in trying to grasp the nature of psychic phenomena (not least when it comes to understanding what it means to be a someone). Indeed, this was the method first used by psychology in the nineteenth century, when it was still in its infancy as a scientific discipline.

The second-person perspective on the self exists primarily through the medium of dialogue and of conversation. As a methodological tool, it is applied in the kind of qualitative interviews, therapeutic interviews and

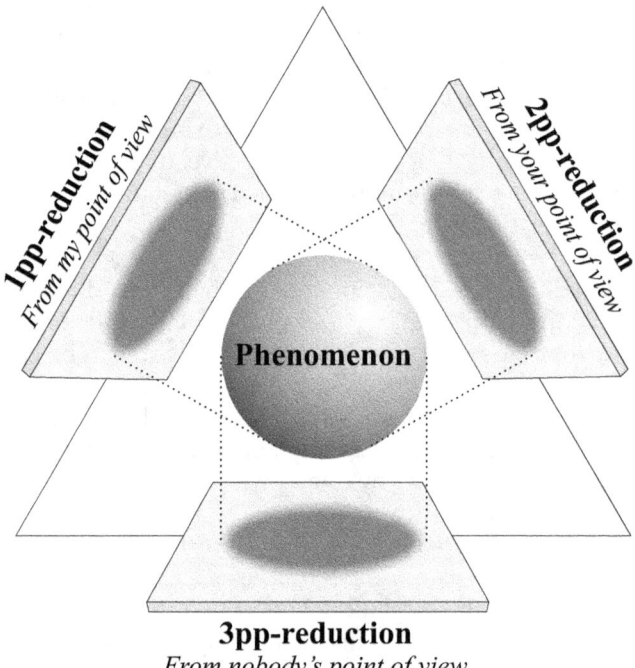

3pp-reduction
From nobody's point of view
(or everybody's point of view)

Figure 8.2 *shows the self (or another psychic phenomenon) from three different methodologically reduced perspectives, each providing a model of the formation of the self in terms of directedness/consciousness. The figure should be read as follows: the sphere casts shadows or projections on the three surfaces – each shadow implies a certain abstracting or reductive approach to the unity.*

existential conversations where one of the interlocutors puts him/herself in the place of the other, and, by taking in what the other expresses, forms an impression of what it is like to be that other. Each of the interlocutors tries to visualise what the other introspects. One may call this substitutional introspection or the assumption of an empathic perspective. The term 'empathy' refers precisely to the ability to understand the perspective of the other (these considerations are inspired by Kohut 1977, 1984).

The third-person perspective can be found in those methods of researching and gaining insight that specifically steer clear of assuming an introspective or empathic perspective. Here, the goal is to produce insights and explanations that are valid from any perspective by taking a universal perspective that is 'purged' of subjectivity. Even when it is difficult to put oneself in the place of the other one may nevertheless produce, from a third-person perspective, useful information concerning the self that can in principle be shared by anyone, regardless of their subjective outlook or their perspective distance from us.

Third aspect: natural history, cultural history, life history

In taking a natural history approach we describe and explain a psychological phenomenon, for example the self, by looking at the natural conditions under which it emerged, and how it developed over time as humankind itself evolved. The natural history approach thus involves considerations concerning the 'nature component' of the self; in other words, the ways in which our personality is formed and influenced by the physical, biochemical and neurophysical constitution laid down by our genetic inheritance.

In taking a cultural history approach, we attempt to describe and explain the self on the basis of how it develops in interaction with the man-made reality, or culture, we are surrounded by. Here we look at how the human self has developed through the various different stages of our cultural history as a species. Further, we look at how the modern self develops in interaction with the given culture that surrounds it. Finally, we look at how the self develops differently in different cultures all over the world, that is, at how cultural differences influence the development of the self.

In taking a life history approach we deal with the course of each individual's particular life-history, and how particular life-historical events contribute to, or, on the contrary, obstruct or slow down, the formation and development of the self.

If one progresses from a (necessary) methodological reduction to a (gross) ontological reduction, mistakenly inferring the latter from the former, one will narrow down one's understanding and explanation of the psyche to one of the following: (1) One may believe that the natural-historical constitution is decisive: we are born with certain inherited

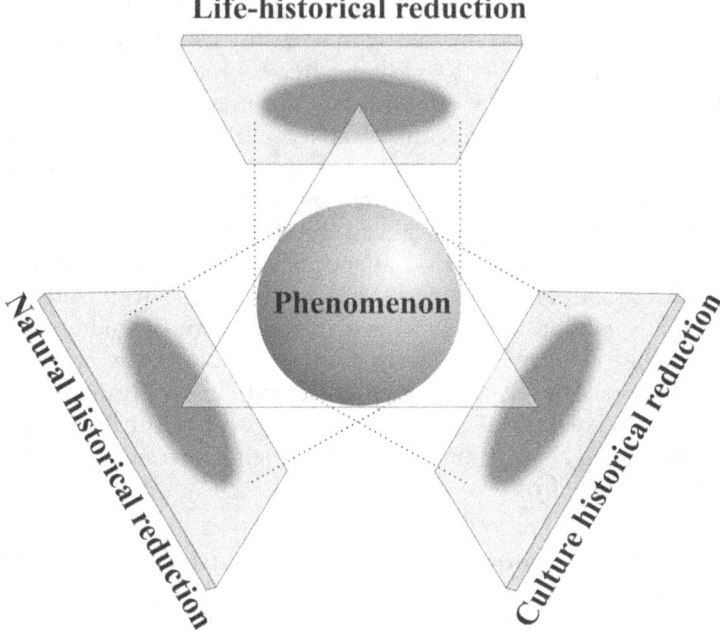

Figure 8.3 *shows the self (or another psychic phenomenon) from three different methodologically reduced perspectives, each providing a model of the fundamental dynamic forces involved in the formation of the self. The figure should be read as follows: the sphere casts shadows or projections on each of the three surfaces – each shadow implies a certain abstracting or reductive approach to the unity.*

dispositions, features, inclinations, and tempers which will continue to characterize us as selves and neither we nor the surrounding culture can modify these characteristics to any appreciable extent. (2) One may believe that, on the contrary, the cultural-historical dimension is decisive in determining our personality, behaviour, and conception of ourselves: although we are born with a certain biological and physical constitution, this does not, except in the most general sense, programme what we will be like as people. The 'personal touch' is conferred only in our interaction with the surrounding culture: it is through this interaction that the self is formed. Thus, a decisive role is played by the specific culture into which we are born: the self is influenced above all by the culture it develops in, while the contribution made by the particular course of an individual's life within that culture and by his/her personal experiences along the way will be marginal and insignificant. (3) Finally, one may believe that the self is primarily influenced by the course of the individual's life history, irrespective of its biological basis or the cultural framework in which the individual has lived. Although it is recognised that nature and culture form the basis for the development of the self, the decisive factor, from this point of view, is how one's personal life history has unfolded: it is this that primarily determines one's destiny, shaping one's personality and development as a human being.

The epigenetic and epidynamic creation of human nature

Throughout the book the taxonomic models have all been structured over the same vertical stratification: centeredness, decentredness, and individuatedness – both in relation to the culture historical and the life historical description of the development of free will, consciousness, and self. This parallel between phylogenesis and ontogenesis is neither strange nor coincidental.

To explain this further we have to look at how developmental dynamics in human nature generally happen. How do we imagine that the forces that shape humans – the inborn mental dispositions and culture's 'project human being' – work together in order to create human nature? Traditionally, one would answer either in an 'Aristotelian' way suggesting that development is 'pushed' by a (genetic) plan, or one would answer 'Platonically' indicating that it is 'pulled' (by a project intended for us by culture or the world spirit). Neither of these explanations prove sufficient when it comes to explaining how human nature can occur.

We are used to imagining that it takes a plan to steer a developmental process in a certain direction. Without a plan, there is only chaos, we imagine. In other words, we think epigenetically about development, as we see, for instance, in the classical developmental, psychological ideas of Freud, Erikson, or Piaget (the prefix epi means on top – so the developmental levels follow one on top of the other, governed by genetically implanted programmes). Strictly speaking, however, if a plan already exists, then it cannot be an actual development (equal to the creation of something completely new or emergent). It can only be an unfolding of principles and shapes that are already anticipated as types of germs in the plan.

If we insist on thinking along genuine developmental paths then it actually turns out to be a fringe benefit that we escape from the quagmire of classical debate of inheritance/environment. This debate has been dominated by the question as to whether one should find such a plan – or at least its essential principles – implanted as inheritance or embedded as a socializing 'project human being'? If however, we insist that in the creation of human nature (whether in the earliest developmental process or in later processes such as therapeutic ones) everything happens as a genuine development, then we simultaneously free ourselves from having to look for a complete developmental plan for the entire human nature. The development of human nature may start on the basis of some elementary inborn basic principles, but the rest (and actual human nature) is developed without a plan.

If no complete developmental plan exists, how come development is not chaotic? How can human nature without a plan still occur with almost unfailing certainty in every new little human? How can most developmental processes still steadily and quietly fall into place in the development of human nature? If we are not to think of systematic development, then how must we think? The answer is: attractors. But first an example.

According to Thelen (1992), the view in modern research on human motor functions is, for example with upright walking, that it does not need to be represented in the brain. Such a motoric pattern of movements simply adjusts itself (without being 'worked out' in the brain) on the optimum mechanical interaction between (1) the conditions for movement in the physical environment (e.g., gravity and even surface), (2) the bodily options for movement (e.g., the joints' flexibility and the body's changing centres of gravity during movement) and (3) the type and purpose of movement (e.g., walking from one place to another). The upright walk for humans is the optimum forward movement, given the output conditions and that the body finds this type of movement by itself. Not because some mystical wisdom is hidden in the body, merely because the body happens to be functionally organized as it is. It is in the body's nature to walk as it does. Man can easily move in other ways, for instance, by jumping to a place or tap dancing to it, but these are not optimum types of movement, and they require more physical and conscious effort (at least for the untrained).

The development of the optimum self-organizing patterns of movement is also seen in small children. Before children can walk, they crawl in all sorts of possible (and impossible) ways: some crawl forward, others sideways, others crawl (to huge annoyance) backwards, and some 'bottom' their way forward. But from each way of moving they all end up walking in more or less the same way (apart from the individual physical differences). It can be said that development is neither pushed nor pulled by any superior plan for developing upright walking, but rather falls into place in a certain way. From a number of different combinatory usages of the dynamic conditions of possibilities, the motoric development falls into place in the upright walk. It takes neither an inborn programme nor an externally inflicted learning programme for the child to walk.

The type of movement by which a dynamic development or movement tends to fall in place is called an attractor. An attractor is the pattern of movement or the path of development which the development tends to follow, given the general dynamic of possibility-conditions and the interaction of forces. Consequently, the concept of attractors marks another principle of explanation besides the 'push/pull' explanations. An attractor is simply the optimum choreography that occurs when dynamic forces interact. The development is not determined by a programme that is unfolded and pushes, or by an acquired compliance to an over-individualized project that pulls. Development is self-organizing. It falls in place with the attractors. Given the existing conditions and forces (including the societal 'project human being') certain development paths occur in all children without being programmed beforehand. It happens all by itself.

Let us look at a more psychological example regarding the core in human nature. The very interactive connectedness that basically produces human nature is, with its intentional bipolarity (S$\Rightarrow$ and $\Rightarrow$O), such an attractor. This means that intentionality is not programmed, inborn, or culture historical. It simply occurs when the initial conditions, the child's genetic output conditions and the responses to these from the surroundings are present. Basically, any living organism is active. On the one hand, it is a striving for life. It is a movement from the organism out at the world (intentio$\Rightarrow$). On the other hand, it is an adjustment as a consequence of the basic conditions of life in the surroundings. It is the same movement but now seen in the light of how it is adjusted by the surrounding conditions ($\Rightarrow$intentum). In human intentionality the same pattern repeats itself. First of all, in the beginning there are a number of attachment projects, an assertive energy that becomes the intentionality's movement from intentio to intentum. It is the active and receiving aspect in humans' direction at/by other directions. Secondly, there is a harmonious adjustment to the societal 'project human being'. This marks the intentionality's movement from intentum to intentio. It is the receiving part in the life project. So the intentionality's bipolar, dynamic form is the optimum form, the attractor, with which active outwardly and inwardly directed forces of movement choreographically fall into place.

The human attractors choreographically match the paths along which the development of human nature moves, given the interaction between physical/biological and cultural/social forces.

So with such an attractor model for development, one does not need to assume that everything in the development of human nature is previously embedded in a developmental plan. It is sufficient to assume that a certain set of initial conditions or boundary conditions exists. Thereby the first developmental paths occur. There is no previously given plan for the emergence of the next higher developmental paths. They develop as a consequence of the way in which the development otherwise falls into place with the first developmental paths. This provides a new and higher level of output or boundary conditions and a new set of human-creating dynamic forces that will later allow the development to fall into place with even higher developmental paths. It happens all by itself – and each time in the same way.

Consequently, there is nothing strange or contradictory in assuming that free will, consciousness, and self in human nature are created on the basis of dynamic forces which initially are 'external' functional forces. These external forces simply fall, without a plan, into place in a freedom-creating, consciousness-creating and self-creating manner.

I call such a development based on dynamic attractor principles epidynamic (in contrast to epigenetic). Dynamic interactions simply and incessantly fall into the necessary higher places, they are attracted to each other in the dynamically necessary ways whereby the dynamic types of interaction between the human organism and the environment develops on top of each other in layers.

This is why the epidynamics of life history must necessarily reflect the epidynamics of culture history. Mankind's genetic foundation and inheritance immediately provide each newly arrived individual with the opportunity to develop a centralized way of living in dynamic interaction with his/her surroundings and a group of members from the same species. Through the culture historical epidynamics, higher-level decentralized, individualized ways of living have developed on this centralized foundation. The culture historical movement simply falls into place in this way, given the centralized foundation's dynamic opportunities.

So when the culture history already exists to every newborn, and when the decentralized and individualized dynamic types of interaction and living are already embedded in the shape of the surrounding culture's significant artefacts and institutions, one can claim that the surrounding culture's world of ideas pulls the individual's life historical development up through the centred, decentred and individuated levels in a 'Platonian' way. Basically, if culture 'suddenly disappeared', mankind would still, in principle recreate its culture history and thereby recreate the human nature of free will, consciousness, and self. This occurs simply because the development of human nature necessarily falls into its epidynamic place.

The distinctive characteristics of the human psyche defined in terms of human resonance

As we have seen, general psychology deals with the psychic, and consequently with the nature of psychology as a discipline. One of its tasks is precisely to organize the various methods, concepts, models, and theories put forward by the different branches of psychology, in order to identify and define the scope and purpose of the discipline as a whole.

Anthropological psychology represents that part of general psychology that takes things a step further in dealing with the distinctive features of the human psyche, and, as such, it too is involved in the endeavour to draw together and organize the contributions made by the various branches of the discipline to our understanding of human psychology. As was pointed out in the first part of this book, general psychology and anthropological psychology are certainly different disciplines, but each comes into play wherever, in the course of research and the development of models and theories relating to particular topics, questions arise concerning the nature of the psyche and the distinctive features of the human psyche in particular.

If we look at the models of the psyche presented in this book, each of which is based on certain selected phenomena – active connectedness, free will, consciousness and the self – it will be apparent that they pertain both to general psychology and to the distinct dimension of anthropological psychology.

The models are constructed on the basic assumption that the psyche is a hierarchical system in which we differentiate, in broad terms, between the lowest proto-psychic levels (the domain of low-level psychology) and the higher genuine psychic levels (the domain of medium-level and high-level psychology – in connection with this (see Chapter 4).

This is illustrated by the survey of the overall taxonomy presented in Figures 8.4 and 8.5. In these figures the different partial taxonomies that have been presented so far has been combined in an overall taxonomy of the central psychological phenomena. The final taxonomy is based on the anthropological-psychological conception that the fundamental, psychological phenomena must be understood as phenomena that have developed and are still developing.

This particular approach is captured by the vertical axis of the taxonomy (recurring in practically all the taxonomies previously presented). Fundamentally, the vertical axis implies a line of fracture in nature at which the genuine psychic forms of connectedness emerge ontologically from the non-psychic or proto-psychic. Low-level psychology deals with the proto-psychic, while medium- and high-level psychology deal with the genuine forms of psychic connectedness. The genuinely psychic emerges, then, at the point where there arises in nature forms of connectedness that are not only the product of causal/functional processes, but of intentional behaviour and intentioned action. Consequently, different kinds of scientific explanation are required above and below the line of fracture: causal and functional explanations are applied to phenomena below the line, and intentional and intentioned explanations to those above.

The genuine psychic phenomena are hierarchically arranged according to the forms of connectedness they are based upon: centred, decentred, and individuated.

With the appearance of intentional and intentioned forms of connectedness, we see the emergence of an ontological world-order that is best described or explained in terms of the double top-down/bottom-up

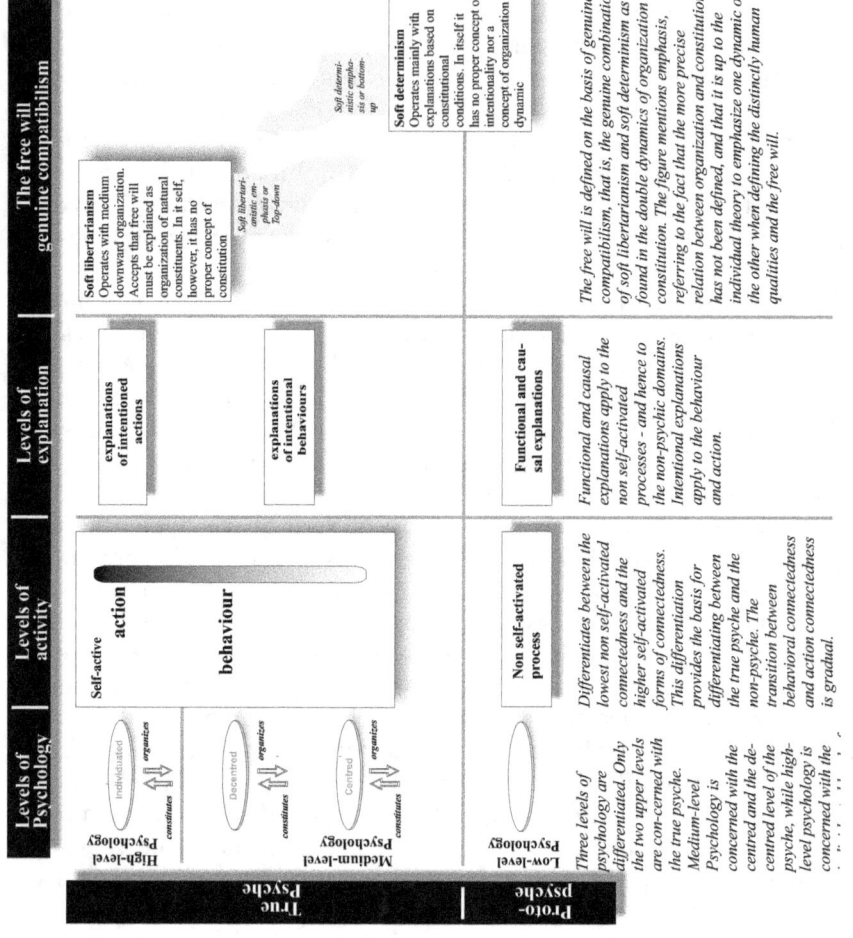

Figure 8.4 The different taxonomies combined – A.

An Anthropological-psychological Taxonomy

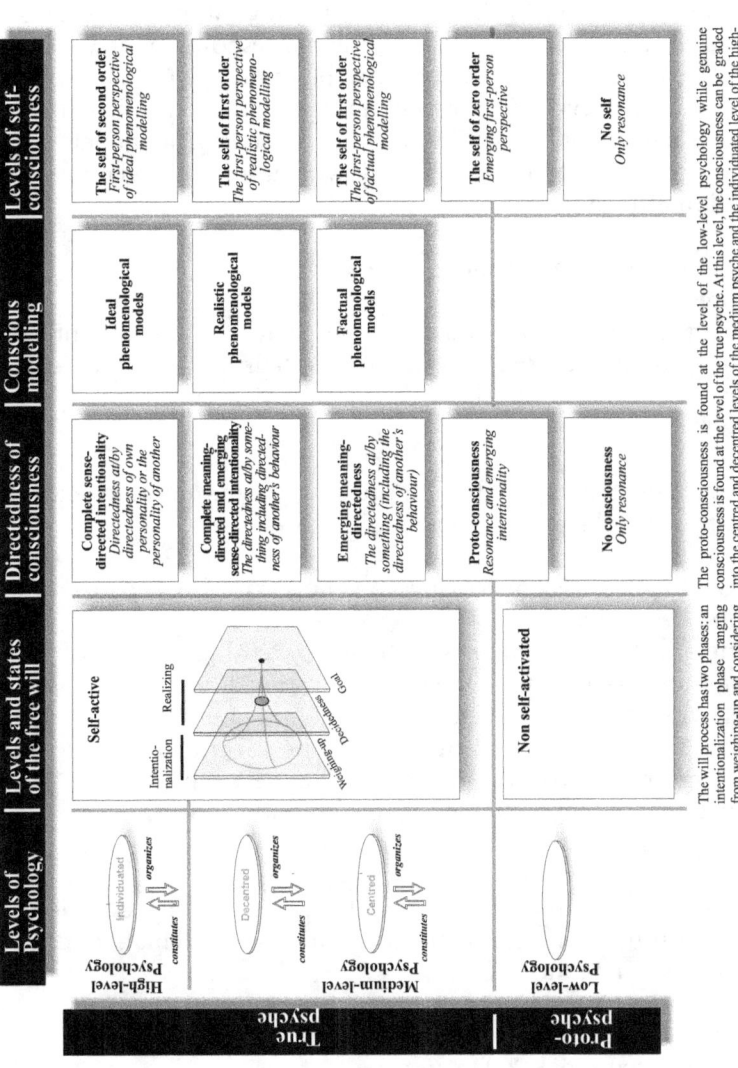

Figure 8.5 *The different taxonomies combined – B.*

perspective and the double dynamic of organization/constitution. This kind of ontological order leads in turn to the emergence of self-organization and, to a certain degree, free will.

As we can see from a horizontal reading of the taxonomy, the central psychic phenomena follow this hierarchical, ontological order: the various levels of directedness in the consciousness thus correspond to certain levels of the consciousness in terms of phenomenological model formation, and, similarly, to various levels of the self, understood as the first-person perspective of these intentionally directed phenomenological models.

Low-level psychology deals with the following taxonomic relations that call for functionalistic types of explanation:

- non self-activated forms of connectedness
- no real directedness
- proto-conscious resonance (which does not have the real, intentional directedness implied by self-activated connectedness, it is not yet real consciousness)
- no real self

Medium-level psychology deals with the following taxonomic relations that call for intentional types of explanation:

- self-activated forms of connectedness in the form of behaviour at the centred and decentred level
- directedness at/by something, in which 'something' refers either to objects or to the behaviour of others, including the directedness manifest in the behaviour of others in actual here-and-now situations
- the directedness of the consciousness in the form of emerging and completed meaning-directedness and emerging sense-directedness
- the production of phenomenological, factual, and realistic models of the surrounding world
- the zero- and first-order self
- a self-organizing dynamic in the form of the free-willed production of models in/through the consciousness, involving factual, and real discourses concerning the self.

High-level psychology deals with the following taxonomic features and calls for genuine intentional explanations:

- self-initiated actions at the individuated level
- directedness towards/by the individual's own directedness and the directedness of a someone: a directedness that can be abstracted from the

individual's own personality and that of the other, since it is relatively constant over time and across situations
- directedness of the consciousness in the form of completed, meaning-directed and sense-directed models
- the formation of ideal phenomenological models
- the second-order self
- a self-organizing dynamic in the form of the free-willed production of models, involving ideal self-directed discourses

How precise a picture, we may now ask, does this overall model of the psyche, and the taxonomy relating the various key phenomena involved, offer us concerning the distinctive features of the human psyche? It would seem that, to a great extent, we can use this model/taxonomy to differentiate between the human and the animal forms of psyche. Animal (or other primitive or artificial) forms of psyche do not involve this kind of hierarchical structure; the level reached by even the most advanced species lies somewhere in the domain of medium-level psychology. The model, however, is constructed from a third-person perspective. It therefore provides a universal 3pp picture of the human psyche, meaning a picture of the universal aspects of the human psyche that we presumably share in common with other (as yet hypothetical) high-level psychic creatures (be they artificial or extraterrestrial). Formulated in this simple way, the distinctively human psyche is thus manifestly distinguished from the low-level psyches, but is not sufficiently characterised to enable us to differentiate it from similar, but non-human, high-level psyches.

It is usually considered that, in order to identify the distinguishing features of the human psyche, as anthropological psychology requires us to do, we must have recourse primarily to first- and second-person methods. These methods are based on pure introspection (an 'I-I' relationship) in the case of the 1pp perspective or, in the case of the 2pp perspective, on the empathetic perspective assumed in conversations between humans (an 'I-you' relationship). This idea is expressed by the so-called Turing-test: that the decision as to whether a machine has a true psyche like ours must be made by a human being who has a conversation with it without knowing whether it is the machine itself or another human being who is actually doing the talking. If this human tester cannot settle the matter, the machine is (sufficiently) human so that any possible differences do not matter in practice. Or, to use the terms adopted in the present book: the perspective distance between the human and the machine is sufficiently small for us to accept that the machine is, to all intents and purposes, human.

What is really at issue here, in fact, is that it is only on the basis of this distinctly human way of being resonant (which is activated when one enters into 1pp or 2pp relations) that one can perceive the distinctively human element of the other. However, a real 3pp methodology may also be used in the identification of the distinctive features of the human psyche – namely, a 3pp methodology that focuses on the role of the irreplaceable in the humanizing or 'self-creating' forms of human connectedness (see Chapter 4 and 7) and on the distinctively human resonances (see Chapter 6) that characterize this connectedness. On the basis of this 3pp perspective we are able to develop objective, theoretical explanations, accessible and, in principle, acceptable from any perspective, concerning the distinctively human forms of resonance: those that result from our unique ability to identify key objects and people in our lives as irreplaceable, and to relate to them as such. These theoretical explanations do not require that this distinctively human resonance be activated (in the researcher) in order that he/she be able to identify, describe, and explain it.

We identify something, or someone, as irreplaceable – in contrast to those objects that can be exchanged, imitated, or copied – through the impressions we make on that thing or person, when we direct ourselves at them: impressions of a kind that enables us to recognize our own selves and in this sense become a someone. The irreplaceable element in our lives also includes all the meaning- and sense-rich elements of our world which we are directed by, which fill our world and render it into a something to which we can relate. As we have seen, it is in this mirroring and idealizing relation that we become a someone and our life a 'something'. This form of humanizing directedness can very well be identified from a universal or objective 3pp perspective.

Nevertheless, the distinctively human qualities of this directedness, and of our sense of irreplaceability, must be found in the distinctly human resonance that is bound up with our deepest constitutions. As we have seen (in Chapter 6), resonance can be found everywhere. Everything, at all levels, resonates with its surroundings: from the deepest, unorganised resonance that is to be found in the way that the lattice structure of a crystal reflects the fundamental, physical laws and conditions in which it was formed; to the biological resonance to be found in the morphology of living organisms, whether this be in the passive interface of plants or in the behavioural interspace between self-activating animals (see Chapter 4); to real psychic resonance in the form of phenomenological qualia, that is, the experiential qualities that emerge in the intentional and intended first-person connectedness of the higher, self-activating biological organisms with their surroundings. The claim is then that, in this sense, resonance is a natural constant to be found in the entire existential continuum. As such, it is certainly accessible and susceptible to scientific 3pp-methodological research. Furthermore – and crucially – our claim is that this resonance is bound up in each case with an organism's particular, constitutive ways of connecting with the surrounding world. Thus, the distinctively human way of being resonant is determined by our specific biological constitution, just as that of a bat, fish or snail is determined by theirs. Indeed, this view is implicit in the entire anthropological psychological taxonomy presented here. As we have emphasised throughout, our self-organization is an organization or orchestration of our constitutive levels, and, this being the case, it is clearly possible to use a 3pp-type of anthropological psychology to identify those features that makes us, and our psyches, specifically human.

An especially 'empathetic' or resonant 1pp or 2pp methodology is, in this sense, not necessary. Or, to put it the other way round: a theoretical and anthropological psychological explanation from a 3pp perspective is actually possible. It is quite a different matter, however, when it comes to a phenomenological understanding of what it is like to be another creature or another human being. This kind of understanding requires a resonance on the part of the observer or the researcher, as well as on the part of the person observed. Such resonance does not emerge from acquiring a universally valid, theoretical explanation; on the contrary, it can result only from the fact that we do enter into this kind of resonant connectedness with one another.

So, the distinguishing characteristics of the human psyche must be explained from a 3pp, on the basis of the distinctive features of and laws governing human resonance – and it must be understood from 2pp and 1pp, using the methods of empathy and introspection involved. This resonance is formed in our basic, constitutive connections with the surrounding world. But, obviously, the distinctive features of human resonance cannot be exhaustively identified, described and explained at the level of low-level psychology alone (in terms merely of our biological constitution as human beings). Resonance does indeed 'reverberate' in, and is formed by, the entire vertical continuum: right up to the self-organizing forms of qualia by means of which we consciously model our world, sense it and let it make an impression on us. Human resonance can be fully explained only on the basis of this kind of overall hierarchical and constitutive/organizing model. It is only by identifying, describing and explaining the distinctively human form of resonance in terms of the entire vertical continuum that we can develop a genuine psychological theory concerning our distinctively human capacity to be and to organize ourselves in such a way that we are conscious of being, and feeling ourselves, a someone while at the same time experiencing the world as a human place to be.

Bibliography

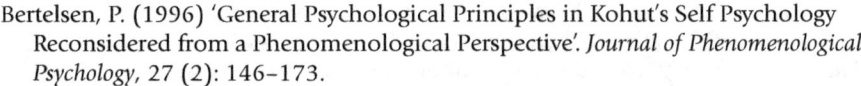

Bertelsen, P. (1996) 'General Psychological Principles in Kohut's Self Psychology Reconsidered from a Phenomenological Perspective'. *Journal of Phenomenological Psychology*, 27 (2): 146-173.
—— (1999a) 'Free Will in Psychology – In the Search of a Genuine Compatibilism'. *Journal of Theoretical and Philosophical Psychology*, 19 (1): 41-77.
—— (1999b) 'Development of Phenomenological Consciousness in Early Childhood'. *Journal of Theoretical and Philosophical Psychology*, 19 (2): 195-216.
—— (2002) 'Will and Self in Augustine: Double-Bind and Taboo'. *Theory & Psychology*, 12 (6): 749-776.
Bertelsen, P. and L. Hem (1986) 'En overordnet forskningsmodel'. *Psyke & Logos*, 109-151.
Boehm, C. (2000) 'Conflict and the Evolution of Social Control'. *Journal of Consciousness Studies*, 7 (1-2): 79-101.
Boss, M. (1990) 'The unconscious: What is it?' In: Hoeller, K. (ed.) *Readings in Existential Psychology and Psychiatry*. Seattle: Review of existential psychology and psychiatry.
Burns, T. R. and E. Engdahl (1998) 'The Social Construction of Consciousness. Part 1: Collective Consciousness and its Socio-cultural Foundations'. *Journal of Consciousness Studies*, 5 (1): 67-85.
Chalmers, D. J. (1996a): *Conscious Mind. In Search of a Fundamental Theory*. Oxford: Oxford University Press.
—— (1996b) 'Facing up to the problem of consciousness'. In: Hameroff, S. R., A. W. Kaszniak and A. Scott, (eds) *Toward a Science of Consciousness. The First Tuscon Discussion and Debates*. Mass.: MIT Press.
Churchland, P. M. (1979) *Scientific Realism and the Plasticity of Mind*. Cambridge: Cambridge University Press
—— (1995): *The Engine of Reason, The Seat of the Soul: A Philosophical Journey into the Brain*. Mass.: MIT Press.
Conrad, M. and D. Conrad (1997) 'Of Maps and Territoriums: A Three Point Landing on the Mind-Body Problem'. In: Årheim, P., H. Liljenström and U. Svedin, *Matter Matters? On the Material Basis of the Cognitive Activity of Mind*. London: Springer.
Crick, F. (1994) *The Astonishing Hypothesis*. New York: Scribners.

Dennett, D. C. (1984) *Elbow Room. The Varieties of Free Will Worth Wanting.* Oxford: Clarendon Press.

Emmeche, C., S. Køppe and F. Stjernfelt (1997) 'Explaining Emergence: Towards an Ontology of Levels'. *Journal for General Philosophy of Science,* 28: 83–119.

—— (1998) 'Levels, Emergence and Three Versions of Downward Causation'. In: Bøgh Andersen, P., C. Emmeche, N. O. Finnemann and P. Voetmann Christiansen, (eds) *Downward Causation - Minds, Bodies and Matter.* Dordrecht: Kluwer Academic Publishers.

Engelsted, N. (1989) *Personlighedens almene grundlag. En teoretisk ekskursion i psykens historie. I-II.* Århus Universitetsforlag,

—— (1994) 'Værdi, verden og virksomhedsteori'. In: *Psykologi i et jubilæumsperspektiv.* Psykologisk Institut, Aarhus Universitet.

—— (1999) *Hvad psykologien i grunden er videnskaben om.* Essay præsenteret på Augustkonferencen 1999, Psykologisk Institut, Aarhus Universitet.

Fink, H. (1995) 'Modet i midten'. *Philosophia,* 24 (3–4): 7–25.

Fingarette, H. (1969) *Self-deception.* London: Routledge and Kegan Paul.

Flack, J. C. and F. B. M. de Waal (2000) '"Any Animal Whatever". Darwinian Building Blocks of Morality in Monkeys and Apes'. *Journal of Consciousness Studies,* 7 (1–2): 1–29.

Flanagan, O. (1992) *Consciousness Reconsidered.* Mass.: MIT Press.

Fog, J. (1998) *Saglig medmenneskelighed. Grundforhold I psykoterapien.* Hans Reitzels forlag. København.

Folke Larsen, S. (1983) 'Erindringens nature og historie'. *Psyke & Logos,* 2: 277–307.

Frege, G. (1975) *Funktion, Begriff, Bedeutung.* Göttingen, Vandenhoeck and Rubrecht.

Fromm, E. (197?) *Kunsten at elske.* Hans Reitzel. København.

Goodall, J. (1986) *The Chimpanzees of Gombe: Patterns of Behavior.* Cambridge, Mass.: Belknap Press of Harvard University Press.

Gullestad, S. (1992) *Å si fra. Autonomibegrepet i psykoanalysen.* Universitetsforlaget. Oslo.

Heckhausen, H. (1987) 'Intentionsgeleitetes Handeln der eigenen Identität'. In: Heckhausen, H. et al. (eds) *Jenseits des Rubikon. Der Wille in den Human-Wissenschaften.* Berlin: Springer Verlag.

Hameroff, S. (1997) 'Quantum Automata in Cytoskeletal Microtubules: A Nanoscale Substrate for Cognition'. In: Årheim, P., H. Liljenström and U. Svedin: *Matter Matters? On the Material Basis of the Cognitive Activity of Mind.* Springer: London.

Isaac, G. (1978) 'The Food-sharing Behavior of Protohuman Hominids'. *Scientific American,* 238 (4): 90–108.

Jaynes, J. (1976) *The Origin of Consciousness in the Break-down of the Bicameral Mind.* Boston: Houghton Mifflin Company.

Jolly, C. and Plog, F. (1987) *Physical Anthropology and Archeology.* New York: Knopf.

Katzenelson, B. (1985) 'Moralens inderside'. *Psyke & Logos,* 6: 354–377.

Katzenelson, B. (1996) 'Handling og adfærd'. *Bulletin fra Forum for Antropologisk Psykologi,* 1 (2–26): 70–84.

Kohut, H. (1984) *How does Analysis Cure?* Anold Goldberg (ed.), with the collaboration of Paul Stepansky. Chicago: The University of Chicago Press.

Kohut, H. (1977) *The Restoration of the Self.* New York: International Universities Press.

Køppe, S. (1990) *Virkelighedens niveauer. De nye videnskaber og deres historie*. Gyldendal. København.
Laland, K. N., J. Odling-Smee and M. W. Feldman (2000) 'Niche Construction, Biological Evolution and Cultural Change'. *Behavioral and Brain Science* 23 (1): 131-146.
Levine, J. (1983) 'Materialism and Qualia: The Explanatory Gap'. *Pacific Philosophical Quarterly* 64: 354.
Libet, B., A. Freeman and K Sutherland (eds) (1999) *The Volitional Brain. Towards a Neuroscience of Free Will*. Exeter: Imprint Academic.
Logan, M. and W. Sanders (1976) 'The Model'. In: Wolf, E: *The Valley of Mexico: Shades in Pre-Hispanic Ecology and Society*. Albuquerque: University of New Mexico Press.
Mammen, J. (1983) *Den menneskelige Sans. Et essay om psykologiens genstandsområde*. Dansk Psykologisk forlag.
—— (1986) Erkendelse som objektrelation. *Psyke og Logos,* 7 (1): 178-202.
—— (1999) *Psyken som 'Res Extensa'*. Essay præsenteret på Augustkonferencen 1999, Psykologisk Institut, Aarhus Universitet.
May, R. (1977) *Kjærlighet og vilje*. Forlaget Forum. Oslo.
Midgley, M. (1994) *The Human Primate. Humans, Freedom and Morality*. London: Routledge.
Nagel, T. (1974) 'What is it Like to be a Bat?' *Philosophical Review,* 83: 435-450.
—— (1986) *'The View From Nowhere'*. Oxford: Oxford University Press.
Poulsen, H. (1991) *Conations*. Aarhus: Aarhus University Press.
Polanyi, M. (1969) *Knowing and Being*. Edited with an introduction by Marjorie Grene. Chicago: University of Chicago Press
Raffman, D. (1995) 'On the Persistence of Phenomenology'. In: Metzinger, T. (ed.) *Conscious Experience*. Schöningh: Paderborn.
Sartre, J-P. (1969) *Being and Nothingness: An Essay on Phenomenological Ontology* (transl. by Hazel E. Barnes from 1945 L'être et le néant). London: Routledge.
Schultz, E. (1998) *Frihed og bånd i menneskelivet*. Dansk Psykologisk Copenhagen: Forlag.
Shapiro, D. (1989): *Psychotherapy of Neurotic Character*. New York: Basic Books.
Taylor, C. (1982) 'Responsibility for Self'. In: Watson, G. (ed.) *Free Will*. Oxford: Oxford University Press.
—— (1983) 'Hegel's Philosophy of Mind'. In: Fløjstad, G. (ed) *Contemporaty philosophy*, 4: 133-155.
—— (1991) *The Ethics of Authenticity*. Harvard: Harvard University Press.
Thelen, E. (1992) 'Development as a Dynamic System'. *Current Directions in Psychological Science*, 1 (6): 189-193.
Wackerhausen, S. (1994) 'Et åbent sundhedsbegreb – mellem fundamentalisme og relativisme'. In: Juul Jensen, U. et al. (eds) *Sundhedsbegreber – filosofi og praksis*. Århus. Philosophia.
Watson, G. (1990) 'Free Agency'. In: Watson, G. (ed.): *Free Will*. Oxford: Oxford University Press.
Weinert, F. E. (1987) ‚Bildhafte Vorstellungen des Willens'. In: Heinz Heckhausen et al. (eds.) *Jenseits des Rubikon. Der wille in den humanwissenschaften*. Berlin: Springer Verlag.

Willert, S. (2000) 'Bevidsthedsfunktionen. Biologiske og psykologiske perspektiver'. *Bulletin fra Forum for Antropologisk Psykologi*, 7: 6-41.
Wittgenstein, L. (1971) *Filosofiske undersøgelser.* Copenhagen: Munksgaard.
Østerberg, D. (1966): *Forståelsesformer.* Oslo: Pax.

Index

1pp, 2pp, 3pp (*see* perspective)

A
accumulation (*see* knowledge accumulation) 2, 3, 14, 17, 30, 37, 38, 39, 44, 46
action, 25, 32, 45, 49, 101, 107–109, 123, 124, 162, 168, 180, 188–189, 217–218
action guide, 8, 37, 78, 94, 194, 205, 207
activity, 3, 24, 57–97, 107–109, 115–116, 144, 152, 168, 169
aggression, 24, 68, 85, 87, 212
agrarian revolution, 77
algorithm, 105–106, 113
alienation, 95
anchoring (*see* empirical anchoring)
anchoring tool (*see* DIT)
anonymous, 70–72, 75–76, 80, 128–130, 145, 183, 192–195, 202, 214, 216
anthropological, anthropological psychology, 47–55, 110, 113, 119, 225–243
applied disciplines, applied psychology, 14, 31–55, 225–243
Aristotle, 81, 128
art, 66, 75, 76, 79, 80, 194, 201
artifact, 29, 65–70, 75–76, 80, 90, 164, 185, 194, 204, 236

attractor, 234–235
Augustine, 91, 128–131, 195
Australopithecus afarensis, 55
authenticity, 53, 93, 96, 100, 109, 117, 123, 134, 210–213, 217–219

B
behavior (vs action), 101–109
binding, the binding problem, 161
biology, 24, 43, 47, 53, 69, 148
body, 24, 29, 32, 52, 164, 222, 234
Bonobo, 149, 150
bottom-up, 4, 46, 111, 113, 124, 126, 132, 153, 178, 179, 182, 188, 210, 229, 240
brain, 24, 29, 32, 52, 164, 222, 234
burial, 76, 77

C
care, 86, 142, 150, 158, 206, 219
causal, causality, 111–115, 126, 132, 220, 221
causality explanation (*see* types of explanations)
cave paintings, 75
centeret, 58–72,
centralization, 77
chimpanzee, 84–89, 116, 158, 194
choice, 5–6, 10–15, 71, 73, 74, 80, 93, 94, 96, 106, 116–117, 123, 127, 142, 220

choice category, 104, 105, 113
city-state, 77, 78, 81, 90, 91, 195
climatic changes, 57, 58, 76
cognition, cognitive, 68, 104, 117, 128, 129, 153, 158, 162, 168, 177, 213
coherence, 23, 25–30, 43, 46, 161, 220
compatibilism (free will), 120–126
compatibility (scientific) intern, extern, 43–44, 226
complexity, 40
conation, 8, 67, 68, 128, 212
conflict, conflict managing by Chimpanzees, 85–88
connected, functional and intentional, 2, 3, 6, 10, 16, 20, 90, 99–109, 146, 160, 184, 185, 187
consciousness,
    phenomenological model building, 174–177, 180, 182, 214, 240, 241
    unconscious, 127, 134, 143, 146, 162, 184, 185, 189, 205
    stream of consciousness, 144, 178
    phenomenological quality, 145, 146, 154, 155, 242
    presentative, 144–146, 154
    representive, 144
construction validity, 42
construction, social, 163–171
continuum, vertical, 96, 179, 203–213
cooperative, 49, 51, 72, 73, 75, 77, 79, 88, 89
correspondence, 43, 109, 240
cross disciplinary, 30, 54–55
cultural history, 55, 74, 89, 127, 167, 191, 192, 221, 231
culture, 65–68

D
Darwin, 84, 178
decentered, 72–76, 82, 88, 89, 192, 194, 233

decision, 127, 132, 137–140, 180
degrees of freedom, 114, 116, 117, 132, 172, 209
Democritus, 157
determinism, soft, hard, 120–125, 142, 221
Diderot, 157
dilemma, 96, 154, 155, 215
directed at/by, 3–5, 68, 107–109
discourse, cultural, societal, discourse of the self, 3, 7, 9, 50, 53, 78, 80, 81, 93, 94, 95, 96, 127–130, 167
DIT (Data Identifying Tool), 33–34, 41

E
empathy, 108, 149, 151, 209, 231, 243
empirical, anchoring, 14, 15, 33–34, 38, 41–42, 167–170, 179, 194, 195, 196–202, 209, 217, 222, 228, 240, 241
engagement, 79, 108, 162, 183, 216, 217, 218, 221, 222
epigenetical, epidynamics, 233, 236
Eros, 128
essentialism, essentialistic, 13, 15, 16, 48, 49, 117
ethics, 15, 47, 69, 71, 72, 73, 77, 78, 80, 135–136, 150, 159, 198
evaluator, weak and strong, 93, 96
evolution, evolutionary theory, 2, 48, 47–55, 57–58, 62–70, 82, 100, 101, 108, 111–115, 120, 178, 195, 227
existential, 174, 195, 212, 215, 217, 219, 230
explanation, types of explanations, 99–214

F
First order self (*see* order)
first person (*see* perspective)

food sharing, 67, 69, 85
foraging, 58, 71, 87
free will, 119–142, 180–182, 212, 213, 214–221, 240
Frege, 15
function, functional, functionalism, 99–109

G

gene pool, 16, 63, 69, 70
general psychology, 23–46, 47, 54, 55, 100, 110, 118, 179, 226, 227
goal directed, 80, 108, 115, 116, 175
God, God as transitional object, 95, 121, 127–131, 142, 195, 196, 214, 220
group hunting, 71, 74

H

habit, 49, 62, 66, 131
hierarchy, hierarchical model, 97, 99, 110, 111, 124, 125, 126, 132, 150, 169, 188, 237, 240, 241, 243
history, historical, 15–16, 48–52
homebase, 62–70
Hominid, 49, 50, 58, 61, 63, 66, 68, 69, 71, 84, 88, 100, 192
humanization, 70, 71
hunting, 59, 61, 62, 66, 67, 71, 74, 75, 76, 102, 106
Huxley, T. H., 84
hyper mobility, 91
hypothesis, 38, 39, 41, 42, 43,

I

idealization, mirroring, 185, 186, 192, 194, 204, 207, 208, 209, 213, 217, 242
inclination, 49, 50, 71, 73, 74, 78, 79, 84, 85, 93, 100, 101, 109, 117, 127, 132, 134, 140, 232
individualism, 7, 8, 9, 53, 90, 94, 95

individuated, 76–82, 88, 89, 90, 91–96, 109, 118, 119, 127, 128, 131, 134, 140, 174, 179, 182, 194, 195, 196, 212, 214, 222, 233, 240
in-group, 69
inheritance, 70, 231, 233, 236
inside-out, 3, 107, 150, 153, 171, 183, 184, 199, 206, 227, 228
institution, 49, 50, 51, 54, 62, 66, 67, 69, 70, 75, 79, 87, 90, 168, 169, 170, 185, 191, 194, 236
instrumentalism, 94, 95
intention, intentio, intentum, 104, 107, 108, 115, 126, 127, 137, 138, 139, 140, 144, 146, 150, 155, 157, 159, 160, 171, 175–178, 180–182, 183–187, 188, 198, 199, 200, 202, 205, 206, 207, 213, 217, 227, 235
intentional explanations (*see* types of explanations)
intentionality, meaning directed, sense directed, 173, 175, 172, 174, 177
intentionalization phase, 137, 180
interdisciplinary, 30, 43, 44–46, 54–55, 118
interface, interspace, 101–108, 113, 242
introspection, 152, 209, 221, 230, 231, 241, 243
irreplaceable, 203–206, 208, 209, 242

K

Kant, 132, 133, 150, 151, 182
knowledge accumulation, 2, 3, 14, 17, 30, 37, 38, 39, 44, 46

L

language, 29, 67, 163, 167, 173
learning, 11, 24, 63, 65, 69, 70, 73, 157, 234

levels, low-, medium-, high-level psychology, 114–118, 119, 140, 152, 153, 169, 176, 180, 182, 190, 210, 237, 240, 241, 243
libertarianism, soft, hard, 120, 121, 123, 124, 125, 214, 220
Libet, 126–127
life form, 16, 90, 193, 215
life history, 54, 55, 69, 70, 136, 184, 204, 205, 217, 221, 222, 231, 232, 230
life project, 5, 10, 12, 51, 54, 71, 72, 76, 80, 81, 90, 93, 96, 123, 124, 128, 129, 130, 131, 136, 151, 169, 183, 188, 189, 190, 198, 209, 215, 218, 219, 221, 222, 235
life world, 1, 162, 184, 191, 202
local, 11, 15, 16, 53, 58, 91, 92
loneliness, 1, 141, 151, 179, 207
Lucy, 58

M

MAT method, 16–21
meaning, 65–70, 76, 79, 80, 114–117, 171–175, 184, 185, 189, 191, 198, 204, 205, 207, 209, 212, 219, 227, 240, 241, 242
mentalism, mentalistic, 104
mesopotamia, 50, 90
metaphor, 133, 159, 172, 174
metascientific, 28, 29
method, 16–21, 27, 35, 40, 42, 45, 46, 48, 54, 55, 151, 152, 167, 225, 226, 231, 236, 241, 242
methodical reductionism, 40, 227, 228, 229, 230, 231
mirroring, (*see also* idealization), 184, 185, 186, 192, 204, 206, 207, 208, 209, 212, 217, 227, 242
mobility, 91–93
model, scientific, 6, 12, 28, 29, 34–40, 91, 164, 228

morality, moral, 1, 2, 6, 7–10, 15, 16, 18, 73, 75, 77, 78, 82, 84–89, 94, 95, 96, 119, 130, 132, 135, 154, 155, 159, 182, 212, 213, 215, 217, 218, 225

N

natural history, 15, 51, 52–53, 54, 55, 69, 70, 221, 222, 231
natural science, 24, 25, 130
neurophysiology, neuropsychology, 24, 25, 40, 114, 115, 117, 158, 168, 171, 231
niche construction, 63–64
non-algorithmic (*see* algorithm)
norms, 49, 23, 24, 49, 62, 78, 136, 191

O

ontological irreducibility, 40, 43
order, of the self, 183–188, 194, 195, 208, 210, 214, 215, 216, 219, 240, 241
order, the world order, 7, 124, 131, 237
organization, 51, 24, 62, 72, 82, 89, 96, 99, 101, 108, 109–116, 124, 132, 133, 155, 178, 182, 188, 189, 196, 210, 218, 220, 243
   downward organization, 111, 132, 140, 180, 214
   self-organization, 4, 12, 16, 20, 127, 142, 179, 195, 196, 208, 209, 214, 215, 218, 219, 234, 235, 240, 241, 243
original sin, 131
out group, 69
outside-in, 3, 107, 153, 171, 183, 199, 227, 228

P

pan-psychism, 156, 157
personality, personality psychology, 25, 29, 30, 35, 36, 40, 54, 55,

84, 86, 96, 123, 136, 141, 177, 179, 189, 199, 207, 209, 210, 217, 218, 224, 231, 232, 241
perspective distance, 149, 150, 151, 157–159, 231, 241
perspective, perspective of first, second and third person, 146, 150, 151, 152, 166, 189, 191, 192, 194, 195, 205, 206, 207, 208, 229, 241, 242, 243
phenomenology, phenomenological, 2, 76, 79, 80, 143, 145, 146, 152, 154, 155, 156, 159, 161, 162, 163, 165, 166, 168, 174, 175, 177, 180, 182, 183, 185, 210, 214, 221, 222, 240, 241, 242, 243
Plato, 81, 128, 130, 195, 205, 233, 236
play, 63, 66, 172, 173, 174
POM, 37–38
preference, 79, 134
project human being, 80, 191, 192, 196, 200, 201, 233, 235
prosocial, 53, 54
proto-consciousness, 160, 167, 168, 169, 182
proto-psyche, 115, 237
psychogenesis, 67, 69, 70, 71
psychotherapy, 3, 5, 96

Q

qualia, 145–147, 154–155, 156, 157, 161, 242, 243

R

realism, 9, 27, 43, 135, 162, 187, 196, 197, 199, 220
realization phase, 138, 180
reason, 132, 134, 154–155
religion, 65, 71, 191, 195
repertoire, practical, therapeutically, 37, 38, 39, 42, 117

reproduction, 63, 100, 113, 116
resonance, 155–159, 160, 164, 165, 166, 171, 179, 182, 210, 212, 213, 214, 221, 222, 236, 240, 242, 243
responsibility, 5, 93, 95, 119, 141, 142, 219

S

Sartre, 123, 141, 214, 216
Schopenhauer, 132, 133
search activity, 101–107, 115, 201, 227
second order self (*see* order)
second person
self-consciousness, 59, 70, 71, 72, 74, 79, 80, 82, 89, 90, 97, 117, 140, 154, 161, 168, 169, 174, 182, 186, 187, 195, 206, 209, 210, 212, 214, 216, 219, 228
sense, 65–70, 76, 79, 80, 114–117, 171–175, 184, 185, 189, 191, 198, 204, 205, 207, 209, 212, 219, 227, 240, 241, 242
sensory category, 104, 105, 113
social psychology, 3, 5, 23, 24, 40, 55, 196, 209, 210
social science, 17, 24, 25, 43
sociogenesis, 67, 69,
Socrates, 81, 195
soft determinism, 120, 121–123, 124, 125, 126, 132, 221
solipsism, 151
somebody, to be someone, 6, 70, 145, 146, 155, 157, 183, 184, 185, 186, 204, 205, 206, 208, 209, 210, 217, 219, 222, 229, 230, 240, 242, 243
something, the world is something, 187, 188, 204, 209, 213, 219, 226, 240, 242
spatiotemporal, 50, 51, 74, 77, 82
specializing (urban), 77, 78

Spencer, H., 84
Spinoza, 157
stratification (urban), 77, 78, 233
sympathy, 149, 150, 151, 212, 213

T
taxonomy, 18, 19, 20, 55, 97, 117, 153, 180, 210, 225, 226, 237, 240, 241, 243
thermostat (consciousness), 156, 157, 159, 161
third order self (*see* order)
third person (*see* perspective)
TOM, 38–39
tool, using of, 62, 65, 67, 75
top-down, 4, 46, 124, 132, 153, 179, 181, 182, 183, 197, 212, 240
transparence, 161, 162
Turing test, 241
types of explanations, 101–109, 110, 111, 115, 122

U
universal pragmatism, 53
urbanization, 77, 78, 79, 80

V
validity, 11, 26, 41, 42, 81, 112, 147
values, 8, 9, 10, 79, 93, 94, 95, 96, 100, 108, 116, 123, 124, 159, 162, 164, 185, 189, 207
vertical continuum (*see* continuum)
Victorian will, 134, 178
violence, 23, 24, 30, 212, 217

W
Wittgenstein, 65, 172
writing, 80, 81, 194

www.ingramcontent.com/pod-product-compliance
Lightning Source LLC
Chambersburg PA
CBHW071337080526
44587CB00017B/2864